Other Books and Series by Jeff Bowen

Applications for Enrollment of Chickasaw Newborn Act of 1905
Volumes I thru VII

Cherokee Intermarried White 1906 Volume I thru X

Applications for Enrollment of Creek Newborn Act of 1905
Volumes I, II, III, IV, V, VI & VII

Visit our website at **www.nativestudy.com** to learn more about these and other books and series by Jeff Bowen

APPLICATIONS FOR ENROLLMENT OF CREEK NEWBORN ACT OF 1905
VOLUME VIII

TRANSCRIBED BY
JEFF BOWEN
NATIVE STUDY
Gallipolis, Ohio
USA

Other Books and Series by Jeff Bowen

1901-1907 Native American Census Seneca, Eastern Shawnee, Miami, Modoc, Ottawa, Peoria, Quapaw, and Wyandotte Indians (Under Seneca School, Indian Territory)

1932 Census of The Standing Rock Sioux Reservation with Births And Deaths 1924-1932

Census of The Blackfeet, Montana, 1897- 1901 Expanded Edition

Eastern Cherokee by Blood, 1906-1910, Volumes I thru XIII

Choctaw of Mississippi Indian Census 1929-1932 with Births and Deaths 1924-1931   Volume I
Choctaw of Mississippi Indian Census 1933, 1934 & 1937, Supplemental Rolls to 1934 & 1935 with Births and Deaths 1932-1938, and Marriages 1936-1938 Volume II

Eastern Cherokee Census Cherokee, North Carolina 1930-1939 Census 1930-1931 with Births And Deaths 1924-1931 Taken By Agent L. W. Page Volume I
Eastern Cherokee Census Cherokee, North Carolina 1930-1939 Census 1932-1933 with Births And Deaths 1930-1932 Taken By Agent R. L. Spalsbury   Volume II
Eastern Cherokee Census Cherokee, North Carolina 1930-1939 Census 1934-1937 with Births and Deaths 1925-1938 and Marriages 1936 & 1938 Taken by Agents R. L. Spalsbury And Harold W. Foght Volume III

Seminole of Florida Indian Census, 1930-1940 with Birth and Death Records, 1930-1938

Texas Cherokees 1820-1839 A Document For Litigation 1921

Choctaw By Blood Enrollment Cards 1898-1914 Volumes I thru XVII

Starr Roll 1894 (Cherokee Payment Rolls) Districts: Canadian, Cooweescoowee, and Delaware Volume One
Starr Roll 1894 (Cherokee Payment Rolls) Districts: Flint, Going Snake, and Illinois   Volume Two
Starr Roll 1894 (Cherokee Payment Rolls) Districts: Saline, Sequoyah, and Tahlequah; Including Orphan Roll   Volume Three

Cherokee Intruder Cases Dockets of Hearings 1901-1909 Volumes I & II

Indian Wills, 1911-1921 Records of the Bureau of Indian Affairs Books One thru Seven;
Native American Wills & Probate Records 1911-1921

Other Books and Series by Jeff Bowen

Turtle Mountain Reservation Chippewa Indians 1932 Census with Births & Deaths, 1924-1932

Chickasaw By Blood Enrollment Cards 1898-1914 Volume I thru V

Cherokee Descendants East An Index to the Guion Miller Applications Volume I
Cherokee Descendants West An Index to the Guion Miller Applications Volume II (A-M)
Cherokee Descendants West An Index to the Guion Miller Applications Volume III (N-Z)

Applications for Enrollment of Seminole Newborn Freedmen, Act of 1905

Eastern Cherokee Census, Cherokee, North Carolina, 1915-1922, Taken by Agent James E. Henderson   Volume I (1915-1916)
Volume II (1917-1918)
Volume III (1919-1920)
Volume IV (1921-1922)

Complete Delaware Roll of 1898

Eastern Cherokee Census, Cherokee, North Carolina, 1923-1929, Taken by Agent James E. Henderson   Volume I (1923-1924)
Volume II (1925-1926)
Volume III (1927-1929)

Applications for Enrollment of Seminole Newborn Act of 1905 Volumes I & II

North Carolina Eastern Cherokee Indian Census 1898-1899, 1904, 1906, 1909-1912, 1914 Revised and Expanded Edition

1932 Hopi and Navajo Native American Census with Birth & Death Rolls (1925-1931) Volume 1 - Hopi
1932 Hopi and Navajo Native American Census with Birth & Death Rolls (1930-1932) Volume 2 - Navajo

Western Navajo Reservation Navajo, Hopi and Paiute 1933 Census with Birth & Death Rolls 1925-1933

Cherokee Citizenship Commission Dockets 1880-1884 and 1887-1889 Volumes I thru V

Copyright © 2012
by Jeff Bowen

ALL RIGHTS RESERVED
No part of this publication may be reproduced
or used in any form or manner whatsoever
without previous written permission from the
copyright holder or publisher.

Originally published:
Baltimore, Maryland
2012

Reprinted by:

Native Study LLC
Gallipolis, OH
www.nativestudy.com
2020

Library of Congress Control Number: 2020917992

ISBN: 978-1-64968-087-7

Made in the United States of America.

This series is dedicated to the descendants of the Creek newborn listed in these applications.

DEPARTMENT OF THE INTERIOR.

Commissioner to the Five Civilized Tribes.

NOTICE.

Opening of Land Office at Wewoka,
IN THE SEMINOLE NATION, INDIAN TERRITORY.

Notice is hereby given that on Monday, September 4, 1905, the Commissioner to the Five Civilized Tribes will establish a land office at Wewoka, in the Seminole Nation, Indian Territory, for the purpose of allowing citizens and freedmen of the Seminole Nation to select allotments of land for their minor children enrolled under the Act of Congress approved March 3, 1905 (33 Stat. L 1060), and for the further purpose of allowing citizens and freedmen of the Seminole Nation, whose allotments are incomplete, to select additional land in order to bring the value of their allotments up to the standard of $309.09, as nearly as may be practicable.

Each child whose enrollment in accordance with the Act of March 3, 1905, has been duly approved by the Secretary of the Interior, is entitled to receive an alllotment of forty acres without regard to the character or value of the land selected.

Selection of allotments for minor children must be made by their citizen or freedmen parents or by a duly appointed guardian, or curator, or by a duly appointed administrator.

TAMS BIXBY,
Commissioner.

Muskogee, Indian Territory,
July 29, 1905.

This particular notice makes mention of the Act of 1905. The Creek and Seminole were closely related tribes. Both tribes' notices were like similar in nature.

DEPARTMENT OF THE INTERIOR,
Commission to the Five Civilized Tribes.

Closing of Citizenship Rolls

OF THE MUSKOGEE OR CREEK NATION.

WHEREAS, on June 13, 1904, the Secretary of the Interior, under the authority in him vested by the provisions of the act of Congress approved March 3, 1901, (31 Stat., 1058) ordered that September 1, 1904, be and the same is hereby fixed as the time when the rolls of the Muskogee or Creek Nation shall be closed:

Notice is hereby given that the Commission to the Five Civilized Tribes will, at its office in Muskogee, Indian Territory, up to and inclusive of September 1, 1904, receive applications for the enrollment of citizens and freedmen of the Muskogee or Creek Nation, and that after that date the application of no person whomsoever for enrollment as a citizen or freedman of said nation will be received by the Commission.

Commission to the Five Civilized Tribes,
TAMS BIXBY, Chairman,
T. B. NEEDLES,
C. R. BRECKINRIDGE,
Commissioners.

Muskogee, Indian Territory,
June 25, 1904.

A notice like this was printed in newspapers and posted throughout Indian Territory.

INTRODUCTION

This series concerns Applications for Enrollment of Creek Newborn, National Archive film M-1301 (Act of 1905), as described in the National Archives publication *American Indians*. It falls under the heading Applications for Enrollment of the Commission to the Five Civilized Tribes, 1898-1914, M-1301 and is transcribed from microfilm rolls 414-419. This shows the application forms filled out by individuals applying for enrollment in the Five Civilized Tribes under the Dawes Commission. These applications contain additional information that wasn't abstracted to the census cards that you find in series M-1186. This particular roll (Creek by Birth) contains its own series of numbers separate from M-1186. To find each party's roll number you would have to reference M-1186. On July 25, 1898, there was an Indian Territory Division created in the Office of the Department of Interior. This division was created because of the increased work caused by what was called the Curtis Act, named after Senator Charles Curtis. Basically, this law stated that the tribal rolls needed to be descriptive and pointed out that each tribal roll was without description and had to be redone. At this point there was such a struggle among the Creeks to accept that the Government was going to change their way of life, again, that their leaders were refusing to cooperate in handing over their census information. The Commission had found that enrolling the Creeks was a difficult task not only because the Creek feared what was coming but also because their tribal structure was consistent with being a confederacy with forty-four different bands whose tribesmen lived in different towns of which each had a king that was supposed to keep track of their citizenry. The Commission reported that there was very little evidence of any census that existed and what there was had been kept carelessly. There were attempts and tribal conflicts along the way, but the Curtis Act would make it so they had to do it again no matter what effort from the past. In 1899, Agent Wesley Smith educated Washington to the fact that it was difficult to verify Creek eligibility. The acts passed by the Creeks themselves concerning enrollment since 1893 had been strewn amongst the archives of the Creek Council in Muskogee, I.T., and there was no provision ever approved for the printing of the those enrollments. There was confusion and difficulty let alone the fact that surnames were practically unknown among the Creek. But there was no confusion on March 9, 1905, when the Commission stated they would come to seven towns in the Creek Nation and accept applications that had to be made on a standardized blank form and contain a notarized affidavit from the mother and the attending doctor or midwife. A few by mail, but most of them were offered to a field party led by Commissioner Needles. The Commission took in applications for 2,410 children by the deadline of midnight, May 2, 1905.

This series contains applications and correspondence from 1,171 of those claimants. Realizing there were over 2,400 applicants originally, it is understood that not all were accepted. Also included are names of doctors, lawyers, mid-wives, and others who attended to the Creek Nation before and during this time in history.

Jeff Bowen
Gallipolis, Ohio
NativeStudy.com

Applications for Enrollment of Creek Newborn
Act of 1905   Volume VIII

NC-584.

Muskogee, Indian Territory, August 10, 1905

Joseph Mingo,
    Wetumka, Indian Territory.

Dear Sir:

    In the matter of the application for the enrollment of your minor daughter Bessie Mingo, born May 28, 1903, as a citizen by blood of the Creek Nation, it will be necessary for you to furnish this office the affidavits of two disinterested persons as to the birth of said child. Said affidavits must set forth said child's name, the date of her birth, the names of her parents and whether or not she was living on March 4, 1905.

        Respectfully,

        Acting Commissioner.

B. H. MILLS   NAT WILLIAMS

Real Estate Agents
and
Notary Public

                            Wetumka, Ind. Ter., Sept 14th 1905

UNITED STATES OF AMERICA,
    INDIAN TERRITORY   SS:
WESTERN JUDICIAL DISTRICT.

I,   Barney Tiger   do solemly[sic] swear that I am a citizen of the Creek Nation, and that I am acquainted with Joseph Mingo and Aggie Mingo and know them to be husband and wife, and know that there was a Female child born to them on the 28th day of May 1903 and the child was named Bessie Ming[sic] and the said Child was liveing[sic] on the 4th day of March 1905.

                                Barney Tiger

Subscribed to in my presence and Sworn to before me this the 14th day of September 1905.
                              B.H. Mills
My Commission Expires Aug 15th 1906.   Notary Public.

Applications for Enrollment of Creek Newborn
Act of 1905 Volume VIII

B. H. MILLS   NAT WILLIAMS

Real Estate Agents
and
Notary Public

Wetumka, Ind. Ter., Sept 14th 190 5

UNITED STATES OF AMERICA,
    INDIAN TERRITORY   SS:
WESTERN JUDICIAL DISTRICT.

I,   Katie Tiger   do solemly[sic] swear that I am a citizen of the Creek Nation, and that I am acquainted with Joseph Mingo and Aggie Mingo and know them to be husband and wife, and know that there was a Female child born to them on the 28th day of May 1903 and the child was named Bessie Ming[sic] and the said Child was liveing[sic] on the 4th day of March 1905.

                                                      Katie Tiger

Subscribed to in my presence and Sworn to before me this the 14th day of September 1905.
                                            B.H. Mills
My Commission Expires Aug 15th 1906.   Notary Public.

BIRTH AFFIDAVIT.
DEPARTMENT OF THE INTERIOR.
COMMISSION TO THE FIVE CIVILIZED TRIBES.

    IN RE APPLICATION FOR ENROLLMENT, as a citizen of the Creek Nation, of Bessie Mingo , born on the 28 day of May, 1903

Name of Father: Joseph Mingo   a citizen of the   Creek   Nation.
Kialigee Town
Name of Mother: Aggie Mingo (nee Yahola)   a citizen of the   Creek   Nation.
Kialigee Town
                                  Postoffice   Wetumka, Ind. Ter.

AFFIDAVIT OF MOTHER.

UNITED STATES OF AMERICA, Indian Territory,
    Western   DISTRICT.   Child is present

    I, Aggie Mingo , on oath state that I am about 22 years of age and a citizen by blood , of the Creek   Nation; that I am the lawful wife of   Joseph Mingo , who is a

Applications for Enrollment of Creek Newborn
Act of 1905   Volume VIII

citizen, by blood of the Creek Nation; that a female child was born to me on 28 day of May , 1903 , that said child has been named Bessie Mingo , and was living March 4, 1905.

her
Aggie x Mingo
mark

Witnesses To Mark:
{ Alex Posey
  DC Skaggs

Subscribed and sworn to before me this 28 day of March , 1905.

Drennan C Skaggs
Notary Public.

Father
AFFIDAVIT OF ~~ATTENDING PHYSICIAN OR MID-WIFE~~.

UNITED STATES OF AMERICA, Indian Territory,
    Western   DISTRICT.

my wife
I, Joseph Mingo , ~~a~~ *(blank)* , on oath state that I attended on ^ Mrs. Aggie Mingo , ~~wife of~~ *(blank)* on the 28 day of May , 1903 ; that there was born to her on said date a female child; that said child was living March 4, 1905, and is said to have been named Bessie Mingo

Joseph Mingo

Witnesses To Mark:
{

Subscribed and sworn to before me this 28 day of March , 1905.

Drennan C Skaggs
Notary Public.

BIRTH AFFIDAVIT.
DEPARTMENT OF THE INTERIOR.
COMMISSION TO THE FIVE CIVILIZED TRIBES.

IN RE APPLICATION FOR ENROLLMENT, as a citizen of the Creek Nation, of Billy Mingo , born on the 16 day of January, 1902

Name of Father: Joseph Mingo   a citizen of the   Creek   Nation.
Kialigee Town
Name of Mother: Aggie Mingo (nee Yahola)   a citizen of the   Creek   Nation.
Kialigee Town

Postoffice   Wetumka, Ind. Ter.

Applications for Enrollment of Creek Newborn
Act of 1905   Volume VIII

AFFIDAVIT OF MOTHER.

UNITED STATES OF AMERICA, Indian Territory,
Western   DISTRICT.

Child is present

I, Aggie Mingo, on oath state that I am about 22 years of age and a citizen by blood, of the Creek Nation; that I am the lawful wife of Joseph Mingo, who is a citizen, by blood of the Creek Nation; that a male child was born to me on 16 day of January, 1902, that said child has been named Billy Mingo, and was not living March 4, 1905.

                                            her
                                    Aggie x Mingo

Witnesses To Mark: mark
   { Alex Posey
     DC Skaggs

Subscribed and sworn to before me this 28 day of March, 1905.

                                  Drennan C Skaggs
                                  Notary Public.

                      Father
AFFIDAVIT OF ~~ATTENDING PHYSICIAN OR MID-WIFE~~.

UNITED STATES OF AMERICA, Indian Territory,
Western   DISTRICT.

                                                      my wife

I, Joseph Mingo, ~~a~~ (blank), on oath state that I attended on ^ Mrs. Aggie Mingo, ~~wife of~~ (blank) on the 16 day of January, 1902; that there was born to her on said date a male child; that said child was not living March 4, 1905, and ~~is said to have been~~ was named Billy Mingo

                                  Joseph Mingo

Witnesses To Mark:
   {

Subscribed and sworn to before me this 28 day of March, 1905.

                                  Drennan C Skaggs
                                  Notary Public.

Applications for Enrollment of Creek Newborn
Act of 1905 Volume VIII

DEPARTMENT OF THE INTERIOR.
COMMISSION TO THE FIVE CIVILIZED TRIBES.

In the matter of the death of Billy Mingo a citizen of the Creek Nation, who formerly resided at or near Wetumka , Ind. Ter., and died on the 18 day of January , 1902

AFFIDAVIT OF RELATIVE.

UNITED STATES OF AMERICA, Indian Territory, }
Western DISTRICT.

I, Joseph Mingo , on oath state that I am 31 years of age and a citizen by blood , of the Creek Nation; that my postoffice address is Wetumka , Ind. Ter.; that I am father of Billy Mingo who was a citizen, by blood , of the Creek Nation and that said Billy Mingo died on the 18 day of January , 1902

Joseph Mingo

Witnesses To Mark:
{

Subscribed and sworn to before me this 28 day of March, 1905.

Drennan C Skaggs
Notary Public.

NC 584 JLD
DEPARTMENT OF THE INTERIOR,
COMMISSIONER TO THE FIVE CIVILIZED TRIBES.

In the matter of the application for the enrollment of , deceased, as a citizen by blood of the Creek Nation.

. . . .

STATEMENT AND ORDER.

The record in this case shows that on March 30, 1905, application was made, in affidavit form, for the enrollment of Billy Mingo, deceased, as a citizen by blood of the Creek Nation, under the provisions of the act of Congress approved March 3, 1905.

It appears from the affidavit filed in this matter that said Billy Mingo, deceased, was born January 16, 1902, and died January 18, 1903.

The Act of Congress approved March 3, 1905, (33 Stats., 1048), provides:

Applications for Enrollment of Creek Newborn
Act of 1905   Volume VIII

"That the Commission to the Five Civilized Tribes is authorized for sixty days after the date of the approval of this act to receive and consider applications for enrollment, of children, <u>born subsequent to May twenty-fifth, nineteen hundred and one, and prior to March fourth, nineteen hundred and five, and living on said latter date, to citi</u>zens of the Creek tribe of Indians whose enrollment has been approved by the Secretary of the Interior prior to the approval of this act; and to enroll and make allotments to such children."

It is, therefore, ordered that the application for the enrollment of Billy Mingo, deceased, as a citizen by blood of the Creek Nation be, and the same is, hereby dismissed.

Tams Bixby   Commissioner.

Muskogee, Indian Territory.
JAN 4 – 1907

C 588

DEPARTMENT OF THE INTERIOR,
COMMISSION TO THE FIVE CIVILIZED TRIBES.
Holdenville, I. T., March 28, 1905.

In the matter of the application for the enrollment of Luther Lewis King as a citizen of the Creek Nation.

MATTIE KING, being duly sworn, testified as follows:

BY COMMISSION:
Q What is your name: A Mattie King.
Q How old are you? A Nineteen.
Q What is your post office address? A Holdenville.
Q Are you a citizen of the Creek Nation? A Yes, sir.
Q To what town do you belong? A Little River Tulsa.
Q Do you make application for the enrollment of your child, Luther Lewis King, as a citizen of the Creek Nation? A Yes, sir.
Q Who is that child's father? A Charlie King.
Q Is he a citizen of the Creek Nation? A No, sir. He is a citizen of the United States.
Q Is he your lawful husband? A Yes, sir.
Q When was your child, Luther Lewis King, born? A The 23rd day of February, 1905.
Q What day was that? A It was Friday I think?
Q Was there any record made of the birth of the child? A Yes, sir.
Q Have you that record with you? A I have it at home.
Q Who made the record? A I did.
Q When did you make that record? A Eight of ten day after the child was born.
Q Is that record made with a pencil or pen? A Pencil.
Q On what is that record made? A On a piece of paper.

Applications for Enrollment of Creek Newborn
Act of 1905 Volume VIII

Q Who attended on you at the time the child was born? A My mother.
Q Would she know when the child was born? A Yes, sir.
Q She swears in her affidavit that the child was born in March? A He was born in February.
Q How old is the child? A He was a month old the 23" of March.
Q Was the child born before or after the people began making application for the enrollment of new-born children? A I couldn't answer that.
Q Was the child born at the first[sic] heard you could make application for the enrollment of new-born children? A Yes, sir., it was born.
Q When did you first hear that applications could be made for new-born children? A In February, along the last of February or First of March.
Q At that time the child was living March 4, 1905? A Yes, sir.
Q How old was the child when you first heard of it? A I don't recollect. It was along the first of March when I heard of it.

CHARLIE KING, bing[sic] duly sworn, testified as follows:

BY COMMISSION:
Q What is your name? A Charlie King.
Q How old are you? A Twenty-four.
Q What is your post office address? A Holdenville.
Q Are you a citizen of the Creek Nation? A No, sir, I am a citizen of the United States.
Q Do you know Mattie King? A Yes, sir., she is my wife.
Q Are you lawfuly[sic] married to her? A Yes, sir.
Q When were you married to her? A I was married in April, 1901.
Q Are you the father of Luther Lewis King? A Yes, ssir[sic].
Q When was he born? A He was born February 23, 1905.
Q How do you fix the date of his birth? A Because I was there.
Q What day of the week was that? A I don't know what day of the week it was.
Q Was it Sunday or Monday? A I don't remember what day it was?[sic] It was Tuesday I believe.
Q Was there any record made as to when the child was born? A No, sir.
Q Did your wife make a record of the birth? A No, sir.
Q Are you positive that she didn't write it down? A Yes, sir.
Q Who attended on your wife at the time the child was born? A Polly Bruner.
Q Would she know when the child was born? A I don't know. She can't hardly tell her age. I don't know whether she can or not.
Q She swears that the child was born in March?[sic] A Well, she disremembered.
Q How old is the child? A He is a month old the 23rd of this month.
Q When did you first hear that Creek Citizens could make application for the enrollment of new-born children? A It has been about three weeks ago I guess.
Q Was Luther Lewis King born at that time? A Yes, sir.
Q Living was he? A Yes, sir.
Q How old was the child at that time? A He was somewhere in four or five days old.
Q Was there any one else present at the time the child was born? A No, sir.
Q Would any of your immediate neighbors know when the child was born? A Yes, sir.

Applications for Enrollment of Creek Newborn
Act of 1905   Volume VIII

Q Name some of them? A Jim Todd, Tom Norman Tom Tyler, and Berry Bruner.
Q What is the post office address of these people? A Holdenville.

POLLIE BRUNER, being duly sworn, testified as follows:

BY COMMISSION:
Q What is your name? A Plly[sic] Bruner.
Q How old are you? A I don't know my age.

Witness appears to be about fifty years old.

Q What is your post office address? A Holdenville.
Q Are you a citizen of the Creek Nation? A Yes, sir.
Q To what town do you belong? A Little River Tulsa.
Q Do you know Mattie and Charlie King? A Yes, sir.
Q What relation are they to you? A Mattie is my daughter.
Q Do you know a child of theirs named Luther Lewis King? A Yes, sir.
Q Do you know when that child was born? A Good as I can make it out it was the 23 of February.
Q Did you attend on Mattie King at the time the child was born? A Yes, sir.
Q Have you executed an affidavit about the birth of this child? A Yes, sir.
Q In that affidavit you swore that that[sic] child was born sometime in March? A Well, I made a mistake there.
Q Do you know of your own knowledge that this child was born February 23? A Yes, sir.
Q How do you fix the date? A That is just as good as I can fix it.
Q Did the parents tell you when the child was born? A No, sir.
Q Why didn't you remember when you executed the affidavit that the child was born February 23? A It looked like I ought but I couldn't.
Q[sic] We was all sick and I was sick myself.
Q On what day was that child born? A It was born on Friday I think.
Q How old is the child? A I can't tell you how old he is.
Q Can you tell how many weeks or how many months old it is? A I can't tell nothing about that. I don't know much. Can't count.
Q Do you know the nature of an oath? A Yes, sir.
Q You saw you were sick at the time the child was born? A Yes, sir., I was sick and could hardly tend on her.
Q Did you attend on Mattie King as mid-wife while you were sick? A Yes, sir., I attended on her then I went to bed.

James TODD, being duly sworn, testified as follows:

BY COMMISSION:
Q What is your name? A James Todd.
Q How old are you? A Thirty-four.
Q What is your post office address? A Holdenville.

Applications for Enrollment of Creek Newborn
Act of 1905   Volume VIII

Q Are you a citizen of the Creek Nation? A No, sir.
Q Are you a United States citizen? A Yes, sir., I think so.
Q Do you know Charlie and Mattie King? A Yes, sir.
Q Do you know a child of theirs named Luther Lewis King? A I don't know it[sic] name. I aksed[sic] them two or three weeks ago if they had named it and they said no.
Q Do you know an infant child of theirs? A Yes, sir.
Q Do you know when that child was born? A I couldn't say just exactly what day it was.
Q To the best of your recollection? A To the best of my recollection it was born in February.
Q About what time in February? A I wont[sic] be positive just what day it was but it was sometime in February it was born.
Q What time in February? A It was along towards the last of February.

L. HIBBARD, being duly sworn, testified as follows:

BY COMMISSION:
Q What is your name? A L. Hibbard.
Q How old are you? A Sixty-five.
Q What is your post office address? A Holdenville.
Q You are a United States citizen are you? A Yes, sir.
Q Did you attend on Mrs. King at the time their child, Luther Lewis King, was born? A No, sir.
Q Did you attend on her any time during her illness? A I was there before and I treated her afterwards.
Q How long before? A About the middle of February.
Q How long after you were there was the child born? A I can't say, but I was there on the 14 of March and the child was born then.
Q How old was the child when you were there the second time? A I guess it was two weeks old. Something like that.
Q You were there just before the child was born and after the child was born? A Yes, sir., I was there about the middle of February and the child I think was born about last of February. I was there again the 14th of March and the child was born then.
Q The child, you say, was about two weeks old the 14th of March? A Yes, sir., I think about that. It might have been a little over that. I never asked them when the child was born.
Q How old would you judge the child to be now? A I would judge the child to be a month or little over now.
Q You are positive that the child was born in February are you? A Yes, sir., I did think so. It was two weeks any way when I was there the second time.

I, D. C. Skaggs, on oath state that the above and foregoing is a full and true transcript of my stenographic notes as taken in said cause on said date.

DC Skaggs

Applications for Enrollment of Creek Newborn
Act of 1905 Volume VIII

Subscribed and sworn to before me this 19" day of July, 1905.

                              Edw C Griesel
                              Notary Public.

BIRTH AFFIDAVIT.

DEPARTMENT OF THE INTERIOR.
COMMISSION TO THE FIVE CIVILIZED TRIBES.

IN RE APPLICATION FOR ENROLLMENT, as a citizen of the Creek Nation, of Claudy J. King, born on the 10 day of December, 1901

Name of Father: Charlie King   a citizen of the United States Nation.
Name of Mother: Mattie King (nee Bruner)   a citizen of the   Creek   Nation.
Little River Tulsa Town
                     Postoffice   Holdenville, I. T.

AFFIDAVIT OF MOTHER.
                              Child present

UNITED STATES OF AMERICA, Indian Territory,
    Western   **DISTRICT.**

I, Mattie King, on oath state that I am 19 years of age and a citizen by blood, of the Creek   Nation; that I am the lawful wife of   Charlie King, who is a citizen, ~~by~~ *(blank)* of the   United States   Nation; that a   male   child was born to me on 10 day of December, 1901, that said child has been named   Claudy J. King, and was living March 4, 1905.

                            Mattie King
Witnesses To Mark:

Subscribed and sworn to before me this 28 day of March, 1905.

                            Drennan C Skaggs
                            Notary Public.

Applications for Enrollment of Creek Newborn
Act of 1905   Volume VIII

AFFIDAVIT OF ATTENDING PHYSICIAN OR MID-WIFE.

UNITED STATES OF AMERICA, Indian Territory,
Western DISTRICT.

I, Mary A. King , a mid-wife , on oath state that I attended on Mrs. Mattie King , wife of Charlie King on the 10 day of December three years ago last December, 1*(blank)* ; that there was born to her on said date a male child; that said child was living March 4, 1905, and is said to have been named Claudy J. King

             her
          Mary A. x King
Witnesses To Mark: mark
 { DC Skaggs
   Alex Posey

Subscribed and sworn to before me this 28 day of March , 1905.

          Drennan C Skaggs
            Notary Public.

BIRTH AFFIDAVIT.

DEPARTMENT OF THE INTERIOR.
COMMISSION TO THE FIVE CIVILIZED TRIBES.

IN RE APPLICATION FOR ENROLLMENT, as a citizen of the Creek Nation, of Berry W. King , born on the 17 day of March , 1902

Name of Father: Charlie King   a citizen of the United States Nation.
Name of Mother: Mattie King   a citizen of the   Creek   Nation.
Little River Tulsa Town
          Postoffice Holdenville, I. T.

AFFIDAVIT OF MOTHER.
            Child present

UNITED STATES OF AMERICA, Indian Territory,
Western DISTRICT.

I, Mattie King , on oath state that I am 19 years of age and a citizen by blood , of the Creek Nation; that I am the lawful wife of Charlie King , who is a citizen, ~~by~~ *(blank)* of the United States Nation; that a male child was born to me on 17 day of March , 1902 , that said child has been named Berry W. King , and was living March 4, 1905.

          Mattie King

Applications for Enrollment of Creek Newborn
Act of 1905   Volume VIII

Witnesses To Mark:
{

Subscribed and sworn to before me this 28 day of March, 1905.

Drennan C Skaggs
Notary Public.

AFFIDAVIT OF ATTENDING PHYSICIAN OR MID-WIFE.

UNITED STATES OF AMERICA, Indian Territory, }
   Western   DISTRICT.

I, Pollie Bruner, a mid-wife, on oath state that I attended on Mrs. Mattie King, wife of Charlie King on or about the 17 day of March two years ago, 1*(blank)* ; that there was born to her on said date a male child; that said child was living March 4, 1905, and is said to have been named Berry W. King

Pollie x Bruner

Witnesses To Mark:
{ DC Skaggs
  Alex Posey

Subscribed and sworn to before me this 28 day of March, 1905.

Drennan C Skaggs
Notary Public.

BIRTH AFFIDAVIT.
DEPARTMENT OF THE INTERIOR.
COMMISSION TO THE FIVE CIVILIZED TRIBES.

IN RE APPLICATION FOR ENROLLMENT, as a citizen of the Creek Nation, of Luther Lewis King, born on the 23 day of February, 1905

Name of Father: Charlie King   a citizen of the United States Nation.
Name of Mother: Mattie King   a citizen of the   Creek   Nation.
Little River Tulsa Town

Postoffice   Holdenville, I. T.

Applications for Enrollment of Creek Newborn
Act of 1905   Volume VIII

AFFIDAVIT OF MOTHER.   Child present

UNITED STATES OF AMERICA, Indian Territory, }
Western   DISTRICT.

I, Mattie King , on oath state that I am 19 years of age and a citizen by blood , of the Creek Nation; that I am the lawful wife of Charlie King , who is a citizen, ~~by~~ *(blank)* of the United States Nation; that a male child was born to me on 23 day of February , 1905 , that said child has been named Luther Lewis King , and was living March 4, 1905.

Mattie King

Witnesses To Mark:
{

Subscribed and sworn to before me this 28 day of March , 1905.

Drennan C Skaggs
Notary Public.

AFFIDAVIT OF ATTENDING PHYSICIAN OR MID-WIFE.

UNITED STATES OF AMERICA, Indian Territory, }
Western   DISTRICT.

I, Pollie Bruner , a mid-wife , on oath state that I attended on Mrs. Mattie King, wife of Charlie King ~~on the (blank) day of~~ sometime in March , 1905 ; that there was born to her on said date a male child; that said child is living and is about a month old ~~was living March 4, 1905~~, and is said to have been named Luther Lewis King

                                       her
                              Pollie x Bruner
Witnesses To Mark: mark
{ DC Skaggs
  Alex Posey

Subscribed and sworn to before me this 28 day of March , 1905.

Drennan C Skaggs
Notary Public.

Applications for Enrollment of Creek Newborn
Act of 1905   Volume VIII

(Note on small piece of paper):

From the testimony of the mother & midwife it appears that the correct name of this child is Cilla Chupco, and she should be so enrolled, but mother & midwife refuse to execute a new affidavit.

NC-586.

Muskogee, Indian Territory August 10, 1905

Rhoda Long (Loday Long)
    Yearger[sic], Indian Territory.

Dear Madam:

    In the matter of the application for the enrollment of your minor daughter Cilla Larney as a citizen by blood of the Creek Nation this office is unable to identify either your[sic] or the father of said child, Tony Larney, upon the final roll of citizens by blood of the Creek Nation. It is necessary, before the rights of said child can be finally determined for you and the father Tony Larney to be identified.

    You are, therefore, requested to inform this office as to whether or not you are finally enrolled under the name of Loday Long and as to the names of your parents and other members of your family.

    You should also inform this office as to under which name the said Tony Larney is finally enrolled, the names of his parents and other members of his family and his final roll number as the same appears upon his allotment certificate and deeds.

                  Respectfully,

                          Acting Commissioner.

NC-586.

Muskogee, Indian Territory, October 17, 1905.

Rhoda (or Loday) Long,
    Yeager, Indian Territory

Dear Madam:

    In the matter of the application for the enrollment of your minor daughter, Cilla Larney, as a citizen by blood of the Creek Nation this office is unable to identify either

Applications for Enrollment of Creek Newborn
Act of 1905   Volume VIII

you or the father of said child, Tony Long, upon the final roll of citizens by blood of the Creek Nation.

It is necessary, before the rights of said child can be finally determined, for you and the father, Tony Long, to be identified. You are, therefore, requested to inform this office as to whether you were finally enrolled under the name of Loday Long and as to the names of your parents and other members of your family.

You should also inform this office as to under which name the father, Tony Long, is finally enrolled, the names of his parents and other members of your family and his final roll number as the same appears upon his allotment certificate and deeds.

Respectfully,

Commissioner.

NC-586

DEPARTMENT OF THE INTERIOR,
COMMISSIONER TO THE FIVE CIVILIZED TRIBES.

Muskogee, Indian Territory, December 6, 1905.

In the matter of the application for the enrollment of Cilla Larney as a citizen by blood of the Creek Nation.

Rhoda Long, being duly sworn, testified as follows (through Jesse McDermott, Official Interpreter):

EXAMINATION BY THE COMMISSIONER:
Q What is your name? A Rhoda Long.
Q Are you sometimes known as Loday? A Yes sir.
Q You are enrolled, I think, as Loday Long--is that your name? A Yes, that's mine.
Q What is the name of your father? A Sam Long.
Q What is the name of your mother? A Kizzie.

The witness is identified as Loday Long on Creek Indian card, Field No. 1713, Roll No. 5512.

Q Ask her the names of some of ther[sic] brothers and sisters. A Hannah is one.
Q Have you a child name Cilla Chupco? A Yes, that's the one, hers.
Q What is the name of the father of that child? A He's known by the name Toney Larney. I don't know whether he ever was called Toney Chupco or not.
Q Were you married to him at the time the child was born? A No.

Applications for Enrollment of Creek Newborn
Act of 1905   Volume VIII

Lawyer Deere, being duly sworn, testified as follows (through Jesse McDermott, Official Interpreter):

EXAMINATION BY THE COMMISSIONER:
Q What is your name? A Lawyer Deere.
Q How old are you? A I am nearly 50 now.
Q What is your post office? A Yeager.
Q Do you know Rhoda or Loday Long? A Yes sir.
Q You know her child, Cilla? A Yes sir.
Q What is the correct name of that child, Cilla Larney, Cilla Long or Cilla Chupco? A Right name would be Cilla Chupco.
Q Her mother called it Cilla Larney. Can you explain that? A His father goes by the name Toney Larney but he is enrolled as Toney Chupco.
Q What is the name of Toney Larney's or Toney Chupco's father? A He goes by the name Micco Chupco or Micco Larney.
Q What is the name of the mother of Toney? A Katie Chupco.

Kizzie Long, being duly sworn, testified as follows (through Jesse McDermott, Official Interpreter):

EXAMINATION BY THE COMMISSIONER:
Q What is your name? A Kizzie Long.
Q What is your postoffice? A Yeager, Indian Territory
Q How old are you? A I don't know.

Witness appears to be about 50 years old.

Q Are you the mother of Loday Long? A Yes sir.
Q Loday and Rhoda are just the same? A Yes sir.
Q What is the name of the child you have in your lap there? A Cilla.
Q What is the name of the father? A Toney.
Q Do you know whether his name is Toney Long or Toney Larney or Toney Chupco? A I always thought that his name was Toney Larney; that is the name that he goes by.
Q He is enrolled here as "Toney Chupco", tell her. A His father was known as Chupco--Micco Chupco. Possibly they enrolled him that way--that the name would be the same as his--
Q Chupco--Cilla Chupco? A Yes sir. I want the child named after me.
Q Tell her she made affidavit here in which she says the child's name is Cilla Larney. A If there is any change to be made in this, the Commission will have to do it.

It is difficult to elicit answers from the witnesses. They seem to be irritated, angry and very reluctant to satisfactorily answer questions. Rhoda (or Loday) Long and the midwife, Kizzie, refuse to sign new affidavits.

Applications for Enrollment of Creek Newborn
Act of 1905 Volume VIII

INDIAN TERRITORY,)
Western District.)
)
)

I, J. Y. Miller, a stenographer to the Commission to the Five Civilized Tribes, do hereby certify that the above and foregoing is a true and complete translation of my notes as same appear in my stenographic report of this case.

                              J Y Miller

Sworn to and subscribed before me
this the 8th day of December, 1905.   J McDermott
                                            Notary Public.

BIRTH AFFIDAVIT.

DEPARTMENT OF THE INTERIOR.
COMMISSION TO THE FIVE CIVILIZED TRIBES.

IN RE APPLICATION FOR ENROLLMENT, as a citizen of the Creek Nation, of Cilla Larney, born on the 25 day of August, 1902

Name of Father: Toney Larney   a citizen of the   Creek   Nation.
Tuckabatche Town
Name of Mother: Rhoda Long   a citizen of the   Creek   Nation.
Tuckabatche Town
                              Postoffice   Yeager, Ind. Ter.

AFFIDAVIT OF MOTHER.

UNITED STATES OF AMERICA, Indian Territory,
    Western   DISTRICT.   Child is present

    I, Rhoda Long, on oath state that I am about 30 years of age and a citizen by blood, of the Creek Nation; that I ~~am~~ was formerly the lawful wife of Toney Larney, who is a citizen, by blood of the Creek Nation; that a female child was born to me on 25 day of August, 1902, that said child has been named Cilla Larney, and was living March 4, 1905. That Kizzie Long attended on me as midwife at the birth of the child, and she cannot appear presently to execute affidavit on account of severe illness.
                                                  her
                                          Rhoda x Long
Witnesses To Mark: mark
  { Alex Posey
    DC Skaggs

Applications for Enrollment of Creek Newborn
Act of 1905   Volume VIII

Subscribed and sworn to before me this 28 day of March, 1905.

                            Drennan C Skaggs
                            Notary Public.

AFFIDAVIT OF ATTENDING PHYSICIAN OR MID-WIFE.

UNITED STATES OF AMERICA, Indian Territory, }
    Western   DISTRICT.

I, Kizzie Long, a midwife, on oath state that I attended on Mrs. Rhoda Long, wife of Tony Larney on the 25 day of August, 1902; that there was born to her on said date a female child; that said child was living March 4, 1905, and is said to have been named Cilla Larney

                                        her
                             Kizzie x Long
Witnesses To Mark: mark
 { Alex Posey
  Edw C Griesel

Subscribed and sworn to before me this 18 day of August, 1905.

                            Edw C Griesel
                            Notary Public.

BIRTH AFFIDAVIT.
                    DEPARTMENT OF THE INTERIOR,
COMMISSIONER TO THE FIVE CIVILIZED TRIBES.

ENROLLMENT OF MINORS.   ACT OF CONGRESS, APPROVED APRIL 26, 1906.

IN RE APPLICATION FOR ENROLLMENT, as a citizen of the Creek Nation, of Cilla Chupco, born on the 25 day of August, 1902

Name of Father: Toney Chupco   a citizen of the   Creek   Nation.
Name of Mother: Loday Long   a citizen of the   "   Nation.

Tribal enrollment of father Roll #I 4918   Tribal enrollment of mother I 5512

                      Postoffice   Yeager I.T.

Applications for Enrollment of Creek Newborn
Act of 1905   Volume VIII

AFFIDAVIT OF MOTHER.

UNITED STATES OF AMERICA, Indian Territory,
Western   District.   child is present

I, Loday Long , on oath state that I am about 30 years of age and a citizen by blood , of the Creek Nation; that I ~~am~~ was formerly the lawful wife of Toney Chupco , who is a citizen, by blood of the Creek Nation; that a female child was born to me on 25" day of August , 1902 , that said child has been named Cilla Chupco , and was living March 4, 1906.

                                            her
                                    Loday x Long
WITNESSES TO MARK: mark
  { HG Hains
    Lona Merrick

Subscribed and sworn to before me this 20" day of July , 1906.

                                    HG Hains
                                      Notary Public.

AFFIDAVIT OF ATTENDING PHYSICIAN OR MID-WIFE.

UNITED STATES OF AMERICA, Indian Territory,
Western   District.

I, Kizzie Long , a midwife , on oath state that I attended on Loday Long , wife of Toney Chupco on the 25" day of August , 1902 ; that there was born to her on said date a female child; that said child was living March 4, 1906, and is said to have been named Cilla Chupco

                                          her
                                   Kizzie x Long
WITNESSES TO MARK: mark
  { HG Hains
    Lona Merrick

Subscribed and sworn to before me this 20 day of July , 1906.

                                    HG Hains
                                      Notary Public.

Applications for Enrollment of Creek Newborn
Act of 1905   Volume VIII

N.C. 587.

DEPARTMENT OF THE INTERIOR,
COMMISSIONER TO THE FIVE CIVILIZED TRIBES.
Muskogee, Indian Territory, January 3, 1906.

In the matter of the application for the enrollment of Willie Compier as a citizen by blood of the Creek Nation.

Mitchell Compier being duly sworn, testified as follows through Alex Posey official interpreter.

Q What is your name? A Mitchell Compier.
Q What is your age? A I think I am about twenty six.
Q What is your post office address? A Yeager.
Q Have you a child named Willie Compier? A Yes, sir.
Q Is it living? A Yes, sir.
Q How old is it? A It was born March 15, 1903
Q This Millie, you give her name as Millie Goat is that her name now? A Yes, sir.
Q What was her name before that? A She was known as Millie Compier before she married Mardle[sic] Goat, before her marriage to him she was known as Millie Thomas.
Q What was the name of her father? A Thomasey
Q What was the name of her mother? A Peepsie
Q Do you know the names of any of her sisters? A Katie and Minnie Thomas. Minnie has been married once and she may have her husband's name now.

Said Millie is identified as Millie Thomas on Creek Indian card field No. 1527, opposite roll No. 4898.

Q Is Millie Goat living? A Yes, sir.

The witness is advised that this office requires the affidavit of Millie Goat in this matter.
I, Anna Garrigues, on oath state that the above and foregoing is a true and correct copy of my stenographic notes taken in said case on said date.

Anna Garrigues

Subscribed and sworn to before me
this 8 day of January 1906.

J McDermott
Notary Public.

Applications for Enrollment of Creek Newborn
Act of 1905 Volume VIII

Western District
Indian Territory   SS

We, the undersigned, on oath state that we are personally acquainted with Millie Goat formerly wife of Mitchell Compier and that on or about the 15 day of March , 1903 , a male child was born to them and has been named Willie Compier ; and that said child was living March 4, 1905.

We further state that we have no interest in this case.

                                        Noah Long
                                             his
                                    Thomas x Long
Witness to mark: mark
  Alex Posey
  EC Griesel

Subscribed and sworn to before
me this 3 day of June 1906.

C 587

DEPARTMENT OF THE INTERIOR,
COMMISSION TO THE FIVE CIVILIZED TRIBES,
Holdenville, I. T., March 31, 1905.

In the matter of the application for the enrollment of Willie Compier as a citizen by blood of the Creek Nation.

MITCHELL COMPIER, being duly sworn, testified as follows:

Through Alex Posey Official Interpreter:

BY COMMISSION:
Q What is your name? A Mitchell Compier.
Q How old are you? A Twenty-five.
Q What is your post office address? A Yeager.
Q Are you a citizen of the Creek Nation? A Yes, sir.
Q To what town do you belong? A Tuckabatche.
Q Do you make application for the enrollment of your minor child, Willie Compier, as a citizen by blood of the Creek Nation? A Yes, sir.
Q Who is his mother? A Millie Goat.
Q Were you lawfully married to Millie Goat at the time this child was born? A The child was born after I was separated from her.

Applications for Enrollment of Creek Newborn
Act of 1905   Volume VIII

Q How long after you separated from her was the child born? A We separated in April, 1902.
Q You stated in your affidavit that the child was born on or about the 15th day of March 1903, according to that the child was born about eleven months after you separated from your wife? A I may be mistaken but that is the way I fixed the dates, according to what all my neighbors say. We were married or began living together in February, 1902, and separated in April of the same year.
Q How long after you separated from your wife was it that Willie was born? A About nine months, and I had always thought the child was born sometime in December by my neighbors all contended that it was born in March.
Q Then the affidavit which you have just executed is not of your own personal knowledge but according to what your neighbors have told you? A Yes, sir.
Q Does the mother of the child recognize you as the father of the child? A Yes, sir. When the child was about eight months old she turned it over to me to rear.
Q Were you lawfully married to Millie Goat? A We were married according to old Indian Custom.
Q Was there any ceremony performed at your marriage to her? A We just lived together. The marriage was arranged by my uncle, John McKenney, and the mother of Millie Goat.
Q How old is the child now? A Must be about three years old.
A Is the child living? A Yes, sir.
Q Can the child walk? A It began walking last summer. It is an a[sic] active child. Can walk and talk and wears breeches and he runs away sometimes.
Q Is the mother of the child a citizen of the Creek Nation? A Yes, sir.
Q To what town does she belong? A Tuckabatche.
Q What caused the separation of yourself and wife? A I separated from her through fear. Miller Bruner, a relative of hers, threatened to kill me if I continued to live with her. That is the reason of our separation.
Q What relation was Miller Bruner to your wife? A An uncle I think. He has since been killed. He had a ~~bad~~ very bad reputation as a man-killer and I didn't care to oppose him and went out of the neighborhood to avoid trouble.

-------O-------

I, D. C. Skaggs, on oath state that the above and foregoing is a full and true transcript of my stenographic notes as taken in said cause on said date.

DC Skaggs

Subscribed and sworn to before me this 20th day of July, 1905.

J McDermott
Notary Public.

Applications for Enrollment of Creek Newborn
Act of 1905   Volume VIII

BIRTH AFFIDAVIT.

DEPARTMENT OF THE INTERIOR,
COMMISSIONER TO THE FIVE CIVILIZED TRIBES.

ENROLLMENT OF MINORS.   ACT OF CONGRESS, APPROVED APRIL 26, 1906.

IN RE APPLICATION FOR ENROLLMENT, as a citizen of the Creek Nation, of Willie Compier, born on the 15 day of March, 1903

Name of Father: Mitchell Compier   a citizen of the   Creek   Nation.
Name of Mother: Millie Goat nee Thomas a citizen of the   Creek   Nation.

Tribal enrollment of father   *(blank)*   Tribal enrollment of mother   *(blank)*

Postoffice   Yager[sic], I.T.

AFFIDAVIT OF MOTHER.

UNITED STATES OF AMERICA, Indian Territory, }
Western   District.

I, Millie Goat nee Thomas, on oath state that I am 23 years of age and a citizen by blood, of the Creek Nation; that I ~~am~~ was the lawful wife of Mitchell Compier, who is a citizen, by Blood of the Creek Nation; that a Male child was born to me on 15th day of March, 1903, that said child has been named Willie Compier, and was living March 4, 1906.

Millie Goat nee Thomas

WITNESSES TO MARK:
{ Alfred F Goat
{ Chas Rider

Subscribed and sworn to before me this 21st day of July, 1906.

Chas Rider
Notary Public.

Applications for Enrollment of Creek Newborn
Act of 1905   Volume VIII

BIRTH AFFIDAVIT.

DEPARTMENT OF THE INTERIOR.
COMMISSION TO THE FIVE CIVILIZED TRIBES.

IN RE APPLICATION FOR ENROLLMENT, as a citizen of the Creek Nation, of Willie Compier, born on or about the 15 day of March, 1903

Name of Father: Mitchell Compier a citizen of the Creek Nation.
Tuckabatche Town
Name of Mother: Millie Goat (nee Thomas) a citizen of the Creek Nation.
Tuckabatche Town
 Postoffice Yeager, Ind. Ter.

AFFIDAVIT OF MOTHER.

UNITED STATES OF AMERICA, Indian Territory,
 Western DISTRICT. Child is not present

I, Mitchell Compier, on oath state that I am 25 years of age and a citizen by blood, of the Creek Nation; that I ~~am~~ was formerly the ~~lawful~~ wife husband, according to Indian custom of Millie Goat, who is a citizen, by blood of the Creek Nation; that a male child was born to ~~me~~ her on or about 15 day of March, 1903, that said child has been named Willie Compier, and was living March 4, 1905. That Millie Goat and I have separated and I have custody of the child. That the midwife, Bipacy Thomas, who attended the mother at the birth of the child is now dead.

 Mitchell Compier

Witnesses To Mark:
{

Subscribed and sworn to before me this 31 day of March, 1905.

 Drennan C Skaggs
 Notary Public.

United States of America)
)
Western District)
)
Indian Territory)

Personall[sic] appeared before me a Notary Public, within and for the western District, Thomas Long, a creek[sic] citizen, and John R Goat and state upon oath, that they both are acquainted with Millie Goat nee Thomas, and that upon the 15th day of

Applications for Enrollment of Creek Newborn
Act of 1905   Volume VIII

March 1903, their[sic] was born to her a male child, who was named Willie Compier, and is now liveing[sic], that the mid-wife who attended her is now dead,
that we are both creek[sic] citizens and have no interst[sic] in the fileing[sic] of this claim.

                                                    his
                                     Thomas Long x

Witness to mark   mark
Alfred F. Goat   John R. Goat
Chas Rider

Subscribed and sworn to before me this 21st day of July 1905

                                        Chas Rider
                                             Notary Public.

My Commission expires July 16th, 1910.

NC-587.

                                   Muskogee, Indian Territory, August 10, 1905.

Mitchell Compier,
    Yeager, Indian Territory.

Dear Sir:

    In the matter of the application for the enrollment of your minor son Willie Compier as a citizen by blood of the Creek Nation it will be necessary for you to file with this office the affidavit of the mother of said child as to his birth and it appearing from your affidavit now on file with this office that the midwife who attended at the birth of said child is now dead, it will be necessary for you to furnish, in lieu of her affidavit the affidavits of two disinterested persons relative to the birth of said children[sic]. Said affidavits must set forth said child's name, the date of his birth, the names of his parents and whether or not he was living on March 4, 1905.

    In order that Millie Goat, the mother of said child may be identified upon the final roll of citizens by blood of the Creek Nation you are requested to state under which name she is finally enrolled, the names of her parents and other members of her family and if possible her final roll number as the same appears upon her allotment certificate and deeds.

                                        Respectfully,

                                        Acting Commissioner.

Applications for Enrollment of Creek Newborn
Act of 1905   Volume VIII

NC-587.

Muskogee, Indian Territory, October 17, 1905.

Millie Thomas,
    Senora[sic], Indian Territory.

Dear Madam:

    There is on file with this office an application for the enrollment of one Willie Compier, born March 15, 1903, child of Mitchell Compier and Millie Goat.

    You are requested to advise this office whether or not you are the same person as Millie Goat the mother of said Willie Compier. In the event that you are the same person as Millie Goat you are requested to execute an affidavit, on the form herewith inclosed, giving the date of birth of said child and whether or not he was living on March 4, 1905.

    You are also requested to furnish this office with the affidavits of two disinterested persons who know the date of the birth of said child and whether or not he was living March 4, 1905.

    Respectfully,

    Commissioner.

B C
Env.

NC-587.

Muskogee, Indian Territory, October 17, 1905.

Mitchell Compier,
    Yeager, Indian Territory.

Dear Sir:

    In the matter of the application for the enrollment of your minor son Willie Compier as a citizen by blood of the Creek Nation it will be necessary for you to file with this office the affidavit of the mother of said child as to his birth, and it appearing from your affidavit, now on file with this office, that the midwife who attended at the birth of said child is now dead it will be necessary for you to furnish in lieu of her affidavit the affidavits of two disinterested persons relative to the birth of said child. Said affidavits must set forth said child's name, the date of his birth, the names of his parents and whether or not he was living on March 4, 1905.

    In order that Millie Goat, the mother of said child, may be identified upon the roll of citizens by blood of the Creek Nation you are requested to state under which name she

Applications for Enrollment of Creek Newborn
Act of 1905   Volume VIII

is finally enrolled, the names of her parents and other members of her family and her final roll number as the same appears upon her allotment certificate and deeds.

      Respectfully,

          Commissioner.

                JWH

N C 587

      Muskogee, Indian Territory, March 1, 1907.

Millie Goat,
  Holdenville, Indian Territory.

Dear Madam :--

  You are hereby advised that on February 15, 1907, the Secretary of the Interior approved the enrollment of your minor child, Willie Compier, as a citizen by blood of the Creek Nation, and that the name of said child appears upon the roll of New Born citizens by blood of the Creek Nation, enrolled under the Act of Congress approved March 3, 1905, as number 1162.

  This child is now entitled to allotment and application therefor should be made without delay at the Creek Land Office, Muskogee, Indian Territory.

      Respectfully,

          Commissioner.

                HGH

REFER IN REPLY TO THE FOLLOWING:
NC-589.

    DEPARTMENT OF THE INTERIOR,
  COMMISSIONER TO THE FIVE CIVILIZED TRIBES.

    Muskogee, Indian Territory, August 9, 1905.

Legus Thompson,
  Brush Hill, Indian Territory.

Dear Sir:

Applications for Enrollment of Creek Newborn
Act of 1905   Volume VIII

In the matter of the application for the enrollment of your minor daughter Ollie Thompson, born August 6, 1904, as a citizen by blood of the Creek Nation, it will be necessary for you to furnish this office the affidavits of two disinterested persons relative to the birth of said child. Said affidavits to set forth said child's name, the date of her birth, the names of her parents and whether or not she was on living March 4, 1905.

Please give this matter your prompt attention.

         Respectfully,

                Wm. O. Beall
                Acting Commissioner.

Cheesie McIntosh,
 Attorney-at-Law.
SUPT. CREEK SCHOOLS.

      Checotah, J. T. Sept. 30   *190* 5.

To the Commissioners of the five[sic] Civilized Tribes
 Sir:-

  We respectfully state to you that at the time our child, Ollie Thompson, was born there was no one present, or for some time afterward. It is therefore absolutely impossible to get a witness to the birth of the child except ourselves. If you require witnesses who know a few days afterwards, we can furnish several of them.

  (The mother)   Lena Thompson
  (The husband)   Legus x Thompson

Witnesses to mark
 John R. Cassingham
 Cheesie McIntosh

NC-589

         Muskogee, Indian Territory, October 3, 1905.

Legus Thompson,
 Brushhill, Indian Territory.

Dear Sir:

  Receipt is acknowledged of your communication of September 30, 1905, enclosing affidavits of yourself, your wife, Lenna[sic] Thompson, and of Sam Richardson[sic] relative to the date of the birth of your minor child, Ollie Thompson; you

Applications for Enrollment of Creek Newborn
Act of 1905   Volume VIII

state that it is absolutely impossible to secure the affidavit of any person who was present at the birth of said child.

In reply you are advised that this Office desires the affidavit of any other disinterested person who knows the month and year in which said Ollie Thompson was born and whether or not she was living March 4, 1905.

Respectfully,

Commissioner.

Commission to the Five Civilized Tribes

In an application for enrollment as a citizen of the Creek Nation of Ollie Thompson, born on the 6th day of August 1904.

I, Simma Thompson, on oath state that I am about fifty-five years of age and a citizen by blood of the Creek Nation, and that I am personally acquainted with Legus Thompson and his wife Lena Thompson; that a female child was born on or about 6th day of August 1904; that I saw said child about two weeks after it was born; that said child was named Ollie Thompson and was living March 4, 1905.

Witnesses to Mark   Simma x Thompson
John R Cassingham
Cheesie McIntosh

Subscribed and sworn to before me this 30 day of Sept 1905

J B Lucas
Notary Public.

I, Sam Richard on oath state that I am about 47 years of age and a citizen by blood of the Creek Nation; that I am personally acquainted with Legus Thompson and his wife, Lena Thompson; that a female child was born to them on or about the 6th day of August 1904; that I saw said child about three weeks after it was born and that said child was named Ollie Thompson and was living March 4, 1905.

Sam Richard

Subscribed and sworn to before me this 30 day of Sept 1905
My Com expires Aug 12-1906.   J B Lucas
Notary Public.

Applications for Enrollment of Creek Newborn
Act of 1905   Volume VIII

Commission to the Five Civilized Tribes.
In re of the Enrollment of Ollie Thompson.

    I, John Fox, being duly sworn, state that my age is 36 years ~~of a~~ That I am a citizen by blood of the Creek Nation and that my post office is Brush Hill. That I am personally acquainted with Legus Thompson and his wife, Lena Thompson That there was a female child born to them on or about the 6th day of August 1904 and that she was named and is called Ollie Thompson That I was at the home of Legus Thompson on the 10th or 11th of August, 1904 and saw the mother and the child and was then told that she was born on the 6th day of August 1904. I further know that said child, Ollie Thompson, was alive March 4, 1905. I state that I have absolutely no interest in this matter but make this statement simply because it is true.

                                                John Fox

Subscribed and sworn to before me this 7th day of October 1905.
                                                Ben D. Gross
                                                            Notary Public.

Commission to the Five Civilized Tribes.
In re of the Enrollment of Ollie Thompson.

    Having been duly sworn I Dave Washington state that I am thirty five years of age and am a citizen by blood of the Creek Nation and that I am personally acquainted with Legus Thompson and his wife Lenna Thompson. That I live about three fourths of a mile from the home of said Legus Thompson. That a female child was born to them on the 6th of August 1904; That I was at their home about three hours after the birth of said child; that said child was named and is called Ollie Thompson and was living March 4, 1905. I further state that I have no interest whatever in this matter and make these statements simply because they are true.

                                            Dave Washington

Subscribed and sworn to before me this 30 day of Sept 1905
My Com expires Aug 12th 1906.   J B Lucas
                                                        Notary Public.

BIRTH AFFIDAVIT.

DEPARTMENT OF THE INTERIOR.
COMMISSION TO THE FIVE CIVILIZED TRIBES.

IN RE APPLICATION FOR ENROLLMENT, as a citizen of the Creek Nation, of Ollie Thompson, born on the 6th day of August, 1904

Name of Father: Legus Thompson   a citizen of the   Creek   Nation.
Name of Mother: Lena Thompson   a citizen of the   Creek   Nation.

Applications for Enrollment of Creek Newborn
Act of 1905   Volume VIII

Postoffice   Brush Hill, Indian Ter

AFFIDAVIT OF MOTHER.

UNITED STATES OF AMERICA, Indian Territory,
Western   DISTRICT.

I, Lena Thompson, on oath state that I am 26 years of age and a citizen by blood, of the Creek Nation; that I am the lawful wife of Legus Thompson, who is a citizen, by blood of the Creek Nation; that a female child was born to me on 6th day of August, 1904, that said child has been named Ollie Thompson, and was living March 4, 1905.

Lena Thompson

Witnesses To Mark:

Subscribed and sworn to before me this 30th day of Sept., 1905.

My Com Expires   J B Lucas
Aug 12th 1906.   Notary Public.

AFFIDAVIT OF ATTENDING PHYSICIAN OR MID-WIFE.

UNITED STATES OF AMERICA, Indian Territory,
Western   DISTRICT.

I, Legus Thompson, a the husband, on oath state that I attended on Mrs. Lena Thompson, wife of Legus Thompson on the 6th day of August, 1904; that there was born to her on said date a female child; that said child was living March 4, 1905, and is said to have been named Ollie Thompson

Legus x Thompson

Witnesses To Mark:
  John R Cassingham
  Cheesie McIntosh

Subscribed and sworn to before me this 30th day of Sept., 1905.

J B Lucas
Notary Public.

My Com Expires Aug 12th 1906.

Applications for Enrollment of Creek Newborn
Act of 1905 Volume VIII

BIRTH AFFIDAVIT.

DEPARTMENT OF THE INTERIOR.
COMMISSION TO THE FIVE CIVILIZED TRIBES.

IN RE APPLICATION FOR ENROLLMENT, as a citizen of the Creek Nation, of Ollie Thompson , born on the 6th day of August , 1904

Name of Father:	Legus Thompson	a citizen of the	Creek Nation.
Name of Mother:	Lena Thompson	a citizen of the	Creek Nation.

Postoffice Brush Hill, I.T.

AFFIDAVIT OF MOTHER.

UNITED STATES OF AMERICA, Indian Territory,
Western   DISTRICT.

I, Lena Thompson , on oath state that I am twenty six years of age and a citizen by blood , of the Creek Nation; that I am the lawful wife of Legus Thompson , who is a citizen, by blood of the Creek Nation; that a female child was born to me on 6th day of August , 1904 , that said child has been named Ollie Thompson , and was living March 4, 1905.

Lena Thompson

Witnesses To Mark:
 S.J. Logan
 Siah Gray

Subscribed and sworn to before me this 27 day of March , 1905.

My Com Expires   Bennie McIntosh
May 16, 1908   Notary Public.

AFFIDAVIT OF ATTENDING PHYSICIAN OR MID-WIFE.

UNITED STATES OF AMERICA, Indian Territory,
Western   DISTRICT.

I, Legus Thompson , a Husband , on oath state that I attended on Mrs. Lena Thompson , ~~wife of~~ my wife on the 6th day of August , 1904 ; that there was born to her on said date a female child; that said child was living March 4, 1905, and is said to have been named Ollie Thompson

his
Legus x Thompson
mark

Applications for Enrollment of Creek Newborn
Act of 1905   Volume VIII

Witnesses To Mark:
{ S.J. Logan
{ Siah Gray

Subscribed and sworn to before me this 27 day of March, 1905.

My Com Expires
May 16, 1908

Bennie McIntosh
Notary Public.

C 590
DEPARTMENT OF THE INTERIOR,
COMMISSION TO THE FIVE CIVILIZED TRIBES.
Holdenville, I. T., March 27, 1905.

In the matter of the application for the enrollment of application for the enrollment of Ella Palmer as a citizen of the Creek Nation.

MARY PALMER, being duly sworn, testified as follows:

BY COMMISSION:
Q What is your name?   A Mary Palmer.
Q How old are you?   A Twenty.
Q What is your post office address?   A Sasakwa.
Q Are you a citizen of the Creek Nation?   A Yes, sir.
Q To what town do you belong?   A Cheyarha.
Q Do you make application for the enrollment of your child, Ella Palmer, as a citizen of the Creek Nation?   A Yes, sir.
Q Who is the father of this child?   A Jim Palmer.
Q Is he a citizen of the Creek Nation?   A No, sir, he is a Seminole.
Q If it should be found that Ella Palmer is entitled to be enrolled in either the Creek or Seminole Nations, in which nation do you elect to have her enrolled?   A In the Creek Nation.

---oooOOOooo---

I, D. C. Skaggs, on oath state that the above and foregoing is a full and true transcript of my stenographic notes as taken in said cause on said date.

DC Skaggs

Subscribed and sworn to before me this 17" day of July, 1905.

J McDermott
Notary Public.

Applications for Enrollment of Creek Newborn
Act of 1905 Volume VIII

BIRTH AFFIDAVIT.

DEPARTMENT OF THE INTERIOR.
COMMISSION TO THE FIVE CIVILIZED TRIBES.

IN RE APPLICATION FOR ENROLLMENT, as a citizen of the Creek Nation, of Ella Palmer, born on the 2 day of April, 1903

Name of Father: Jim Palmer   a citizen of the   Seminole   Nation.
Name of Mother: Mary Palmer (nee Frank)   a citizen of the   Creek   Nation.
Cheyarka Town
                          Postoffice   Sasakwa, I.T.

AFFIDAVIT OF MOTHER.   Child present
Testimony 3/27/05

UNITED STATES OF AMERICA, Indian Territory,
  Western   DISTRICT.

I, Mary Palmer, on oath state that I am 20 years of age and a citizen by blood, of the Creek Nation; that I am the lawful wife of Jim Palmer, who is a citizen, by blood of the Seminole Nation; that a female child was born to me on 2 day of April, 1903, that said child has been named Ella Palmer, and was living March 4, 1905.

                                        Mary Palmer
Witnesses To Mark:

Subscribed and sworn to before me this 27 day of March, 1905.

                                        Drennan C Skaggs
                                            Notary Public.

AFFIDAVIT OF ATTENDING PHYSICIAN OR MID-WIFE.

UNITED STATES OF AMERICA, Indian Territory,
  Western   DISTRICT.

I, Jane Frank, a mid-wife, on oath state that I attended on Mrs. Mary Palmer, wife of Jim Palmer on the 2 day of April, 1903; that there was born to her on said date a female child; that said child was living March 4, 1905, and is said to have been named Ella Palmer

                                        Jane Frank

Applications for Enrollment of Creek Newborn
Act of 1905   Volume VIII

Witnesses To Mark:
{

Subscribed and sworn to before me this 27 day of March, 1905.

Drennan C Skaggs
Notary Public.

NC. 590.

Muskogee, Indian Territory, July 14, 1905.

Commissioner to the Five Civilized Tribes,
Seminole Enrollment Division,
Muskogee, Indian Territory.

Gentlemen:

March 30, 1905, application was made to the Commission to the Five Civilized Tribes for the enrollment of Ella Palmer, born April 2, 1903, as a citizen by blood of the Creek Nation. It is stated in said application that the father of said child is Jim Palmer, a citizen of the Seminole Nation, and that the mother is Mary Palmer, a citizen of the Creek Nation.

You are requested to inform the Creek Enrollment Division as to whether application has been made for the enrollment of said Ella Palmer as a citizen of the Seminole Nation, and if so, what disposition has been made of the same.

Respectfully,

Commissioner.

DEPARTMENT OF THE INTERIOR.
COMMISSION TO THE FIVE CIVILIZED TRIBES.

Muskogee, Indian Territory, July 18, 1905.

Chief Clerk,
Creek Enrollment Division.

Dear Sir:

Receipt is acknowledged of your letter of July 14, 1905 (NC-590) stating that application was made to the Commission to the Five Civilized Tribes for the enrollment

Applications for Enrollment of Creek Newborn
Act of 1905 Volume VIII

of Ella Palmer, born April 2, 1903, child of Jim Palmer, a citizen of the Seminole Nation, and Mary Palmer, a citizen of the Creek Nation, as a citizen by blood of the Creek Nation and requesting to be informed as to whether application was made for the enrollment of said Ella Palmer as a citizen of the Seminole Nation.

In reply to your letter you are advised that it does not appear from an examination of the records of this office that any application was made to the Commission to the Five Civilized Tribes for the enrollment of said Ella Palmer as a citizen of the Seminole Nation.

Respectfully,

Tams Bixby   Commissioner.

ND 590

Muskogee, Indian Territory, November 12, 1906

Chief Clerk,
    Seminole Enrollment Division,
        General Office.

Dear Sir:

You are hereby advised that the name of Ella Palmer born April 2, 1903 to Jim Palmer, an alleged citizen of the Seminole Nation and Mary Palmer a citizen by blood of the Creek Nation, is contained in schedule of minor children by blood of the Creek Nation, approved by the Secretary of the Interior, September 17, 1905, opposite Roll number 564.

Respectfully,

Commissioner.

NC. 591.

Muskogee, Indian Territory, July 14, 1905.

Commissioner to the Five Civilized Tribes,
    Cherokee Enrollment Division,
        Muskogee, Indian Territory.
Gentlemen:

April 4, 1905, application was made to the Commission to the Five Civilized Tribes for the enrollment of Willie Eva Flowers, born August 22, 1902, as a citizen by blood of the Creek Nation. It is stated in said application that the father of said child is

Applications for Enrollment of Creek Newborn
Act of 1905 Volume VIII

Joseph Flowers, a citizen of the Creek Nation, and that the mother is Alice Flowers, a citizen of the Cherokee Nation.

You are requested to inform the Creek Enrollment Division as to whether application has been made for the enrollment of said Willie Eva Flowers, as a citizen of the Cherokee Nation, and if so, what disposition has been made of the same.

Respectfully,

Commissioner.

REFER IN REPLY TO THE FOLLOWING:

DEPARTMENT OF THE INTERIOR,
COMMISSIONER TO THE FIVE CIVILIZED TRIBES.

Muskogee, Indian Territory, July 18, 1905.

Chief Clerk,
    Creek Enrollment Division,
        Muskogee, Indian Territory.

Dear Sir:

Replying to your letter of July 14, 1905, (NC. 591) asking to be advised whether or not any application has ever been made for the enrollment, as a citizen of the Cherokee Nation, of Willie Eva Flowers, a child of Joseph Flowers, a citizen of the Creek Nation, and Alice Flowers, a citizen of the Cherokee Nation, you are advised that from an examination of the records of the Cherokee Enrollment Division it does not appear that any application has ever been made for the enrollment of said child as a citizen of that nation.

Respectfully,

Tams Bixby   Commissioner.

GRL

NC 591.

Muskogee, Indian Territory, November 12, 1906.

Chief Clerk,
    Cherokee Enrollment Division,
        General Office.

Dear Sir:

You are hereby advised that the name of Willie Eva Flowers, born August 22, 1902 to Joseph Flowers a citizen by blood of the Creek Nation and Alice Flowers an alleged citizen of the Cherokee Nation, is contained in schedule of minor citizens by

Applications for Enrollment of Creek Newborn
Act of 1905 Volume VIII

blood of the Creek Nation, approved by the Secretary of the Interior, September 27, 1905, opposite Roll number 565.

Respectfully,

Commissioner.

DEPARTMENT OF THE INTERIOR,
COMMISSION TO THE FIVE CIVILIZED TRIBES.

In Re Application for Enrollment, as citizen of the Creek Nation, of Willie Eva Flowers, born on the 28[sic] day of August 1902.

Name of Father Joseph Flowers   a citizen of the Creek Nation.
Name of Mother, Alice Flowers (deceased) a citizen of the Creek Nation.

Postoffice   Coweta, I. T.

Affidavit of Attending Midwife

United States of America,
Indian Territory,
Western District.

I, Caroline Fletcher, a midwife, on oath state that i attended on Mrs. Alice Flowers, wife of Joseph Flowers, on the 28" day of August, 1902; that there was born to her on said date a female child; that said child is now living and is said to have been named Willie Eva Flowers.

Caroline Fletcher

Witnesses to mark:

Subscribed and sworn to before me this "1 day of April, A.D. 1905.
(SEAL)

Z.I.J. Holt
Notary Public.

My commission expires May 9", 1907.

BIRTH AFFIDAVIT.

DEPARTMENT OF THE INTERIOR.
COMMISSION TO THE FIVE CIVILIZED TRIBES.

IN RE APPLICATION FOR ENROLLMENT, as a citizen of the CREEK Nation, of Willie Eva Flowers , born on the 22   day of August , 1902

Applications for Enrollment of Creek Newborn
Act of 1905   Volume VIII

Name of Father: Joseph Flowers   a citizen of the   Creek   Nation.
Name of Mother: Alice   "   a citizen of the   Cherokee   Nation.

Postoffice   Coweta

(child present)

AFFIDAVIT OF ~~MOTHER~~.
father

UNITED STATES OF AMERICA, Indian Territory, ⎫
   WESTERN   DISTRICT. ⎭

    I, Joseph Flowers , on oath state that I am 25 years of age and a citizen by ~~Freedman~~ blood, of the Creek Nation; that I am the lawful ~~wife~~ husband of Alice Flowers (dc'd) , who is a citizen, by ~~Freedman~~ of the Cherokee Nation; that a female child was born to me on 22" day of Aug. , 1902 , that said child has been named Willie Eva Flowers , and is now living.

                             Joseph Flowers

Witnesses To Mark:
{

    Subscribed and sworn to before me this 21" day of April, 1905.

                             Edw C Griesel
                                Notary Public.

BIRTH AFFIDAVIT.
DEPARTMENT OF THE INTERIOR.
COMMISSION TO THE FIVE CIVILIZED TRIBES.

    IN RE APPLICATION FOR ENROLLMENT, as a citizen of the Creek Nation, of Alice Pense, born on the 2nd day of May , 1903

Name of Father: J H Pense   a citizen of the   U.S.   Nation.
Name of Mother: Malissa Pense   a citizen of the   Creek   Nation.

Postoffice   Stone Bluff - I.T.

(child present)
HGH
APR 5- 1905

39

Applications for Enrollment of Creek Newborn
Act of 1905 Volume VIII

AFFIDAVIT OF MOTHER.

UNITED STATES OF AMERICA, Indian Territory, }
   Western   DISTRICT.

    I, Malissa Pense , on oath state that I am 31 years of age and a citizen by Blood, of the Creek Nation; that I am the lawful wife of J H Pense , who is a citizen, by *(blank)* of the US Nation; that a female child was born to me on 2nd day of May, 1903 , that said child has been named Alice Pense , and is now living.

                                        Malissa Pense

Witnesses To Mark:

    Subscribed and sworn to before me this 24th day of March, 1905.

                                        Ralph Dresback
                                        Notary Public.

AFFIDAVIT OF ATTENDING PHYSICIAN OR MID-WIFE.

UNITED STATES OF AMERICA, Indian Territory, }
   Western   DISTRICT.

    I, Mrs M.D. Dotson , a Midwife , on oath state that I attended on Mrs. Malissa Pense , wife of J H Pense on the 2nd day of May , 1903 ; that there was born to her on said date a female child; that said child is now living and is said to have been named Alice Pense

                                          her
                                      M A x Dotson

Witnesses To Mark: mark
    Nellie Dresback
    (Name Illegible)

    Subscribed and sworn to before me this 24th day of March, 1905.

                                        Ralph Dresback
                                        Notary Public.

Cr NC-593

                              Muskogee, Indian Territory, July 19, 1905.

Eliza Hendrickson,
    Krebs, Indian Territory.

Dear Madam:

Applications for Enrollment of Creek Newborn
Act of 1905   Volume VIII

There are on file in this office affidavits executed by you and G. S. Turner, a physician, in which the date of the birth of your minor child, Sarah Jane Hendrickson, is given as December 17, 1902 and December 17, 1903.

You are requested to have the enclosed affidavits properly filled out, signed and executed, and return same to this office in the enclosed envelope.

Respectfully,

Commissioner.

JYM-19-2

BIRTH AFFIDAVIT.

DEPARTMENT OF THE INTERIOR,
COMMISSION TO THE FIVE CIVILIZED TRIBES.

In Re Application for Enrollment, as a citizen of the Creek Nation, of Sarrah[sic] Hendrickson, born on the 17 day of Dec., 1902

Name of Father: James Hendrickson   a citizen of the United States Nation.
Name of Father: Eliza Hendrickson   a citizen of the   Creek   Nation.

Post-office   Krebs I.T.

AFFIDAVIT OF MOTHER.

UNITED STATES OF AMERICA,
   INDIAN TERRITORY,
   Central   District.

I, Eliza Hendrickson, on oath state that I am 26 years of age and a citizen by Blood, of the Creek Nation; that I am the lawful wife of James Hendrickson, who is a citizen, by Birth of the United States Nation; that a Female child was born to me on Dec. 17 day of Dec, 1902, that said child has been named Sarrah Hendrickson, and is now living.

her
Eliza x Hendrickson
mark

WITNESSES TO MARK:
{ Harry Oglesby
{ R. L. Green

Subscribed and sworn to before me this 29 day of Sept, 1904.

W. J. Oglesby
NOTARY PUBLIC.

Applications for Enrollment of Creek Newborn
Act of 1905 Volume VIII

AFFIDAVIT OF ATTENDING PHYSICIAN OR MID-WIFE.

UNITED STATES OF AMERICA,
INDIAN TERRITORY,
Central   District.

I, G. S. Turner , a Physician , on oath state that I attended on Mrs. Eliza Hendrickson , wife of James Hendrickson on the 17 day of Dec , 1904 ; that there was born to her on said date a Female child; that said child is now living and is said to have been named Sarrah Hendrickson

G. S. Turner M.D.

WITNESSES TO MARK:

Subscribed and sworn to before me this 1st day of Oct. , 1904.

W. J. Oglesby
NOTARY PUBLIC.

BIRTH AFFIDAVIT.

DEPARTMENT OF THE INTERIOR.
COMMISSION TO THE FIVE CIVILIZED TRIBES.

IN RE APPLICATION FOR ENROLLMENT, as a citizen of the Creek Nation, of Sarrah Jane Hendrickson , born on the 17 day of Dec , 1903

Name of Father: James Hendrickson   a citizen of the U. S.   Nation.
Name of Mother: Eliza Hendrickson   a citizen of the Creek   Nation.

Postoffice   Krebs, I. T.

AFFIDAVIT OF MOTHER.

UNITED STATES OF AMERICA, Indian Territory,
Central   DISTRICT.

I, Eliza Hendrickson , on oath state that I am 26 years of age and a citizen by Blood , of the Creek Nation; that I am the lawful wife of James Hendrickson , who is a citizen, by Birth of the U S Nation; that a Female child was born to me on 17 day of Dec , 1903, that said child has been named Sarrah Jane Hendrickson , and is now living.

Eliza x Hendrickson

Applications for Enrollment of Creek Newborn
Act of 1905   Volume VIII

Witnesses To Mark:
- George Fisher
- Laura Brown

Subscribed and sworn to before me this 31 day of March, 1905.

W. J. Oglesby
Notary Public.

AFFIDAVIT OF ATTENDING PHYSICIAN OR MID-WIFE.

UNITED STATES OF AMERICA, Indian Territory,
Central   DISTRICT.

I, G. S. Turner, a Physician, on oath state that I attended on Mrs. Eliza Hendrickson, wife of James Hendrickson on the 17 day of Dec, 1903; that there was born to her on said date a Female child; that said child is now was living March 5, 1905 living[sic] and is said to have been named Sarrah Jane Hendrickson

G. S. Turner M.D.

Witnesses To Mark:

Subscribed and sworn to before me this 31 day of March, 1905.

W.J. Oglesby
Notary Public.

BIRTH AFFIDAVIT.

DEPARTMENT OF THE INTERIOR.
COMMISSION TO THE FIVE CIVILIZED TRIBES.

IN RE APPLICATION FOR ENROLLMENT, as a citizen of the Creek Nation, of Sarrah Jane Hendrickson, born on the 17 day of Dec, 1902

Name of Father:	James Hendrickson	a citizen of the	U. S.	Nation.
Name of Mother:	Eliza Hendrickson	a citizen of the	Creek	Nation.

Postoffice   Krebs, I. T.

Applications for Enrollment of Creek Newborn
Act of 1905   Volume VIII

AFFIDAVIT OF MOTHER.

UNITED STATES OF AMERICA, Indian Territory, ⎫
Central   DISTRICT.   ⎭

I, Eliza Hendrickson , on oath state that I am Twenty Six years of age and a citizen by Blood , of the Creek Nation; that I am the lawful wife of James Hendrickson , who is a citizen, by *(blank)* of the United States Nation; that a female child was born to me on the 17 day of December , 1902 , that said child has been named Sarrah Jane Hendrickson , and is now living.

                                        Eliza x Hendrickson

Witnesses To Mark:
⎰ *(Name Illegible)*
⎱ Joe Dye

Subscribed and sworn to before me this 31 day of July , 1905.

                                        W.J. Oglesby
                                              Notary Public.

AFFIDAVIT OF ATTENDING PHYSICIAN OR MID-WIFE.

UNITED STATES OF AMERICA, Indian Territory, ⎫
Central   DISTRICT.   ⎭

I, G. S. Turner , a physician , on oath state that I attended on Mrs. Eliza Hendrickson , wife of James Hendrickson on the 17 day of Dec , 1902 ; that there was born to her on said date a female child; that said child ~~is now living and is said to have been named~~ was living March 5, 1905 and is said to have been named Sarrah Jane Hendrickson.

                                        GS Turner M.D.

Witnesses To Mark:
⎰
⎱

Subscribed and sworn to before me this 31 day of July, 1905.

                                        W.J. Oglesby
                                          Notary Public.

Applications for Enrollment of Creek Newborn
Act of 1905   Volume VIII

DEPARTMENT OF THE INTERIOR,
COMMISSION TO THE FIVE CIVILIZED TRIBES.
HENRYETTA, I.T. April 18, 1905.

In the matter of the application for the enrollment of certain new borns as citizens of the Creek Nation.

Alex Posey being duly sworn, testified as follows:

By Commission:

Q What is your name, age and post office address?
A. Alex Posey, 31, Muskogee.
Q Are you a citizen of the Creek Nation? A Yes, sir.
Q Got your land, have you? A Yes, sir.
Q You have been engaged recently in the field for the Dawes Commission securing evidence about Creek citizens or new borns? A Yes, sir.
Q Have you a list of children for whom application could not be made and about whom you have succeeded in obtaining some information? A Yes, sir.
Q You may state the conditions and the names of these children? You desire to make application for them? A Yes, sir.
Q Name them. A John Lewis, Hutchechuppa, Nona Lewis, Hutchechuppa, have three children--one over three years old named Eddie-- another (a girl) over two years old--still another (also a girl) about one year old. Post Office, Henryetta, Indian Territory.
Q This is the information you received from relatives right around Henryetta, Indian Territory, on April 18, 1905? A Yes, sir.
Q Were you informed that the parents of these children were unwilling to make application for their enrollment? A Yes, sir.
Q This was the only way that the rights of these children would be saved? A Yes sir. I made every effort to obtain direct information from the parents but in every instance they refused to give their testimony.

Lona Merrick, being duly sworn, states that the above and foregoing is a true and correct transcript of her stenographic notes as taken in said cause on said date.

(signed) Lona Merrick

Subscribed and sworn to before me this 9 day of May 1905.

Edw C Griesel
Notary Public.

Anna Garrigues on oath states that the above is a true copy of the original on file in this office.

Anna Garrigues

Applications for Enrollment of Creek Newborn
Act of 1905   Volume VIII

Subscribed and sworn to before me this 8th day of August 1905

          Edw C Griesel
            Notary Public.

DEPARTMENT OF THE INTERIOR,
COMMISSION TO THE FIVE CIVILIZED TRIBES.
HENRYETTA, I.T. April 18, 1905.

In the matter of the application for the enrollment of certain new borns as citizens of the Creek Nation.

Alex Posey being duly sworn, testified as follows:

By Commission:
Q What is your name, age and post office address?
A. Alex Posey, 31, Muskogee.
Q Are you a citizen of the Creek Nation? A Yes, sir.
Q Got your land, have you? A Yes, sir.
Q You have been engaged recently in the field for the Dawes Commission securing evidence about Creek citizens or new borns? A Yes, sir.
Q Have you a list of children for whom application could not be made and about whom you have succeeded in obtaining some information? A Yes, sir.
Q You may state the conditions and the names of these children? You desire to make application for them? A Yes, sir.
Q Name them. A John Lewis, Hutchechuppa, Nona Lewis, Hutchechuppa, have three children--one over three years old named Eddie-- another (a girl) over two years old--still another (also a girl) about one year old. Post Office, Henryetta, Indian Territory.
Q This is the information you received from relatives right around Henryetta, Indian Territory, on April 18, 1905? A Yes, sir.
Q Were you informed that the parents of these children were unwilling to make application for their enrollment? A Yes, sir.
Q This was the only way that the rights of these children would be saved? A Yes sir. I made every effort to obtain direct information from the parents but in every instance they refused to give their testimony.

  Lona Merrick, being duly sworn, states that the above and foregoing is a true and correct transcript of her stenographic notes as taken in said cause on said date.

            Lona Merrick

Subscribed and sworn to before me this 9 day of May 1905.

          Edw C Griesel
            Notary Public.

Applications for Enrollment of Creek Newborn
Act of 1905   Volume VIII

BIRTH AFFIDAVIT.

DEPARTMENT OF THE INTERIOR.
COMMISSION TO THE FIVE CIVILIZED TRIBES.

IN RE APPLICATION FOR ENROLLMENT, as a citizen of the Creek Nation, of Lillie Lewis, born ~~on the (blank) day of~~ June , 1902

Name of Father: John Lewis   a citizen of the   Creek   Nation.
   Hutchachuppa Town
Name of Mother: Mona Lewis   a citizen of the   Creek   Nation.
   Hutchachuppa Town
                              Postoffice   Henryetta, I.T.

AFFIDAVIT OF ATTENDING PHYSICIAN OR MID-WIFE.

UNITED STATES OF AMERICA, Indian Territory,
   Western   DISTRICT.

I, Leslie Fields , a mid-wife , on oath state that I attended on Mrs. Mona Lewis, wife of John Lewis ~~on the (blank) day of~~ sometime in June , 1902 ; that there was born to her on said date a female child; that said child was living March 4, 1905, and is said to have been named Lillie Lewis
                                       her
                                 Leslie x Fields
Witnesses To Mark: mark
   DC Skaggs
   Alex Posey

Subscribed and sworn to before me this 26 day of June, 1905.

                              Drennan C Skaggs
                                 Notary Public.

BIRTH AFFIDAVIT.

DEPARTMENT OF THE INTERIOR.
COMMISSION TO THE FIVE CIVILIZED TRIBES.

IN RE APPLICATION FOR ENROLLMENT, as a citizen of the Creek Nation, of Lillie Lewis , born on the 2 day of July, 1902

Name of Father: John Lewis   a citizen of the   Creek   Nation.
   Hutchechubbie[sic] Town

Applications for Enrollment of Creek Newborn
Act of 1905   Volume VIII

Name of Mother: Monnah Lewis (Fields)   a citizen of the   Creek   Nation.
Hutchechubbie Town
                                Postoffice   Henryetta I.T.

AFFIDAVIT OF MOTHER.   (Child present) 4/13-05

UNITED STATES OF AMERICA, Indian Territory,
   Western   DISTRICT.

    I, Monnah Lewis, on oath state that I am 29 years of age and a citizen by blood, of the Creek Nation; that I am the lawful wife of John Lewis, who is a citizen, by blood of the Creek Nation; that a female child was born to me on 2 day of July, 1902, that said child has been named Lillie Lewis, and is now living.

                                          her
                                 Monnah x Lewis
                                     mark

Witnesses To Mark:
   EC Griesel
   Jesse McDermott

    Subscribed and sworn to before me this 13" day of April, 1905.

    (Seal)   J. McDermott
                                      Notary Public.

              No one present
        ~~AFFIDAVIT OF ATTENDING PHYSICIAN OR MID-WIFE.~~

N.C. 594.
              DEPARTMENT OF THE INTERIOR,
     COMMISSIONER TO THE FIVE CIVILIZED TRIBES?[sic]
                Senora, I. T., October 11, 1905.

    In the matter of the application for the enrollment of Lillie Lewis as a citizen by blood of the Creek Nation.

         LESLIE FIELDS, being duly sworn, testified as follows:

    Through Alex Posey Official Interpreter:

    BY THE COMMISSIONER:
Q What is your name? A Leslie Fields.
Q How old are you? A I was a young girl during the Civil War.
Q What is your post office address? A Henryetta.

Applications for Enrollment of Creek Newborn
Act of 1905 Volume VIII

Q Are you a citizen by bloood[sic] of the Creek Nation? A Yes, sir.
Q To what town do you belong? A Hutchechuppa.
Q Do you know John and Mona Lewis? A Yes, sir. Mona is my daughter.
Q Have they a child named Lillie? A Yes, sir.
Q Is Lillie a boy or girl? A A girl.
Q You executed an affidavit as to the birth of this child did you not? A Yes, sir.
Q According to the affidavit executed by you, June 21, 1905, Lillie was born sometime in June, 1902. The mother's affidavit, executed June 13, 1905, states that Lillie was born July 2, 1902. Which of the two dates is correct? A The date given in the mother's affidavit is correct. I was mistaken as to the month.
Q Did you attned[sic] on Mona at the birth of this child? A Yes, sir.

---oooOOOooo---

I, D. C. Skaggs, on oath state that the above and foregoing is a full and true transcript of my stenographic notes as taken in said cause on said date.

D C Skaggs

Subscribed and sworn to before me this 30 day of Dec, 1905.

Edw C Griesel
Notary Public.

BIRTH AFFIDAVIT.

DEPARTMENT OF THE INTERIOR.
COMMISSION TO THE FIVE CIVILIZED TRIBES.

IN RE APPLICATION FOR ENROLLMENT, as a citizen of the Creek Nation, of Eddie Lewis, born on the 7 day of July , 1901

Name of Father: John Lewis   a citizen of the   Creek   Nation.
    Hutchachuppa Town
Name of Mother: Mona Lewis   a citizen of the   Creek   Nation.
    Hutchachuppa Town
                     Postoffice   Henryetta, I.T.

Applications for Enrollment of Creek Newborn
Act of 1905 Volume VIII

AFFIDAVIT OF MOTHER.

UNITED STATES OF AMERICA, Indian Territory,
Western DISTRICT. }

I, Mona Lewis , on oath state that I am 21 years of age and a citizen by blood , of the Creek Nation; that I am the lawful wife of John Lewis , who is a citizen, by blood of the Creek Nation; that a male child was born to me on 7 day of July , 1901 , that said child has been named Eddie Lewis , and was living March 4, 1905.

            her
          Mona x Lewis
Witnesses To Mark: mark
{ DC Skaggs
  Alex Posey

Subscribed and sworn to before me this 21st day of June , 1905.

         Drennan C Skaggs
           Notary Public.

AFFIDAVIT OF ATTENDING PHYSICIAN OR MID-WIFE.

UNITED STATES OF AMERICA, Indian Territory,
Western DISTRICT. }

I, Leslie Fields , a mid-wife , on oath state that I attended on Mrs. Mona Lewis, wife of John Lewis on the 7 day of July , 1901 ; that there was born to her on said date a male child; that said child was living March 4, 1905, and is said to have been named Eddie Lewis

           her
         Leslie x Fields
Witnesses To Mark: mark
{ DC Skaggs
  Alex Posey

Subscribed and sworn to before me this 21 day of June , 1905.

         Drennan C Skaggs
           Notary Public.

Applications for Enrollment of Creek Newborn
Act of 1905 Volume VIII

BIRTH AFFIDAVIT.

DEPARTMENT OF THE INTERIOR.
COMMISSION TO THE FIVE CIVILIZED TRIBES.

IN RE APPLICATION FOR ENROLLMENT, as a citizen of the Creek Nation, of Mose Lewis, born on the 28 day of June, 1904

Name of Father: John Lewis   a citizen of the   Creek   Nation.
Hutchechubbie[sic] Town
Name of Mother: Monnah Lewis (Fields)   a citizen of the   Creek   Nation.
Hutchechubbie Town
                        Postoffice   Henryetta I.T.

AFFIDAVIT OF MOTHER.   (Child present) 4/13-05

UNITED STATES OF AMERICA, Indian Territory, ⎫
       Western   DISTRICT.   ⎭

I, Monnah Lewis, on oath state that I am 29 years of age and a citizen by blood, of the Creek Nation; that I am the lawful wife of John Lewis, who is a citizen, by blood of the Creek Nation; that a male child was born to me on 28 day of June, 1904, that said child has been named Mose Lewis, and is now living.

                                her
                        Monnah x Lewis
Witnesses To Mark: mark
 ⎧ EC Griesel
 ⎩ Jesse McDermott

Subscribed and sworn to before me this 13" day of April, 1905.

(Seal)   J. McDermott
                                        Notary Public.

BIRTH AFFIDAVIT.

DEPARTMENT OF THE INTERIOR.
COMMISSION TO THE FIVE CIVILIZED TRIBES.

IN RE APPLICATION FOR ENROLLMENT, as a citizen of the Creek Nation, of Mosey Lewis, born on the 28 day of June, 1904

Name of Father: John Lewis   a citizen of the   Creek   Nation.
Name of Mother: Manna Lewis   a citizen of the   Creek   Nation.

Applications for Enrollment of Creek Newborn
Act of 1905   Volume VIII

Postoffice   Henryetta, Ind. Terr.

AFFIDAVIT OF MOTHER.

UNITED STATES OF AMERICA, Indian Territory,
Western DISTRICT.

I, Manna Lewis, on oath state that I am 27 years of age and a citizen by Blood, of the Creek Nation; that I am the lawful wife of John Lewis, who is a citizen, by Blood of the Creek Nation; that a male child was born to me on 28th day of June, 1904, that said child has been named Mosey Lewis, and was living March 4, 1905.

                                    her
                           Manna x Lewis
Witnesses To Mark: mark
{ Charles Powell
  John Bastable

Subscribed and sworn to before me this 25th day of March, 1905.

                            J. O. Hamilton
                            Notary Public.

AFFIDAVIT OF ATTENDING PHYSICIAN OR MID-WIFE.

UNITED STATES OF AMERICA, Indian Territory,
Western DISTRICT.

I, Rosanna Brown, a midwife, on oath state that I attended on Mrs. Manna Lewis, wife of John Lewis on the 28th day of June, 1904; that there was born to her on said date a male child; that said child was living March 4, 1905, and is said to have been named Mosey Lewis

                            Rosanna Brown
Witnesses To Mark:
{

Subscribed and sworn to before me this 1st day of April, 1905.

                            J. O. Hamilton
                            Notary Public.

Applications for Enrollment of Creek Newborn
Act of 1905 Volume VIII

CERTIFICATE OF RECORD.

United States of America,
INDIAN TERRITORY, } ss.
Northern District.

I, *CHARLES A. DAVIDSON*, Clerk of the United States Court in the Northern District, Indian Territory, do hereby certify that the instrument hereto attached was filed for record in my office the 1 day of Mch 1902 at M., and duly recorded in Book 226, Marriage Record, Page 171

WITNESS my hand and seal of said Court at Muscogee, in said Territory, this 2 day of Mch A. D. 190 2

Chas. A. Davidson   Clerk.
By   Deputy.

MARRIAGE LICENSE

United States of America,
INDIAN TERRITORY, } ss.   *No.* **368**
Northern District.

To Any Person Authorized by Law to Solemnize Marriage---Greeting:

You are Hereby Commanded to Solemnize the Rite and publish the Banns of Matrimony between Mr. Joseph Vance of Red Fork, in the Indian Territory, aged 20 years and Miss Ora M. Austin of Red Fork in the Indian Territory aged 16 years according to law, and do you officially sign and return this License to the parties therein named.

WITNESS my hand and official seal at Muscogee Indian Territory this 25" day of January A.D. 190 2

Chas. A. Davidson
Clerk of the U.S. Court

By T. A. Chandler   Deputy

Applications for Enrollment of Creek Newborn
Act of 1905   Volume VIII

CERTIFICATE OF MARRIAGE.

United States of America,
   INDIAN TERRITORY, } ss.
   Northern District.

I, Marion Baker , *a Minister of the Gospel, DO HEREBY CERTIFY that on the* 28 *day of* January *A. D.* 1902, *I did duly and according to law as commanded in the foregoing License, solemnize the Rite and publish the Banns of Matrimony between the parties therein named.*

WITNESS my hand this 28 *day of* January A. D. 1902

My credentials are recorded in the office of the Clerk of the United States Court, Indian Territory, Northern District, Book B *, Page* 44 .

Marion Baker
A Minister of the Gospel

Note—This License and Certificate of Marriage must be returned to the Office of the Clerk of the United States Court in the Northern District, Indian Territory, from whence it was issued, within sixty days from the date thereof, or the party to whom the license was issued will be liable in the amount of the One Hundred Dollars ($100.00)

BIRTH AFFIDAVIT.

DEPARTMENT OF THE INTERIOR.
COMMISSION TO THE FIVE CIVILIZED TRIBES.

IN RE APPLICATION FOR ENROLLMENT, as a citizen of the Creek Nation, of William Mellette Vance, born on the 31 day of January, 1904

Name of Father: Joseph Vance   a citizen of the Creek Nation.
Name of Mother: Ora Myrtle Vance   ~~a citizen of the~~ no a citizen Nation.

Postoffice   Red Fork, Indian Territory

AFFIDAVIT OF MOTHER.

UNITED STATES OF AMERICA, Indian Territory,
   Western Judicial   DISTRICT. }

I, Ora Myrtle Vance , on oath state that I am 20 years of age ~~and a citizen by~~ (blank) , ~~of the~~ (blank) ~~Nation~~; that I am the lawful wife of Joseph Vance , who is a citizen, by blood of the Creek Nation; that a male child was born to me on 31th[sic] day of January , 1904 , that said child has been named William Mellette Vance , and was living March 4, 1905.

Applications for Enrollment of Creek Newborn
Act of 1905   Volume VIII

                                        Mrs Ora Myrtle Vance
Witnesses To Mark:
{

Subscribed and sworn to before me this   12 day of May , 1905.

                                        W. S. McCluskey
My Commission Expires April 28th, 1907   Notary Public.

AFFIDAVIT OF ATTENDING PHYSICIAN OR MID-WIFE.

UNITED STATES OF AMERICA, Indian Territory, ⎫
     Western Judicial   DISTRICT.   ⎬
                                           ⎭

I, John C. W. Bland , a Practicing Physician , on oath state that I attended on Mrs. Ora Myrtle Vance, wife of Joseph Vance on the 31th[sic] day of January , 1904; that there was born to her on said date a male child; that said child was living March 4, 1905, and is said to have been named William Mellette Vance

                                        John C. W. Bland, M.D.
Witnesses To Mark:
{

Subscribed and sworn to before me this 17th day of May , 1905.

                                        W. S. McCluskey
My Commission Expires April 28th, 1907   Notary Public.

(The above Birth Affidavit given again.)

NC-595.

                         Muskogee, Indian Territory, August 10, 1905.

Ora Myrtle Vance,
     c/o Joseph Vance,
          Red Fork, Indian Territory.

Dear Madam:

In the matter of the application for the enrollment of your minor son Mellette Vance as a citizen by blood of the Creek Nation it will be necessary for you to file with this office either the original or a certified copy of the marriage license and certificate showing marriage between you and Joseph Vance, the father of said child.

Applications for Enrollment of Creek Newborn
Act of 1905 Volume VIII

Respectfully,

Acting Commissioner.

BIRTH AFFIDAVIT.

DEPARTMENT OF THE INTERIOR.
COMMISSION TO THE FIVE CIVILIZED TRIBES.

IN RE APPLICATION FOR ENROLLMENT, as a citizen of the Creek Nation, of Cleller Brown, born on the 22nd day of June, 1904

Name of Father: Jackson Brown   a citizen of the   Creek   Nation.
Name of Mother: Laura Brown   a citizen of the United States Nation.

Postoffice   Krebs, Ind. Ter.

AFFIDAVIT OF MOTHER.

UNITED STATES OF AMERICA, Indian Territory,
Central   DISTRICT.

I, Laura Brown, on oath state that I am 22 years of age and a citizen by *(blank)*, of the United States ~~Nation~~; that I am the lawful wife of Jackson Brown, who is a citizen, by blood of the Creek Nation; that a female child was born to me on 22nd day of June, 1904, that said child has been named Cleller Brown, and was living March 4, 1905.

laura[sic] Brown

Witnesses To Mark:
{

Subscribed and sworn to before me this 16 day of Aug, 1905.

W.J. Oglesby
Notary Public.

Applications for Enrollment of Creek Newborn
Act of 1905   Volume VIII

AFFIDAVIT OF ATTENDING PHYSICIAN OR MID-WIFE.

UNITED STATES OF AMERICA, Indian Territory,
  Central   DISTRICT.

I, Dollie Hill , a mid-wife , on oath state that I attended on Mrs. Laura Brown , wife of Jackson Brown on the 22 day of June , 1904 ; that there was born to her on said date a female child; that said child was living March 4, 1905, and is said to have been named Cleller Brown

x   Dollie Hill

Witnesses To Mark:
  A Harrington
  J H Elliott

Subscribed and sworn to before me this 21st day of Aug, 1905.

J H Elliott
Notary Public.
My com exp. July 4, 1908.

BIRTH AFFIDAVIT.

DEPARTMENT OF THE INTERIOR.
COMMISSION TO THE FIVE CIVILIZED TRIBES.

IN RE APPLICATION FOR ENROLLMENT, as a citizen of the Creek Nation, of Cleller Brown, born on the 22 day of June , 1904

Name of Father:	Jackson Brown	a citizen of the	Creek	Nation.
Name of Mother:	Laura Brown	a citizen of the	U.S.	Nation.

Postoffice   Krebs, I. T.

AFFIDAVIT OF MOTHER.

UNITED STATES OF AMERICA, Indian Territory,
  Central   DISTRICT.

I, Laura Brown , on oath state that I am 22 years of age and a citizen by birth , of the United States Nation; that I am the lawful wife of Jackson Brown , who is a citizen, by blood of the Creek Nation; that a Female child was born to me on 22 day of June , 1905[sic] , that said child has been named Cleller Brown , and is now living.

Laura x Brown

Applications for Enrollment of Creek Newborn
Act of 1905 Volume VIII

Witnesses To Mark:
  { Sallie B Oglesby
  { Eliza Hendrickson

Subscribed and sworn to before me this 29 day of March , 1905.

          W.J. Oglesby
            Notary Public.

AFFIDAVIT OF ATTENDING PHYSICIAN OR MID-WIFE.

UNITED STATES OF AMERICA, Indian Territory,
  Central   DISTRICT.

  I, Dollie Hill , a Midwife , on oath state that I attended on Mrs. Laura Brown , wife of Jackson Brown on the 22 day of   June , 1904 ; that there was born to her on said date a Female child; that said child ~~is now~~ was living March 4, 1905, and is said to have been named Cleller[sic]

          x Dollie Hill

Witnesses To Mark:
  { Lynn Glover
  { Wm Barry

Subscribed and sworn to before me this 29 day of March, 1905.

          J.W. Oglesby
            Notary Public.

Applications for Enrollment of Creek Newborn
Act of 1905 Volume VIII

On Cr. Card 44348

CERTIFICATE OF RECORD OF MARRIAGES

UNITED STATES OF AMERICA
THE INDIAN TERRITORY ⎬ SCT.
CENTRAL DISTRICT

I, E. J FANNIN, Clerk of the United States Court in the Indian Territory and District aforesaid, DO HEREBY CERTIFY that the License for and Certificate of the Marriage of

Mr. Jack Brown   and Miss Laura Harrington

were filed in my office in said Territory and District the 13 day of   June A.D. 1899   and duly recorded in Book 8 of Marriage Record, Page 418

WITNESS my hand and seal of said Court, at South McAlester this 6 day of   July   A. D. 1899

E. J. FANNIN, Clerk.
By   Deputy.

MARRIAGE LICENSE

UNITED STATES OF AMERICA
THE INDIAN TERRITORY ⎬ SS.
CENTRAL DISTRICT.

To Any Person Authorized by Law to Solemnize Marriage---GREETING:

You are hereby commanded to solemnize the Rite and publish the Bans of Matrimony between Mr. Jack Brown   *of*   Krebs , *in the Indian Territory, aged* 25   *years and Miss* Laura Harrington   *of*   Krebs   *in the Indian Territory aged*   18   *years according to law, and do you officially sign and return this License to the parties therein named.*

WITNESS, My hand and official seal this   10   *day of*   June   *A.D. 189*9

(No name given)
Clerk of the U.S. Court

Applications for Enrollment of Creek Newborn
Act of 1905 Volume VIII

(No name given)
            Deputy

CERTIFICATE OF MARRIAGE.

UNITED STATES OF AMERICA ⎫   *I,* A.B.S. Hunkapillar
THE INDIAN TERRITORY ⎬ ss.   *a*   Minister of the Gospel
CENTRAL DISTRICT. ⎭

DO HEREBY CERTIFY That on the   10   *day of*   June   *A. D. 189* 9
I did duly and according to law, as commanded in the foregoing License, solemnize the Rite and publish the Bans of MATRIMONY *between the parties therein named.*

Witness my hand this   10   *day of*   June   *A. D. 189* 9

My credentials are recorded in the office of the Clerk of the United States Court, Indian Territory, Central District, Book   A   *, Page*   32   .

                                    A.B.S. Hunkapillar
                                      a Minister

Note—This License and Certificate of Marriage must be returned to the Office of the Clerk of the United States Court of the Indian Territory, from whence it was issued, within sixty days from the date thereof, or the party to whom the license was issued will be liable in the amount of the One Hundred Dollars ($100.00)

NC-596.

                    Muskogee, Indian Territory, August 10, 1905.

Laura Brown,
     c/o Jackson Brown,
          Krebs, Indian Territory.

Dear Madam:

In the matter of the application for the enrollment of your minor daughter Cleller Brown as a citizen by blood of the Creek Nation it will be necessary for you to file with this office either the original or a certified copy of the marriage license and certificate showing marriage between you and Jackson Brown, the father of said child.

There is a discrepancy as to the date of the birth of said child in the evidence now on file in this office, it appearing from your affidavit that she was born on June 22, 1906 and from the affidavit of Dollie Hill, midwife, that she was born June 22, 1904.

For the purpose of correcting this discrepancy there is inclosed herewith a blank for proof of birth which has been properly filled out. You are requested to have the same

Applications for Enrollment of Creek Newborn
Act of 1905 Volume VIII

properly executed and return it to this office in the inclosed envelope together with the evidence of marriage above referred to.

         Respectfully,

CTD-41. Env.   Acting Commissioner.

N.C. 596.

         Muskogee, Indian Territory, October 26, 1905.

Jackson Brown,
  Krebs, Indian Territory.

Dear Sir:

  Receipt is acknowledged of your letter of October 21, 1905, asking when you can file for your new-born child Cleler[sic] Brown.

  In reply you are advised that the matter of the application for the enrollment of said Cleler Brown is pending before this office and that when final action is had in the matter, you will be duly notified.

         Respectfully,

              Commissioner.

BIRTH AFFIDAVIT.

DEPARTMENT OF THE INTERIOR.
COMMISSION TO THE FIVE CIVILIZED TRIBES.

  IN RE APPLICATION FOR ENROLLMENT, as a citizen of the Creek Nation, of David Cornell, born on the 28 day of February , 1903

Name of Father: Willie Cornell   a citizen of the Creek Nation.
Tulsa Little River Town
Name of Mother: Manie Cornell (nee Lovett) a citizen of the Creek Nation.
Tulsa Little River Town
        Postoffice Holdenville, Ind. Ter.

Applications for Enrollment of Creek Newborn
Act of 1905   Volume VIII

AFFIDAVIT OF MOTHER.

UNITED STATES OF AMERICA, Indian Territory,
Western DISTRICT.   Child is present

I, Manie Cornell, on oath state that I am 22 years of age and a citizen by blood, of the Creek Nation; that I am the lawful wife of Willie Cornell, who is a citizen, by blood of the Creek Nation; that a male child was born to me on 28 day of February, 1903, that said child has been named David Cornell, and was living March 4, 1905.

Manie Cornell

Witnesses To Mark:

Subscribed and sworn to before me this 27 day of March, 1905.

Drennan C Skaggs
Notary Public.

AFFIDAVIT OF ATTENDING PHYSICIAN OR MID-WIFE.

UNITED STATES OF AMERICA, Indian Territory,
Western DISTRICT.

I, Mary Harjo, a midwife, on oath state that I attended on Mrs. Manie Cornell, wife of Willie Cornell on the 28 day of February, 1903; that there was born to her on said date a male child; that said child was living March 4, 1905, and is said to have been named David Cornell

her
Mary x Harjo
mark

Witnesses To Mark:
  Alex Posey
  DC Skaggs

Subscribed and sworn to before me this 27 day of March, 1905.

Drennan C Skaggs
Notary Public.

Applications for Enrollment of Creek Newborn
Act of 1905   Volume VIII

NC-598.

Muskogee, Indian Territory, August 9, 1905.

Nettie G. Colmon,
   Mounds, Indian Territory.

Dear Madam:

In the matter of the application for the enrollment of your minor daughter Gladdys, the full name of said child is stated in one affidavit as Gladdys May Colmon and in another as Gladdys Leuna Colmon.

You are requested to immediately inform this office as to which of the above names, if either of them, is the correct name of said child.

Respectfully,

Acting Commissioner.

BIRTH AFFIDAVIT.

DEPARTMENT OF THE INTERIOR.
COMMISSION TO THE FIVE CIVILIZED TRIBES.

IN RE APPLICATION FOR ENROLLMENT, as a citizen of the C R E E K - - - - - - Nation, of Nettie Alice Colmon - - - - -, born on the 12th day of January, 1902
Name of Father: W.E. Colmon - - - - - - - - - - - - a ^non citizen of the C R E E K - - Nation.
Name of Mother: Nettie G. Colmon - - - - - - - - - a citizen of the   C R E E K - - Nation.

Postoffice   Mounds, I.T.

AFFIDAVIT OF MOTHER.

UNITED STATES OF AMERICA, Indian Territory, ⎱
  W E S T E R N - - - - - DISTRICT. ⎰

I, Nettie G. Colmon - - - - - - - - - - - - , on oath state that I am twenty four years of age and a citizen by Blood - - - - , of the C R E E K - - - - - - - - - - - Nation; that I am the lawful wife of W.E. Colmon - - - - - - - - - - - - - , who is a citizen, by not a citizen of the C R E E K - - - - - - - - Nation; that a female   child was born to me on 12th - - -- day of January - - - - - -- - - , 1902 , that said child has been named Nettie Alice Colmon - - - - - -, and was living March 4, 1905.

Applications for Enrollment of Creek Newborn
Act of 1905 Volume VIII

Nettie G. Colmon

Witnesses To Mark:
{

Subscribed and sworn to before me this first day of April - - - - -, 1905.

R Banton
Notary Public.

My Commission expires Feb. 21, 1907

AFFIDAVIT OF ATTENDING PHYSICIAN OR MID-WIFE.

UNITED STATES OF AMERICA, Indian Territory, }
W E S T E R N - - - - - DISTRICT.

I, Mrs E.A. Glenn - -- - - - - - - - - - - , a acting midwife, on oath state that I attended on Mrs. Nettie G. Colmon - - - - - -, wife of W.E. Colmon - - - - - - - - on the 12th day of January - - - -- , 1902 ; that there was born to her on said date a female child; that said child was living March 4, 1905, and is said to have been named Nettie Alice Colmon - - - -

Mrs E A Glenn

Witnesses To Mark:
{

Subscribed and sworn to before me this first day of April - - - - -, 1905.

R Banton
Notary Public.

My Commission expires Feb. 21, 1907

BIRTH AFFIDAVIT.

DEPARTMENT OF THE INTERIOR.
COMMISSION TO THE FIVE CIVILIZED TRIBES.

IN RE APPLICATION FOR ENROLLMENT, as a citizen of the C R E E K - - - - - - Nation, of Nettie Alice Colmon - - - - - -, born on the 12th day of January ---, 1902
                                  non
Name of Father: W.E. Colmon - - - - - - - - - - - - a ^ citizen of the C R E E K---- Nation.
                              nee Barber
Name of Mother: Nettie G. Colmon - - - - - - - - - a citizen of the C R E E K - - - Nation.

Postoffice MOUNDS, INDIAN TERRITORY

Applications for Enrollment of Creek Newborn
Act of 1905 Volume VIII

AFFIDAVIT OF MOTHER.

Child Present

UNITED STATES OF AMERICA, Indian Territory,
    WESTERN   DISTRICT.

      I, Nettie G. Colmon - - - - - - - - - - - - , on oath state that I am twenty three years of age and a citizen by Blood - - - - , of the C R E E K - - - - - - - - - - - Nation; that I am the lawful wife of W.E. Colmon - - - - - - - - - - - - - , who is a not citizen, by Blood - -- of the C R E E K - - - - - - - - Nation; that a female - - child was born to me on 12th -- day of January - - - - - - - , 1902 , that said child has been named Nettie Alice Colmon - - - - - - , and was living March 4, 1905.

Nettie G. Colmon

Witnesses To Mark:
{

      Subscribed and sworn to before me this 26 day of April , 1905.

Edw C Griesel

(Seal)   Notary Public.

AFFIDAVIT OF ATTENDING PHYSICIAN OR MID-WIFE.

UNITED STATES OF AMERICA, Indian Territory,
    WESTERN   DISTRICT.

      I, Mrs E.A. Glenn , a acting midwife , on oath state that I attended on Mrs. Nettie G. Colmon - - - - - - , wife of W.E. Colmon - - - - - - - - on the 12th day of January , 1902 ; that there was born to her on said date a female child; that said child was living March 4, 1905, and is said to have been named Nettie Alice Colmon

Mrs E A Glenn

Witnesses To Mark:
{

      Subscribed and sworn to before me this 25th day of April - - - - , 1905.

R Banton

My Commission expires Feb. 21, 1907   Notary Public.

Applications for Enrollment of Creek Newborn
Act of 1905 Volume VIII

BIRTH AFFIDAVIT.

DEPARTMENT OF THE INTERIOR.
COMMISSION TO THE FIVE CIVILIZED TRIBES.

IN RE APPLICATION FOR ENROLLMENT, as a citizen of the C R E E K - - - - - - Nation, of Gladys May Colmon - - - - - , born on the 20th day of January, 1904

Name of Father: W.E. Colmon - - - - - - - - - - - - a ^non citizen of the C R E E K - - Nation.
Name of Mother: Nettie G. Colmon - - - - - - - - - a citizen of the C R E E K - - Nation.

Postoffice   Mounds, Ind. Ter.

AFFIDAVIT OF MOTHER.

UNITED STATES OF AMERICA, Indian Territory,
W E S T E R N - - - - - DISTRICT.

I, Nettie G. Colmon - - - - - - - - - - - - , on oath state that I am twenty four years of age and a citizen by Blood - - - - , of the C R E E K - - - - - - - - - - - Nation; that I am the lawful wife of W.E. Colmon - - - - - - - - - - - - , who is ~~a citizen, by~~ not a citizen of the C R E E K - - - - - - - - Nation; that a female child was born to me on 20th - - -- day of January - - - - - -- - , 1904 , that said child has been named Gladys May Colmon - - - - - - , and was living March 4, 1905.

Nettie G. Colmon

Witnesses To Mark:

Subscribed and sworn to before me this first day of April - - - - - , 1905.

R Banton
My Commission expires Feb. 21, 1907   Notary Public.

AFFIDAVIT OF ATTENDING PHYSICIAN OR MID-WIFE.

UNITED STATES OF AMERICA, Indian Territory,
W E S T E R N - - - - - DISTRICT.

I, M.D. Taylor - - - - - - - - - - - , a Physician - - - , on oath state that I attended on Mrs. Nettie G. Colmon - - - - - - , wife of W.E. Colmon - - - - - - - - on the 20th day of January - - - - , 1904 ; that there was born to her on said date a female child; that said child was living March 4, 1905, and is said to have been named Gladys May Colmon - - - -

M.D. Taylor, M.D.

Applications for Enrollment of Creek Newborn
Act of 1905 Volume VIII

Witnesses To Mark:

{

Subscribed and sworn to before me this first day of April - - - - - , 1905.

R Banton

My Commission expires Feb. 21, 1907 Notary Public.

BIRTH AFFIDAVIT.

DEPARTMENT OF THE INTERIOR.
COMMISSION TO THE FIVE CIVILIZED TRIBES.

IN RE APPLICATION FOR ENROLLMENT, as a citizen of the C R E E K - - - - - - Nation, of
        u a
Gladdys L~~eony~~ Colmon - - - -- , born on the 20th day of January, 1904
                                  non
Name of Father: W.E. Colmon - - - - - - - - - - - - a ^ citizen of the C R E E K - - Nation.
                            nee Barber
Name of Mother: Nettie G. Colmon - - - - - - - - - a citizen of the C R E E K - - Nation.
(Broken Arrow)
                           Postoffice   Mounds, Indian Territory.

AFFIDAVIT OF MOTHER.   Child Present

UNITED STATES OF AMERICA, Indian Territory,
    WESTERN   DISTRICT.

I, Nettie G. Colmon - - - - - - - - - - - - , on oath state that I am twenty three years of age and a citizen by Blood - - - - - , of the C R E E K - - - - - - - - - - - Nation; that I am the lawful wife of W.E. Colmon - - - - - - - - - - - - , who is not a citizen by Blood - - - of the C R E E K - - - - - - - - Nation; that a female child was born to me on 20th day of January - - - - - - -- , 1904 , that said child has been named Gladdys ~~Leony~~ Leuna Colmon - - - - - - , and was living March 4, 1905.

                                            Nettie G. Colmon

Witnesses To Mark:

{

Subscribed and sworn to before me this 26 day of April , 1905.

(Seal)   Edw C Griesel
                                          Notary Public.

Applications for Enrollment of Creek Newborn
Act of 1905   Volume VIII

AFFIDAVIT OF ATTENDING PHYSICIAN OR MID-WIFE.

UNITED STATES OF AMERICA, Indian Territory, ⎫
   WESTERN   DISTRICT.   ⎬

I, M.D. Taylor - - - - - - - - - - - , a Physician - -, on oath state that I attended on Mrs. Nettie G. Colmon - - - - - -, wife of W.E. Colmon - - - - - - - - on the 20th day of January - -, 1904 ; that there was born to her on said date a female child; that said child was living March 4, 1905, and is said to have been named Gladdys ~~Leony~~ Leuna Colmon - - - -

M.D. Taylor, M.D.

Witnesses To Mark:

{

Subscribed and sworn to before me this 25th day of April - - - - -, 1905.

R Banton

My Commission expires Feb. 21, 1907   Notary Public.

N.C. 599

DEPARTMENT OF THE INTERIOR,
COMMISSIONER TO THE FIVE CIVILIZED TRIBES.
Muskogee, Indian Territory, August 12, 1905.

In the matter of the application for the enrollment of Ella and Leo Roberson as citizens by blood of the Creek Nation.

Philip Roberson, being duly sworn, testified as follows:

By Commissioner.

Q What is your name? A Philip Roberson.
Q How old are you? A I don't know. (Witness appears to be about forty five years of age.)
Q Can you read and write? A Yes, sir.
Q How do you spell your name? A R O B E R S O N.
Q Your children then are named Roberson? A Yes, sir.
Q And your wife is named Mary Roberson? A Yes, sir.

Witness is identified as Philip Roberson, roll No. 4846 Card No. 1470.

Mary Roberson is identified on Creek Indian care 2001, opposite roll No. 6231.

Applications for Enrollment of Creek Newborn
Act of 1905   Volume VIII

Q You are a Creek freedman are you? A Yes, sir.
Q And your wife is a Creek by blood? A Yes, sir.
Q Are these two children living? A Yes, sir.

I, Anna Garrigues, on oath state that the above and foregoing is a true and correct copy of my stenographic notes taken in said case on said date.

                                           Anna Garrigues

Subscribed and sworn to before
me this 12th day of August, 1905.   Edw C Griesel
                                                 Notary Public.

BIRTH AFFIDAVIT.

DEPARTMENT OF THE INTERIOR.
COMMISSION TO THE FIVE CIVILIZED TRIBES.

(Child present)
    IN RE APPLICATION FOR ENROLLMENT, as a citizen of the CREEK Nation, of Leo Robinson , born on the 2 day of August , 1901

Name of Father: Philip Robinson   a citizen of the   Creek   Nation.
Name of Mother: Mary   "   a citizen of the   "   Nation.

                                Postoffice   Bristow

AFFIDAVIT OF MOTHER.

UNITED STATES OF AMERICA, Indian Territory, ⎫
      WESTERN   DISTRICT. ⎭

    I, Mary Roberson , on oath state that I am 28 years of age and a citizen by blood , of the Creek Nation; that I am the lawful wife of Philip Robinson , who is a citizen, by Freedman of the Creek Nation; that a male child was born to me on 2 day of Aug. , 1901 , that said child has been named Leo Robinson , and is now living.

                                       Her
                                Mary x Roberson
Witnesses To Mark: mark
  { JY Miller
    EC Griesel

    Subscribed and sworn to before me this 17 day of March , 1905.

                                  Edw C Griesel
                                         Notary Public.

Applications for Enrollment of Creek Newborn
Act of 1905   Volume VIII

AFFIDAVIT OF ATTENDING PHYSICIAN OR MID-WIFE.

UNITED STATES OF AMERICA, Indian Territory,　}
　　WESTERN　　DISTRICT.

I, Cilla Miller, a midwife, on oath state that I attended on Mrs. Mary Robinson, wife of Philip Robinson on the 2 day of Aug, 1901; that there was born to her on said date a male child; that said child is now living and is said to have been named Leo Robinson

　　　　　　　　　　　　　　　　Her
　　　　　　　　　　　Cilla x Miller
Witnesses To Mark:　　　mark
　{ JY Miller
　 EC Griesel

Subscribed and sworn to before me this 17 day of March, 1905.

　　　　　　　　　　Edw C Griesel
　　　　　　　　　　　　　Notary Public.

BIRTH AFFIDAVIT.

DEPARTMENT OF THE INTERIOR.
COMMISSION TO THE FIVE CIVILIZED TRIBES.

IN RE APPLICATION FOR ENROLLMENT, as a citizen of the CREEK Nation, of Ellen Robinson, born on the 15 day of Sept., 1904

Name of Father: Philip Robinson　　　a citizen of the Creek Nation.
Name of Mother: Mary "　　　　　　a citizen of the   "   Nation.

　　　　　　　Postoffice　Bristow

Child present

AFFIDAVIT OF MOTHER.

UNITED STATES OF AMERICA, Indian Territory,　}
　　WESTERN　　DISTRICT.

I, Mary Robinson, on oath state that I am 28 years of age and a citizen by blood, of the Creek Nation; that I am the lawful wife of Philip Robinson, who is a citizen, by ~~blood~~ Freedman of the Creek Nation; that a female child was born to me on 15 day of Sept., 1904, that said child has been named Ellen Robinson, and is now living.

Applications for Enrollment of Creek Newborn
Act of 1905 Volume VIII

                                    Her
                              Mary x Roberson

Witnesses To Mark: mark
{   JY Miller
       EC Griesel

Subscribed and sworn to before me this 17" day of March, 1905.

                                  Edw C Griesel
                                      Notary Public.

AFFIDAVIT OF ATTENDING PHYSICIAN OR MID-WIFE.

UNITED STATES OF AMERICA, Indian Territory,
      WESTERN   DISTRICT.

    I, Cilla Miller, a midwife, on oath state that I attended on Mrs. Mary Robinson, wife of Philip Robinson on the 15 day of Sept., 1904; that there was born to her on said date a female child; that said child is now living and is said to have been named Ellen Robinson

                                    Her
                              Cilla x Miller

Witnesses To Mark: mark
{   JY Miller
       EC Griesel

Subscribed and sworn to before me this 17 day of March, 1905.

                                  Edw C Griesel
                                      Notary Public.

BIRTH AFFIDAVIT.
DEPARTMENT OF THE INTERIOR.
COMMISSION TO THE FIVE CIVILIZED TRIBES.

    IN RE APPLICATION FOR ENROLLMENT, as a citizen of the Creek Nation, of Maggie Ophelia Self, born on the 8 day of September, 1901

Name of Father: William J. Self   a citizen of the   Creek   Nation.
Broken Arrow Town
Name of Mother: Delila Self   a citizen of the United States Nation.

Applications for Enrollment of Creek Newborn
Act of 1905   Volume VIII

Postoffice   Morse, Indian Territory

AFFIDAVIT OF MOTHER.

UNITED STATES OF AMERICA, Indian Territory,
Western   DISTRICT.   Child is present

I, Delila Self , on oath state that I am 31 years of age and a citizen by *(blank)* , of the United States ~~Nation~~; that I am the lawful wife of William J. Self , who is a citizen, by blood of the Creek Nation; that a female child was born to me on 8 day of September , 1901 , that said child has been named Maggie Ophelia Self , and was living March 4, 1905.

Delila Self

Witnesses To Mark:

Subscribed and sworn to before me this 15 day of March , 1905.

Drennan C Skaggs
Notary Public.

AFFIDAVIT OF ATTENDING PHYSICIAN OR MID-WIFE.

UNITED STATES OF AMERICA, Indian Territory,
Western   DISTRICT.

I, Lucinda M. Parker , a mid-wife , on oath state that I attended on Mrs. Delila Self , wife of William J. Self on the 8th day of September , 1901 ; that there was born to her on said date a female child; that said child was living March 4, 1905, and is said to have been named Maggie Ophelia Self

Lucinda M Parker

Witnesses To Mark:
 EL Parker
 Clark Self

Subscribed and sworn to before me this 20th day of March, 1905.

My Commission Expires May 4 1907   Arthur *(Illegible)*
Notary Public.

Applications for Enrollment of Creek Newborn
Act of 1905   Volume VIII

BIRTH AFFIDAVIT.

DEPARTMENT OF THE INTERIOR.
COMMISSION TO THE FIVE CIVILIZED TRIBES.

IN RE APPLICATION FOR ENROLLMENT, as a citizen of the Creek Nation, of Golie Ray Self, born on the 17 day of February, 1904

Name of Father: William J. Self   a citizen of the   Creek   Nation.
Broken Arrow Town
Name of Mother: Delila Self   a citizen of the United States Nation.

Postoffice   Morse, Indian Territory

AFFIDAVIT OF MOTHER.

UNITED STATES OF AMERICA, Indian Territory, ⎫
         Western   DISTRICT.   ⎬   Child is present

I, Delila Self , on oath state that I am 31 years of age and a citizen ~~by~~ *(blank)* , of the United States ~~Nation~~; that I am the lawful wife of William J. Self , who is a citizen, by blood of the Creek Nation; that a female child was born to me on 17 day of February , 1904 , that said child has been named Golie Ray Self , and was living March 4, 1905.

                              Delila Self
Witnesses To Mark:
 {

Subscribed and sworn to before me this 15 day of March , 1905.

                              Drennan C Skaggs
                              Notary Public.

AFFIDAVIT OF ATTENDING PHYSICIAN OR MID-WIFE.

UNITED STATES OF AMERICA, Indian Territory, ⎫
         (blank)   DISTRICT.   ⎬

I, N. Stutsman , a Physician , on oath state that I attended on Mrs. Delila Self , wife of William J. Self on the 17 day of February , 1904 ; that there was born to her on said date a female child; that said child was living March 4, 1905, and is said to have been named Golie Ray Self

                              N. Stutsman M.D.

Applications for Enrollment of Creek Newborn
Act of 1905   Volume VIII

Witnesses To Mark:
- Elmer Everett
- Nettie Stutsman

Subscribed and sworn to before me this 22 day of Mach[sic] , 1905.

H. Witmore
Notary Public.
My Commission expires May 12 1908

N.C. 600

Muskogee, Indian Territory, August 29, 1905.

Chief Clerk,
Creek Land Office.

Dear Sir:

In compliance with your verbal request, you are hereby advised that the matter of the application for the enrollment of Maggie Ophelia Self, as a citizen of the Creek Nation, is now pending before the Department of the Interior the Interior.

Respectfully,

Commissioner.

N.C. 600

Muskogee, Indian Territory, August 29, 1905.

Chief Clerk,
Creek Land Office.

Dear Sir:

In compliance with your verbal request you are hereby advised that the matter of the application for the enrollment of Golie Ray Self as a citizen of the Creek Nation, is now pending before the Department of the Interior the Interior.

Respectfully,

Commissioner.

Applications for Enrollment of Creek Newborn
Act of 1905   Volume VIII

DEPARTMENT OF THE INTERIOR.
COMMISSION TO THE FIVE CIVILIZED TRIBES.

Muskogee, Indian Territory, September 6, 1905.

Henry G. Hains,
    Chief Clerk, Creek Enrollment Division,
    Muskogee, Indian Territory.
Dear Sir:

    In the matter of the application for the enrollment of Maggie Ophelia Self, as a citizen of the Creek Nation, you are advised that Creek Land Contest No. 837, entitled Maggie Ophelia Self, a minor, by her father and natural guardian, William O[sic]. Self, contestant, versus Rufus Cheestell Burton, by his mother and natural guardian, Mary Burton, contestee, has been held open pending the determination of said application.

    As soon as the application has been finally passed upon by the Honorable Secretary of the Interior, you will advise the allotment contest division so that the contest above referred to may be disposed of in the regular way.

                  Respectfully,

                            Wm. O. Beall
                            Acting Commissioner.

REFER IN REPLY TO THE FOLLOWING:

DEPARTMENT OF THE INTERIOR,
COMMISSIONER TO THE FIVE CIVILIZED TRIBES.

Muskogee, Indian Territory, September 6, 1905.

Henry G. Hains,
    Chief Clerk, Creek Enrollment Division,
    Muskogee, Indian Territory.
Dear Sir:

    In the matter of the application for the enrollment of Golie Ray Self, as a citizen of the Creek Nation, you are advised that Creek Land Contest No. 838, entitled Golie Ray Self, a minor, by his[sic] father and natural guardian, William O[sic]. Self, contestant, versus Annie Lila McIntosh, by her father and natural guardian, D. N. McIntosh, Jr., contestee, has been held open pending the determination of said application.

Applications for Enrollment of Creek Newborn
Act of 1905   Volume VIII

As soon as the application has been finally passed upon by the Honorable Secretary of the Interior, you will advise the Allotment Contest Division so that the contest above referred to may be disposed of in the regular way.

Respectfully,

Wm. O. Beall
Acting Commissioner.

BIRTH AFFIDAVIT.

DEPARTMENT OF THE INTERIOR.
COMMISSION TO THE FIVE CIVILIZED TRIBES.

IN RE APPLICATION FOR ENROLLMENT, as a citizen of the Muskogee Nation, of Hattie Lunsford, born on the 17 day of Sept, 1903

Name of Father: John C. Lunsford   a citizen of the   Muskogee   Nation.
Name of Mother: Martha Lunsford   a citizen of the   Muskogee   Nation.

Postoffice   Beggs, I.T.

AFFIDAVIT OF MOTHER.

UNITED STATES OF AMERICA, Indian Territory,
Western   DISTRICT.

I, Martha Lunsford, on oath state that I am 38 years of age and a citizen by Blood, of the Muskogee Nation; that I am the lawful wife of John C Lunsford, who is a citizen, by Blood of the Muskogee Nation; that a female child was born to me on 17th day of September, 1903, that said child has been named Hattie Lunsford, and was living March 4, 1905.

Martha Lunsford

Witnesses To Mark:
{ Al *(Illegible)*
{ Joe Friday

Subscribed and sworn to before me this 1st day of April, 1905.

O.K Peck
Notary Public.

Applications for Enrollment of Creek Newborn
Act of 1905 Volume VIII

AFFIDAVIT OF ATTENDING PHYSICIAN OR MID-WIFE.

UNITED STATES OF AMERICA, Indian Territory,
   Western   DISTRICT.

   I, A.H. Culp , a Physician , on oath state that I attended on Mrs. Martha Lunsford , wife of John C. Lunsford on the 17 day of Sept , 1903 ; that there was born to her on said date a female child; that said child was living March 4, 1905, and is said to have been named Hattie Lunsford

A.H. Culp M.D.

Witnesses To Mark:
   M.H. Hushfield
   D.H. Watson

   Subscribed and sworn to before me this 1st day of April , 1905.

O.K Peck
Notary Public.

NC-602

Muskogee, Indian Territory, August 10, 1905.

Nancy Kelly,
   Care of Reuben Kelly,
      Coweta, Indian Territory.

Dear Madam:

   In the matter of the application for the enrollment of your minor son, Perry Kelly, as a citizen by blood of the Creek Nation, this Office is unable to identify you upon the final roll of citizens by blood of the Creek Nation. It will be necessary, before the rights of said child can be finally determined, that you be so identified.

   You are therefore requested to immediately inform this Office as to under which name you are finally enrolled, the names of your parents and other members of your family, the Creek Indian Town to which you belong, and your final roll number as same appears upon your allotment certificate and deeds.

   Please give this matter your prompt attention.

Respectfully,

Acting Commissioner.

Applications for Enrollment of Creek Newborn
Act of 1905 Volume VIII

BIRTH AFFIDAVIT.

DEPARTMENT OF THE INTERIOR.
COMMISSION TO THE FIVE CIVILIZED TRIBES.

IN RE APPLICATION FOR ENROLLMENT, as a citizen of the Creek Nation, of Perry Kelly, born on the 14 day of December, 1904

Name of Father: Reuben Kelly   a citizen of the   Creek   Nation.
Name of Mother: Nancy Kelly   a citizen of the   Creek   Nation.

Postoffice   Coweta, I.T.

AFFIDAVIT OF MOTHER.

UNITED STATES OF AMERICA, Indian Territory, ⎫
     Western District[sic]   DISTRICT. ⎭

     I, Nancy Kelly, on oath state that I am 21 years of age and a citizen by birth, of the Creek Nation; that I am the lawful wife of Reuben Kelly, who is a citizen, by birth of the Creek Nation; that a male child was born to me on 14 day of December, 1904, that said child has been named Perry Kelly, and was living March 4, 1905.

                             Nancy Kelley[sic]

Witnesses To Mark:
{

     Subscribed and sworn to before me this 1st day of April, 1905.

                             R.C. Allen
                                     Notary Public.
My Com. Ex. Mch. 15, 1908.

AFFIDAVIT OF ATTENDING PHYSICIAN OR MID-WIFE.

UNITED STATES OF AMERICA, Indian Territory, ⎫
     Western   DISTRICT. ⎭

     I, Mary Bruner, a mid-wife, on oath state that I attended on Mrs. Nancy Kelly, wife of Reuben Kelly on the 14 day of December, 1904; that there was born to her on said date a male child; that said child was living March 4, 1905, and is said to have been named Perry Kelly

                             Mary Bruner

Applications for Enrollment of Creek Newborn
Act of 1905   Volume VIII

Witnesses To Mark:
{

    Subscribed and sworn to before me this 1st day of April, 1905.

R.C. Allen
Notary Public.

My Com. Ex. Mch. 15, 1908.

United States of America, Indian Territory, :
                                    ss.
    Western District.   :

    Before me, B. J. Beavers, a Notary Public, within and for the aforesaid District and Territory, this day personally appeared Phillip Perryman, to me well known for the last six months, who on oath, being first duly sworn, testified as follows sworn, declares that he is a Citizen by blood of the Creek Nation and 33 years of age; that he knows Nancy Kelly and that she was the wife of Reuben Kelley, deceased; that he has known the said Nancy Kelly for 10 years last past; that her maiden name was Nancy Warlecy; that her father's name was Warlecy sometimes called Warlecy Mitchell and her mother's name was Jennetta Warlecy; that the said Nancy Kelly, nee Warlecy, was a member of Coweta town and the mother of Perry Kelly and that the said Nancy Kelly, nee Warlecy, is a member of the Creek Nation by blood, all of which is true of my own personall[sic] knowledge.

Phillip Perryman

Subscribed and sworn to before me this 22nd day of August, A.D. 1905.

B.J. Beavers
Notary Public.

My commission expires December 19, 1908.

United States of America, Indian Territory, :
                                    ss.
    Western District.   :

    Before me, B. J. Beavers, a Notary Public, within and for the aforesaid, before me this day personally appeared Nancy Kelly, to me well known, who on oath declared that she is a Citizen of the Creek Nation by blood and about twenty-one or twenty-two years of age and a resident at the present time of Coweta, Indian Territory; that she is a member of Coweta Town; that she is the wife of Reuben Kelly, deceased and the mother of Perry Kelly, the son of Reuben Kelly; that her fathers[sic] name was Warlecy alias Warlecy Mitchell, a member of Locharpokar Town and lives near Red Fork at the present time; that her mother's name was Jennetta Warlecy; that this affiant enrolled under the name of

Applications for Enrollment of Creek Newborn
Act of 1905   Volume VIII

Nancy Warlecy and on the Creek Indian Roll No. 3080, all of which is true of my own knowledge; and that my brother's names are Jimmie Warlecy.

Nancy Kelly

Subscribed and sworn to before me this 22nd day of August, A.D. 1905.

B.J. Beavers
Notary Public.

My commission expires December 19th, 1908.

N.C. 603.

DEPARTMENT OF THE INTERIOR,
COMMISSIONER TO THE FIVE CIVILIZED TRIBES.
Muskogee, Indian Territory, January 25, 1906.

In the matter of the application for the enrollment of Nora Watson as a citizen by blood of the Creek Nation.

CHARLES S. SMITH, being duly sworn, testified as follows:

Q What is your name? A Charles S. Smith.
Q What is your age? [sic] Fifty six.
Q What is your post office address? A Eufaula.
Q Do you know Homer Watson? A No, sir
Q Do you know Emma McGirt? A Yes, sir.
Q Any kin to you? A My niece.
Q Is she living? A Yes, sir.
Q Do you know a child of hers named Nora Watson? A Yes, sir.
Q Is the child living? A Yes, sir.
Q Was it ever known by any other name than Nora? A Yes, Senora, Senora, Aurora and four or five other names.
Q Do you think Nora and Aurora are the same child? A Yes, sir.
Q Did you ever see the child? A Yes, sir.

Q We have an affidavit here by the mother she says the child's name is Aurora and was born June 1, 1901, this child Nora was born on the same day; you think this is the same child? A Yes, sir.
Q She didn't have two children born June 1, 1901 did she? A No, sir.
Q Are you sure of that? A Yes, sir.

I, Anna Garrigues, on oath state that the above and foregoing is a true and correct copy of my stenographic notes taken in said case on said date.

Applications for Enrollment of Creek Newborn
Act of 1905   Volume VIII

                                            Anna Garrigues
Subscribed and sworn to before me
this 25 day of January 1906.
                                            J McDermott
                                              Notary Public.

N.C. 603.

DEPARTMENT OF THE INTERIOR,
COMMISSIONER TO THE FIVE CIVILIZED TRIBES.
Muskogee, Indian Territory, February 12, 1906/[sic]

In the matter of the application for the enrollment of Nora Watson as a citizen by blood of the Creek Nation.

Emma McGirt, being duly sworn, testified as follows through Alex Posey official interpreter.

Q What is your name? A Emma McGirt.
Q What was your name before it was McGirt? A Watson; my maiden name was Smith.
Q Then you married Watson and now you are married to a man named McGirt?
A Yes, sir.
Q When did you marry McGirt? A Been married to him not quite three years.
Q What is the name of that child in your arms? A The proper name of the child is Nora Watson.
Q Did you ever call it anything else? A At first we called the child Aurora but decided on Nora as the name of the child.
Q Aurora and Nora are the same child and the proper name is Nora? A Yes, sir.
Q You didn't have two children born June 1, 1901? A No, sir only one.
Q How many children have you had altogether? A Three.
Q What are their names? A The oldest child was Louisa Morrison.
Q Is that child living? A Dead.
Q What is the name of the next one? A Nora Watson. The third is named George McGirt.
Q Is George enrolled? A Yes, sir.
Q When did Louisa die? A I stated awhile ago that she was dead. I have forgotten the time of the child's death but it was after they began filing.
Q How old was she when she died? A About three years old.
Q Is your child George McGirt living? A George died last September.
Q How old was he when he died? A About a year old.

I, Anna Garrigues, on oath state that the above and foregoing is a true and correct copy of my stenographic notes taken in said case on said date.

                                            Anna Garrigues

Applications for Enrollment of Creek Newborn
Act of 1905   Volume VIII

Subscribed and sworn to before me
this 12 day of February 1906.

                                        J. McDermott
                                        Notary Public.

United States of America   )
Indian Territory   )
)
Western Judicial District)

      Palmer Mickey   being duly sworn on oath, deposes and says that   he   is a citizen of the Creek Nation, Indian Territory and   30   years of age, and state[sic] that he has known Emma McGirt nee Smith for many years, and that on the 1st day of June 1901 there was born to the said   Emma McGirt nee Smith, a female child who is named Nora Watson the name of her mother is Emma McGirt, and the said child is now liveing[sic], and the mother of Nora Watson was enrolled as Emma ~~McGirt~~, Smith and her fathers[sic] name is Holmer[sic] Watson, all Creek citizens. Emma Smith McGirt father,s[sic] name is John Smith, her mother,s[sic] name is Loisa[sic] Smith. I further state that I have no claim and make this statement only as a disinterested party.   his
Witness to mark   Palmer Mickey x
E.K. Nix   mark
  Alfred F. Goat
      Subscribed and sworn to before me this the 9th day of October, 1905

                                        Chas Rider
                                        Notary Public.
My Commission expires July 11th, 1906

                        Roll Number 8086

United States of America   )
Indian Territory   )
)
Western Judicial District)

     Mollie Palmer   being duly sworn on oath, deposes and says that   she   is a citizen of the Creek Nation, Indian Territory and   35   years of age, and state[sic] that he[sic] has known Emma McGirt nee Smith for many years, and that on the 1st day of June 1901 there was born to the said Emma McGirt nee Smith, a female child who is named Nora Watson the name of her mother is Emma McGirt, and the said child is now liveing[sic], and the mother of Nora Watson was enrolled as Emma ~~McGirt~~, Smith and her fathers[sic] name is Holmer[sic] Watson, all Creek citizens.

Applications for Enrollment of Creek Newborn
Act of 1905   Volume VIII

Emma McGirt nee Smith father,s[sic] name is John Smith, her mother,s[sic] name is Loisa[sic] Smith. I further state that I have no claim and make this statement only as a disinterested party.

                                              his

Witness to mark   Palmer Mickey x

Alfred F. Goat   mark

   David Herrod

      Subscribed and sworn to before me this the 9th day of October, 1905

                                      Chas Rider

                                              Notary Public.

My Commission expires July 11th, 1906

                              Roll Number 8086

BIRTH AFFIDAVIT.

                         DEPARTMENT OF THE INTERIOR.
COMMISSION TO THE FIVE CIVILIZED TRIBES.

      IN RE APPLICATION FOR ENROLLMENT, as a citizen of the Creek Nation, of Nora Watson, born on the 1st day of June, and will be four (4) years old the 1st day of next June

Name of Father: Homer Watson   a citizen of the Creek Nation.
   Eufaula Canadian Town

Name of Mother: Emma McGirt   a citizen of the Creek Nation.
   Tuckabatche Town

                      Postoffice   Holdenville, I.T.

                      AFFIDAVIT OF MOTHER.

                                           Child present

UNITED STATES OF AMERICA, Indian Territory,
    Western   DISTRICT.

     I, Emma McGirt , on oath state that I am about 30 years of age and a citizen by blood , of the Creek   Nation; that I am not the lawful wife of Homer Watson, deceased, , who is were[sic] a citizen, by blood of the Creek Nation; that a female child was born to me on 1st   day of June and will be 4 years old the , 1 1st day of next June , that said child has been named Nora Watson , and was living March 4, 1905. That no one attended on me as physician or midwife at the time the child was born.

                                       Emma McGirt

Witnesses To Mark:

Applications for Enrollment of Creek Newborn
Act of 1905   Volume VIII

Subscribed and sworn to before me this 27 day of March , 1905.

         Drennan C Skaggs
         Notary Public.

BIRTH AFFIDAVIT.

DEPARTMENT OF THE INTERIOR.
COMMISSION TO THE FIVE CIVILIZED TRIBES.

IN RE APPLICATION FOR ENROLLMENT, as a citizen of the Creek Nation, of Aurora Watson, born on the 1st day of June, 1901

Name of Father: Homer Watson	a citizen of the Creek	Nation.
Name of Mother: Emma McGirt	a citizen of the Creek	Nation.

      Postoffice Eufaula, I.T.

AFFIDAVIT OF MOTHER.

UNITED STATES OF AMERICA, Indian Territory, ⎱
  Northern   DISTRICT. ⎰

  I, Emma Watson , on oath state that I am about 23 years of age and a citizen by blood , of the Creek   Nation; that I am the lawful wife of Homer Watson, who is a citizen, by blood of the Creek   Nation; that a female   child was born to me on 1st day of June , 1901; that said child has been named Aurora Watson , and is now living.

         Emma Watson

Witnesses To Mark:
{
   1904[sic]
Subscribed and sworn to before me this 18th day of January , 1902.

         Thos F. *(Illegible)*
         Notary Public.

AFFIDAVIT OF ATTENDING PHYSICIAN OR MID-WIFE.

UNITED STATES OF AMERICA, Indian Territory, ⎱
  Northern   DISTRICT. ⎰

  I, Jennie Barnett , a mid wife , on oath state that I attended on Mrs. Emma Watson , wife of Homer Watson on the 1st day of June , 1901 ; that there was born to

Applications for Enrollment of Creek Newborn
Act of 1905   Volume VIII

her on said date a female child; that said child is now living and is said to have been named Aurora Watson

                                          Jennie Barnett

Witnesses To Mark:

{

    Subscribed and sworn to before me this 18 day of January, 1902.

                                      Thos F. *(Illegible)*
                                            Notary Public.

NC-603

                                Muskogee, Indian Territory, August 10, 1905.

Emma McGirt,
    Holdenville, Indian Territory.

Dear Madam:

    In the matter of the application for the enrollment of your minor daughter, Nora Watson, born June 1, 1901, as a citizen by blood of the Creek Nation, it will be necessary for you to furnish this Office with the affidavits of two disinterested persons as to the birth of said child. Said affidavits must set forth said child's name, the date of her birth, the names of her parents and whether or not she was on living March 4, 1905.

    From the evidence on file, this Office, is unable to identify you upon the final roll of citizens by blood of the Creek Nation. It is necessary that you be so identified before the rights of your said child can be finally determined. You are therefore requested to immediately inform this office as to the name under which you were finally enrolled, the names of your parents and other members of your family and your final roll number as the same appears upon your allotment certificates and deeds.

    Please give this matter your immediate attention.

                                Respectfully,

                                                  Acting Commissioner.

NC-603.

                                Muskogee, Indian Territory, October 17, 1905.

Emma McGirt,
    Holdenville, Indian Territory.

Applications for Enrollment of Creek Newborn
Act of 1905   Volume VIII

Dear Madam:

In the matter of the application for the enrollment of your minor daughter, Nora Watson, born June 1, 1901, as a citizen by blood of the Creek Nation it will be necessary for you to furnish this office with the affidavits of two disinterested persons as to the birth of said child. Said affidavits must set forth said child's name, the date of her birth, the names of her parents and whether or not she was on living March 4, 1905.

From the evidence now on file this office is unable to identify you upon the final roll of citizens by blood of the Creek Nation. It is necessary that you be so identified before the rights of your said child can be finally determined.

You are, therefore, requested to immediately inform this office as to the name under which you were finally enrolled, the names of your parents and other members of your family and your final roll number as the same appears upon your allotment certificate and deeds.

Respectfully,

Commissioner.

BIRTH AFFIDAVIT.

DEPARTMENT OF THE INTERIOR.
COMMISSION TO THE FIVE CIVILIZED TRIBES.

IN RE APPLICATION FOR ENROLLMENT, as a citizen of the Creek Nation, of Nettie Sands, born on the 13th day of December, 1904

Name of Father: Phillip H. Sands   a citizen of the   Creek   Nation.
Name of Mother: Martha Sands   a citizen of the   Creek   Nation.

Postoffice   Sonora, I.T.

AFFIDAVIT OF MOTHER.

UNITED STATES OF AMERICA, Indian Territory,
Western   DISTRICT.

I, Martha Sands, on oath state that I am Twenty Two years of age and a citizen by Blood, of the Creek Nation; that I am the lawful wife of Philip H. Sands, who is a citizen, by Blood of the Creek Nation; that a Female child was born to me on 13th

Applications for Enrollment of Creek Newborn
Act of 1905   Volume VIII

day of December, 1904, that said child has been named Nettie Sands, and was living March 4, 1905.

Martha Sands

Witnesses To Mark:
{ J.W.V. Watson
  Sam Fowler

Subscribed and sworn to before me this 23rd day of March, 1905.

MY COMMISSION EXPIRES JULY 13th, 1908.   J.W. Fowler
                                                Notary Public.

AFFIDAVIT OF ATTENDING PHYSICIAN OR MID-WIFE.

UNITED STATES OF AMERICA, Indian Territory, }
    Western   DISTRICT.

I, Mulliah Yarhola, a Mid Wife, on oath state that I attended on Mrs. Martha Sands, wife of Phillip H. Sands on the 13th day of December, 1904; that there was born to her on said date a Female child; that said child was living March 4, 1905, and is said to have been named Nettie Sands

her
Mulliah x Yarhola
mark

Witnesses To Mark:
{ J.W.V. Watson
  Sam Fowler

Subscribed and sworn to before me this 23rd day of March, 1905.

MY COMMISSION EXPIRES JULY 13th, 1908.   J.W. Fowler
                                                Notary Public.

Applications for Enrollment of Creek Newborn
Act of 1905   Volume VIII

BIRTH AFFIDAVIT.

DEPARTMENT OF THE INTERIOR.
COMMISSION TO THE FIVE CIVILIZED TRIBES.

IN RE APPLICATION FOR ENROLLMENT, as a citizen of the Creek Nation, of John Reed, born on the 10 day of August, 1902
Name of Father: Porter Reed   a citizen of the   Creek   Nation. Tuckabatche Town
Name of Mother: Jennie Reed (nee Bruner)   a citizen of the   Creek   Nation. Weogufky Town

Postoffice   Holdenville, Ind. Ter.

AFFIDAVIT OF MOTHER.

UNITED STATES OF AMERICA, Indian Territory, } Child is present
Western   DISTRICT.

I, Jennie Reed, on oath state that I am about 22 years of age and a citizen by blood, of the Creek Nation; that I am the lawful wife of Porter Reed, who is a citizen, by blood of the Creek Nation; that a male child was born to me on 10 day of August, 1902, that said child has been named John Reed, and was living March 4, 1905.

Jennie Reed

Witnesses To Mark:
{

Subscribed and sworn to before me this 27 day of March, 1905.

Drennan C Skaggs
Notary Public.

AFFIDAVIT OF ATTENDING PHYSICIAN OR MID-WIFE.

UNITED STATES OF AMERICA, Indian Territory, }
Western   DISTRICT.

I, Leister Reed, a midwife, on oath state that I attended on Mrs. Jennie Reed, wife of Porter Reed on the 10 day of August, 1902; that there was born to her on said date a *(blank)* child; that said child was living March 4, 1905, and is said to have been named John Reed

Leister Reed

Witnesses To Mark:
{

Applications for Enrollment of Creek Newborn
Act of 1905   Volume VIII

Subscribed and sworn to before me this 27 day of March, 1905.

         Drennan C Skaggs
         Notary Public.

BIRTH AFFIDAVIT.

DEPARTMENT OF THE INTERIOR.
COMMISSION TO THE FIVE CIVILIZED TRIBES.

IN RE APPLICATION FOR ENROLLMENT, as a citizen of the Creek Nation, of Fanny Davis, born on the 11 day of August, 1903

Name of Father: Sampson Davis   a citizen of the Creek Nation. Tulmochussee Town
Name of Mother: Bettie Davis (nee Sullivan)   a citizen of the Creek Nation. Kialigee Town
       Postoffice Mellette, Ind. Ter.

AFFIDAVIT OF MOTHER.

UNITED STATES OF AMERICA, Indian Territory,
  Western   **DISTRICT.**   Child is present

  I, Bettie Davis, on oath state that I am about 21 years of age and a citizen by blood, of the Creek Nation; that I am the lawful wife of Sampson Davis, who is a citizen, by blood of the Creek Nation; that a female child was born to me on 11 day of August, 1903, that said child has been named Fanny Davis, and was living March 4, 1905.
            her
          Bettie x Davis
Witnesses To Mark: mark
 { Alex Posey
 { DC Skaggs

  Subscribed and sworn to before me this 4 day of April, 1905.

         Drennan C Skaggs
         Notary Public.

Applications for Enrollment of Creek Newborn
Act of 1905   Volume VIII

AFFIDAVIT OF ATTENDING PHYSICIAN OR MID-WIFE.

UNITED STATES OF AMERICA, Indian Territory, }
    Western   DISTRICT.

I, Annie Givens , a midwife , on oath state that I attended on Mrs. Bettie Davis , wife of Sampson Davis on the 11 day of August , 1903 ; that there was born to her on said date a *(blank)* child; that said child was living March 4, 1905, and is said to have been named Fanny Davis

                                    her
                            Annie x Givens
Witnesses To Mark: mark
{ Alex Posey
  DC Skaggs

Subscribed and sworn to before me this   4 day of April , 1905.

                            Drennan C Skaggs
                              Notary Public.

BIRTH AFFIDAVIT.

DEPARTMENT OF THE INTERIOR.
COMMISSION TO THE FIVE CIVILIZED TRIBES.

IN RE APPLICATION FOR ENROLLMENT, as a citizen of the Creek Nation, of Minnie Davis, born on the 4 day of December , 1901

Name of Father: Sampson Davis   a citizen of the   Creek   Nation.
Tulmochussee Town
Name of Mother: Bettie Davis (nee Sullivan)   a citizen of the   Creek   Nation.
Kialigee Town
                    Postoffice   Mellette, Ind. Ter.

AFFIDAVIT OF MOTHER.

UNITED STATES OF AMERICA, Indian Territory, }
    Western   DISTRICT.   Child is present

I, Bettie Davis , on oath state that I am about 21 years of age and a citizen by blood , of the Creek Nation; that I am the lawful wife of Sampson Davis , who is a citizen, by blood of the Creek Nation; that a female child was born to me on 4 day of December , 1901 , that said child has been named Minnie Davis , and was living March 4, 1905.
                                    her
                            Bettie x Davis
                                    mark

Applications for Enrollment of Creek Newborn
Act of 1905   Volume VIII

Witnesses To Mark:
{ Alex Posey
  DC Skaggs

    Subscribed and sworn to before me this 4 day of April , 1905.

                               Drennan C Skaggs
                               Notary Public.

AFFIDAVIT OF ATTENDING PHYSICIAN OR MID-WIFE.

UNITED STATES OF AMERICA, Indian Territory,
    Western   DISTRICT.

    I, Annie Givens , a midwife , on oath state that I attended on Mrs. Bettie Davis , wife of Sampson Davis on the 4 day of December , 1901 ; that there was born to her on said date a *(blank)* child; that said child was living March 4, 1905, and is said to have been named   Minnie Davis

                                 her
                          Annie x Givens
Witnesses To Mark: mark
{ Alex Posey
  DC Skaggs

    Subscribed and sworn to before me this 4 day of April , 1905.

                               Drennan C Skaggs
                               Notary Public.

BIRTH AFFIDAVIT.

DEPARTMENT OF THE INTERIOR.
COMMISSION TO THE FIVE CIVILIZED TRIBES.

    IN RE APPLICATION FOR ENROLLMENT, as a citizen of the Creek Nation, of Johnnie Stubblefield , born on the 7 day of September , 1903

Name of Father: John Stubblefield   a citizen of the United States Nation.
Name of Mother: Ida Stubblefield   a citizen of the   Creek   Nation.
Tulsa Little River Town

                        Postoffice   Holdenville, Ind. Ter.

Applications for Enrollment of Creek Newborn
Act of 1905   Volume VIII

AFFIDAVIT OF MOTHER.

UNITED STATES OF AMERICA, Indian Territory, } Child is present
Western   DISTRICT.

I, Ida Stubblefield, on oath state that I am 23 years of age and a citizen by blood, of the Creek Nation; that I am the lawful wife of John Stubblefield, who is a citizen, ~~by~~ *(blank)* of the United States Nation; that a male child was born to me on 7 day of September, 1903, that said child has been named Johnnie Stubblefield, and was living March 4, 1905.

                                        Ida Stubblefield
Witnesses To Mark:
{

Subscribed and sworn to before me this 27 day of March, 1905.

                                        Drennan C Skaggs
                                        Notary Public.

AFFIDAVIT OF ATTENDING PHYSICIAN OR MID-WIFE.

UNITED STATES OF AMERICA, Indian Territory, }
Western   DISTRICT.

I, Ella Hutson, a midwife, on oath state that I attended on Mrs. Ida Stubblefield, wife of John Stubblefield on the 7 day of September, 1903; that there was born to her on said date a *(blank)* child; that said child was living March 4, 1905, and is said to have been named Johnnie Stubblefield

                                        Ella Hutson
Witnesses To Mark:
{
Subscribed and sworn to before me this 27 day of March, 1905.

                                        Drennan C Skaggs
                                        Notary Public.

BIRTH AFFIDAVIT.

DEPARTMENT OF THE INTERIOR.
COMMISSION TO THE FIVE CIVILIZED TRIBES.

IN RE APPLICATION FOR ENROLLMENT, as a citizen of the Creek Nation, of Minnie Stubblefield, born on the 24 day of February, 1902

Applications for Enrollment of Creek Newborn
Act of 1905   Volume VIII

Name of Father: John Stubblefield   a citizen of the United States Nation.
Name of Mother: Ida Stubblefield (nee Hulsey) a citizen of the   Creek   Nation.
Tulsa Little River Town
                        Postoffice   Holdenville, Ind. Ter.

AFFIDAVIT OF MOTHER.

UNITED STATES OF AMERICA, Indian Territory, } <u>Child</u> is present
    Western   DISTRICT.

    I, Ida Stubblefield , on oath state that I am 23 years of age and a citizen by blood , of the Creek Nation; that I am the lawful wife of John Stubblefield , who is a citizen, ~~by~~ *(blank)* of the United States Nation; that a female child was born to me on 24 day of February , 1902 , that said child has been named Minnie Stubblefield , and was living March 4, 1905.

                                    Ida Stubblefield

Witnesses To Mark:
{

    Subscribed and sworn to before me this 27 day of March , 1905.

                                    Drennan C Skaggs
                                    Notary Public.

AFFIDAVIT OF ATTENDING PHYSICIAN OR MID-WIFE.

UNITED STATES OF AMERICA, Indian Territory, }
    Western   DISTRICT.

    I, Ella Hutson , a midwife , on oath state that I attended on Mrs. Ida Stubblefield , wife of John Stubblefield on the 24 day of February , 1902 ; that there was born to her on said date a *(blank)* child; that said child was living March 4, 1905, and is said to have been named Minnie Stubblefield

                                    Ella Hutson

Witnesses To Mark:
{
    Subscribed and sworn to before me this 27 day of March, 1905.

                                    Drennan C Skaggs
                                    Notary Public.

Applications for Enrollment of Creek Newborn
Act of 1905 Volume VIII

NC-608

Muskogee, Indian Territory, August 10, 1905.

Limbo Carr,
    Lenna, Indian Territory

Dear Sir:

    You are advised that it will be necessary for you to furnish this Office, in the matter of the application for the enrollment of your minor son, Washington Carr, born June 18, 1901, as a citizen by blood of the Creek Nation, the affidavits of two disinterested persons as to the birth of said child. Said affidavits must set forth the name of said child, the date of his birth, the names of his parents, and whether or not he was living March 4, 1905.

                        Respectfully,

                                      Acting Commissioner.

NC-608

Muskogee, Indian Territory, October 17, 1905.

Limbo Carr,
    Lenna, Indian Territory.

Dear Sir:

    You are advised that it will be necessary for you to furnish this office, in the matter of the application for the enrollment of your minor son Washington Carr, born June 18, 1901, as a citizen by blood of the Creek Nation, the affidavits of two disinterested persons as to the birth of said child. Said affidavits must set forth the name of said child, the date of his birth, the names of his parents and whether or not he was living March 4, 1905.

                        Respectfully,

                                      Commissioner.

BIRTH AFFIDAVIT.

DEPARTMENT OF THE INTERIOR.
COMMISSION TO THE FIVE CIVILIZED TRIBES.

    IN RE APPLICATION FOR ENROLLMENT, as a citizen of the Creek Nation, of Washington Carr, born on the 18 day of June, 1901

Applications for Enrollment of Creek Newborn
Act of 1905   Volume VIII

Name of Father: Limbo Carr   a citizen of the   Creek   Nation.
Coweta Town
Name of Mother: Millie Carr   a citizen of the   Creek   Nation.
Tuskegee Town

                Postoffice   Lenna, Ind. Ter.

AFFIDAVIT OF MOTHER.

UNITED STATES OF AMERICA, Indian Territory, }
   Western   DISTRICT.   Child is present

      I,   Millie Carr , on oath state that I am about 45 years of age and a citizen by blood , of the Creek Nation; that I am the lawful wife of Limbo Carr , who is a citizen, by blood of the Creek Nation; that a male child was born to me on 18 day of June , 1901 , that said child has been named Washington Carr , and was living March 4, 1905.

                              her
                          Millie x Carr
Witnesses To Mark: mark
   { Alex Posey
   { DC Skaggs

Subscribed and sworn to before me this   4 day of April , 1905.

                     Drennan C Skaggs
                          Notary Public.

AFFIDAVIT OF ATTENDING PHYSICIAN OR MID-WIFE.

UNITED STATES OF AMERICA, Indian Territory, }
   Western   DISTRICT.

                                                    my wife
      I, Limbo Carr , a (blank) , on oath state that I attended on ^ Mrs. Millie Carr , wife of (blank) on the 18 day of June , 1901 ; that there was born to her on said date a (blank) child; that said child was living March 4, 1905, and is said to have been named Washington Carr   his
                         Limbo x Carr
Witnesses To Mark: mark
   { Alex Posey
   { DC Skaggs

Subscribed and sworn to before me this   4 day of April , 1905.

                     Drennan C Skaggs
                          Notary Public.

Applications for Enrollment of Creek Newborn
Act of 1905 Volume VIII

United States of America } SS
Indian Territory
Western District

I Sissie Barnette[sic] on oath state that I was at Limbo Carr on June 18th 1901 That there was a male child there and I am sadisfied[sic] that it was borned[sic] to Mrs. ~~Limbo Carr~~ Mille[sic] Carr wife of Limbo Carr and it is now libing and is said to have been named Washington Carr.

                                        her   (Seal)
                           Sissie Barnette x
                                        mark

Witness to mark
    (Name Illegible)
    (Name Illegible)

Sworn and subscribed to before me this the 9 day of November 1905

                                      Preston Janway
                                          Notary Public

BIRTH AFFIDAVIT.

DEPARTMENT OF THE INTERIOR.
COMMISSION TO THE FIVE CIVILIZED TRIBES.

IN RE APPLICATION FOR ENROLLMENT, as a citizen of the Creek Nation, of Washington Carr, born on the 18 day of June, 1901

Name of Father: Limbo Carr   a citizen of the   Creek   Nation.
town *(Illegible)*
Name of Mother: Millie Carr   a citizen of the   Creek   Nation.
town Tuskegee
                              Postoffice   Lenna, Ind. Ter.

AFFIDAVIT OF MOTHER.

UNITED STATES OF AMERICA, Indian Territory,
    Western   **DISTRICT.**   Child present

    I, Millie Carr, on oath state that I am about 45 years of age and a citizen by Blood, of the Creek Nation; that I am the lawful wife of Limbo Carr, who is a citizen, by Blood of the Creek Nation; that a male child was born to me on 18 day of June, 1901, that said child has been named Washington Carr, and was living March 4, 1905.

Applications for Enrollment of Creek Newborn
Act of 1905   Volume VIII

                                      her
                                Millie Carr x
Witnesses To Mark: mark
{ T.J. Ingram
{ N B Clifton

Subscribed and sworn to before me this 9 day of November , 1905.

My Commission   Preston Janway
Expires May 19 1908   Notary Public.

AFFIDAVIT OF ATTENDING PHYSICIAN OR MID-WIFE.

UNITED STATES OF AMERICA, Indian Territory,
       Western   DISTRICT.

    I, Anna M Sitton , a midwife , on oath state that I attended on Mrs. Millie Carr, wife of Limbo Carr on the 18 day of June , 1901 ; that there was born to her on said date a male child; that said child was living March 4, 1905, and is said to have been named Washington Carr

                                      Anna Margaret Sitton

Witnesses To Mark:

{

    Subscribed and sworn to before me this 9 day of November, 1905.

                                      Preston Janway
                                        Notary Public.

NC-610

                          Muskogee, Indian Territory, August 10, 1905.

Charlie Reynolds,
    Cathay, Indian Territory.

Dear Sir:

    In the matter of the application for the enrollment of your minor son, Clarence Andrew Reynolds, born September 11, 1903, as a citizen by blood of the Creek Nation, it will be necessary for you to furnish this Office with the affidavits of two disinterested persons as to the birth of said child. Said affidavits must set forth said child's name, the

Applications for Enrollment of Creek Newborn
Act of 1905   Volume VIII

date of his birth, the names of his parents and whether or not he was living March 4, 1905.

Respectfully,

Acting Commissioner.

BIRTH AFFIDAVIT.

DEPARTMENT OF THE INTERIOR.
COMMISSION TO THE FIVE CIVILIZED TRIBES.

IN RE APPLICATION FOR ENROLLMENT, as a citizen of the Creek Nation, of Clarence Andrew Reynolds , born on the 11 day of September , 1903

Name of Father: Charley Reynolds   a citizen of the United States Nation.
Name of Mother: Ada Reynolds (nee Murray)   a citizen of the   Creek   Nation.
Broken Arrow Town
Postoffice   Cathay, Ind. Ter.

AFFIDAVIT OF MOTHER.

UNITED STATES OF AMERICA, Indian Territory, } Child is present
       Western   DISTRICT.

I, Ada Reynolds , on oath state that I am 17 years of age and a citizen by blood , of the Creek   Nation; that I am the lawful wife of Charley Reynolds , who is a citizen, ~~by~~ *(blank)* of the United States ~~Nation~~; that a male child was born to me on 11 day of September , 1903 , that said child has been named Clarence Andrew Reynolds , and was living March 4, 1905.

Ada Reynolds

Witnesses To Mark:
{

Subscribed and sworn to before me this 4 day of April , 1905.

Drennan C Skaggs
Notary Public.

Applications for Enrollment of Creek Newborn
Act of 1905 Volume VIII

AFFIDAVIT OF ATTENDING PHYSICIAN OR MID-WIFE.

UNITED STATES OF AMERICA, Indian Territory, }
    Western   DISTRICT.

my wife
I, Charley Reynolds , a~~—~~ *(blank)*, on oath state that I attended on ^ Mrs. Ada Reynolds , ~~wife of~~ *(blank)* on the 11 day of September , 1903 ; that there was born to her on said date a male child; that said child was living March 4, 1905, and ~~is said to have~~ has been named Clarence Andrew Reynolds

Charle[sic] Reynolds

Witnesses To Mark:
{

Subscribed and sworn to before me this 4 day of April , 1905.

Drennan C Skaggs
Notary Public.

DPARTMENT[sic] OF THE INTERIOR,
Commission to the five[sic] Civilized Tribes.

In Re Application for enrollment as a citizen of the Creek Nation, of Clarence Andrew Reynolds, born on the 11th day of September, 1903.
Name of Father: Charlie Reynolds, a citizen of the United States.
Name of Mother: Ada Reynolds, nee Ada Murray, a citizen of the Creek Nation.

United States of America,)
                          :
Indian Territory   ) ss.   Affidavit of witness to date of birth
                          :   etc. of Clarence Andrew Reynolds.
Western District   )

I, A. T. Brasher, on oath state that I am 63 years old and a citizen of the United States; that I have been well acquainted with Ada Murray, now Ada Reynolds, for about 9 years; that about 4 years ago she was married to Charlie Reynolds, a white man; that on or about the 11th day of September 1903 there was born unto the said Ada Reynolds, nee Ada Murray, a male child, that this child has been named Clarence Andrew Reynolds and was living on the 4th day of March 1905 and is living at the present time; that the said Ada Reynolds, nee Ada Murray, is a citizen by blood of the Creek Nation. I als[sic] on oath state that I have been acquainted with Charlie Reynolds, the husband of Ada Reynolds and the father of Clarence Andrew Reynolds for more than 4 years last past; that my post office address is Cathay, Creek Nation, Indian Territory.

A.T. Brasher

Applications for Enrollment of Creek Newborn
Act of 1905 Volume VIII

Subscribed and sworn to before me this 5th day of September, A.D. 1905.

                                                          Charles Buford

My commission expires   Notary Public.
July 3rd 1906.

United States of America,)
                                  :
Indian Territory   ) ss.   Affidavit of witness to date of birth etc.
                                  :   of Clarence Andrew Reynolds.
Western District   )

     I, A. J. Wiley, on oath state that I am 33 years old and a citizen of the United States; that I have been well acquainted with Ada Murray, now Ada Reynolds, for about 5 years; that about 4 years ago she was married to Charlie Reynolds, a white man; that the said Ada Reynolds, nee Ada Murray, is a citizen by blood of the Creek Nation; that on or about the 11th day of September 1903 there was born to the said Ada Reynolds, nee Ada Murray, a male child, that the same has been named Clarence Andrew Reynolds and was living on the 4th day of March 1905 and is living at the present time; that the father of the said child Clarence Andrew Reynolds is Charlie Reynolds, a white man, with whom I have been well acquainted for more than 5 years; that I have lived in the immediate neighborhood of the said Charlie Reynolds and Ada Reynolds, nee Ada Murray, his wife, for the last 5 years.

                                                  A. J. Wiley

Subscribed and sworn to before me this 5th day of September, A.D. 1905.

                                                 Charles Buford

My commission expires   Notary Public.
July 3rd 1906.

NC-611

                                 Muskogee, Indian Territory, August 10, 1905.

Carrie Morrison,
     Lenna, Indian Territory.

Dear Madam:

     In the matter of the application for the enrollment of your minor daughter, Hettie Ola Morrison, as a citizen by blood of the Creek Nation, it will be necessary for you to furnish this office with either the original or a certified copy of the marriage license, showing the marriage between you and Major Morrison, father of said child.

Applications for Enrollment of Creek Newborn
Act of 1905 Volume VIII

Respectfully,

Acting Commissioner.

CERTIFICATE OF RECORD.

United States of America, ⎫
   INDIAN TERRITORY,   ⎬ ss.
   Western District. ⎭

    I, **ROBERT P. HARRISON**, Clerk of the United States Court in the Western District, Indian Territory, do hereby certify that the instrument hereto attached was filed for record in my office the   3   day of   Nov   1902 at 2 P. M., and duly recorded in Book   N , Marriage Record, Page   316

    WITNESS my hand and seal of said Court at Muscogee, in said Territory, this   3   day of   Nov.   A. D. 1902

                            R P Harrison   Clerk.
By   R. S. Bayne   Deputy.

MARRIAGE LICENSE.
•••••••

United States of America, ⎫
   Indian Territory,   ⎬ ss.   No. **379**
   Western District. ⎭

To Any Person Authorized by Law to Solemnize Marriage---Greeting:

    You are Hereby Commanded to Solemnize the Rite and publish the Banns of Matrimony between Mr.   Major Morrison   of   Burney , in the Indian Territory, aged   18   years and Miss   Carrie Woods   of   Burney   in the Indian Territory aged   17   years according to law, and do you officially sign and return this License to the parties therein named.

    WITNESS my hand and official seal at Muscogee Indian Territory this   29"   day of   October   A.D. 1902

                            R.P. Harrison
                            Clerk of the U.S. Court
By   A.Z. English   Deputy

Applications for Enrollment of Creek Newborn
Act of 1905   Volume VIII

CERTIFICATE OF MARRIAGE.

••••••

United States of America,
   INDIAN TERRITORY, } ss.
   Western District.

    I, W.H. Colvard   , *a Minister of the Gospel, DO HEREBY CERTIFY that on the* 31   *day of*   October   *A. D.* 1902, *I did duly and according to law as commanded in the foregoing License, solemnize the Rite and publish the Banns of Matrimony between the parties therein named.*

    WITNESS my hand this 1st *day of*   November   *A. D.* 1902

    My credentials are recorded in the office of the Clerk of the United States Court, Indian Territory, Northern District, Book   (blank)   *, Page*   (blank)   .

A Minister of the Gospel

Elder, Wm H. Colvard

Note—This License and Certificate of Marriage must be returned to the Office of the Clerk of the United States Court in the Northern District, Indian Territory, from whence it was issued, within sixty days from the date thereof, or the party to whom the license was issued will be liable in the amount of the One Hundred Dollars ($100.00)

BIRTH AFFIDAVIT.

DEPARTMENT OF THE INTERIOR.
COMMISSION TO THE FIVE CIVILIZED TRIBES.

    IN RE APPLICATION FOR ENROLLMENT, as a citizen of the Creek Nation, of Hettie Ola Morrison , born on the 2 day of January, 1905

Name of Father: Major Morrison   a citizen of the   Creek   Nation.
Coweta Town
Name of Mother: Carrie Morrison   a citizen of the United States Nation.

              Postoffice   Lenna, Ind. Ter.

AFFIDAVIT OF MOTHER.

UNITED STATES OF AMERICA, Indian Territory,
    Western   **DISTRICT.** } Child is present

    I, Carrie Morrison   , on oath state that I am 18 years of age and a citizen by (blank) , of the United States Nation; that I am the lawful wife of Major Morrison , who is a citizen, by blood of the Creek   Nation; that a female   child was born to me

Applications for Enrollment of Creek Newborn
Act of 1905 Volume VIII

on 2 day of January, 1905, that said child has been named Hettie Ola Morrison, and was living March 4, 1905.

Carrie Morrison

Witnesses To Mark:
{

Subscribed and sworn to before me this 4 day of April, 1905.

Drennan C Skaggs
Notary Public.

AFFIDAVIT OF ATTENDING PHYSICIAN OR MID-WIFE.

UNITED STATES OF AMERICA, Indian Territory, }
    Western   DISTRICT.

I, Mary McCombs, a midwife, on oath state that I attended on Mrs. Carrie Morrison, wife of Major Morrison on the 2 day of January, 1905; that there was born to her on said date a female child; that said child was living March 4, 1905, and is said to have been named Hettie Ola Morrison

Mary McCombs

Witnesses To Mark:
{

Subscribed and sworn to before me this 4 day of April, 1905.

Drennan C Skaggs
Notary Public.

NC-612

Muskogee, Indian Territory, August 10, 1905.

Sophie Collins,
    Care of Lewis Collins,
        Lenna, Indian Territory.

Dear Madam:

It appears from your affidavit on file with the records of this Office as to the birth of your minor child, Noah Collins, born February 6, 1905, that there was no attending physician or midwife at the birth of said child.

Applications for Enrollment of Creek Newborn
Act of 1905   Volume VIII

You are advised that in lieu of an affidavit of the attending physician or midwife, it will be necessary for you to furnish this Office, in the matter of the application for the enrollment of said child as a citizen by blood of the Creek Nation, with the affidavits of two disinterested persons relative to his birth. Said affidavits must set forth said child's name, the date of his birth, the names of his parents, and whether or not he was living on March 4, 1905.

This matter should receive your prompt attention.

                Respectfully,

                        Acting Commissioner.

BIRTH AFFIDAVIT.

DEPARTMENT OF THE INTERIOR.
COMMISSION TO THE FIVE CIVILIZED TRIBES.

NC 612

IN RE APPLICATION FOR ENROLLMENT, as a citizen of the Creek Nation, of Noah Collins , born on the 6 day of february[sic] , 1905

Name of Father: Lewis Collins   a citizen of the   Creek   Nation.
    Coweta
Name of Mother: Sophie Collins   a citizen of the   *(blank)*   Nation.
    fish pond
                    Postoffice   Lenna

AFFIDAVIT OF MOTHER.

UNITED STATES OF AMERICA, Indian Territory, ⎫
    Western   **DISTRICT.**   ⎭   Child. present

    I, Sophie Collins , on oath state that I am 25 years of age and a citizen by Blood , of the Creek Nation; that I am the lawful wife of Lewis Collins , who is a citizen, by Blood of the Creek Nation; that a male child was born to me on 6 day of february[sic] , 1905 , that said child has been named Noah Collins , and was living March 4, 1905.   her

                                Sophie x Collins
Witnesses To Mark: mark
  { V.E. Hill
     Zun Ott

Applications for Enrollment of Creek Newborn
Act of 1905   Volume VIII

Subscribed and sworn to before me this 6 day of August , 1905.

              Preston Janway
                Notary Public.

AFFIDAVIT OF ATTENDING PHYSICIAN OR MID-WIFE.

UNITED STATES OF AMERICA, Indian Territory, }
 Western   DISTRICT.

  I, Louise Morrison , a midwife , on oath state that I attended on Mrs. Sophie Collins , wife of Lewis Collins on the 6 day of february[sic] , 1905 ; that there was born to her on said date a male child; that said child was living March 4, 1905, and is said to have been named Noah Collins The child was borned[sic] when I got there but I attended to the child and woman

              Louise Morrison

Witnesses To Mark:
{

Subscribed and sworn to before me 24 day of August, 1905.

 My Commission   Preston Janway
  Expires May 19 1908   Notary Public.

BIRTH AFFIDAVIT.
        DEPARTMENT OF THE INTERIOR.
      COMMISSION TO THE FIVE CIVILIZED TRIBES.

  IN RE APPLICATION FOR ENROLLMENT, as a citizen of the Creek Nation, of Noah Collins , born on the 6 day of February , 1905

Name of Father: Lewis Collins   a citizen of the Creek Nation.
 Coweta Town
Name of Mother: Sophie Collins   a citizen of the Creek Nation.
 Fish Pond Town
        Postoffice Lenna, Ind. Terr.

Applications for Enrollment of Creek Newborn
Act of 1905   Volume VIII

AFFIDAVIT OF MOTHER.

UNITED STATES OF AMERICA, Indian Territory,
Western DISTRICT.   Child. present

    I, Sophie Collins , on oath state that I am about 25 years of age and a citizen by blood , of the Creek Nation; that I am the lawful wife of Lewis Collins , who is a citizen, by blood of the Creek Nation; that a male child was born to me on 6 day of February , 1905 , that said child has been named Noah Collins , and was living March 4, 1905. That there was no one in attendance at the birth of the child.

                                             her
                                  Sophie x Collins
Witnesses To Mark: mark
  { DC Skaggs
    Alex Posey

    Subscribed and sworn to before me this 4 day of April , 1905.

                              Drennan C Skaggs
                                  Notary Public.

NC-613

                        Muskogee, Indian Territory, August 11, 1905.

Mulsie Beaver,
    Care of Byer Beaver.
        Eufaula, Indian Territory.

Dear Madam:

    In the matter of the application for the enrollment of your minor son, Walter Beaver, as a citizen by blood of the Creek Nation, it will be necessary for you to furnish this Office with the affidavit of the attending midwife relative to his birth. The date of the birth of this child is omitted from the affidavit of Lucy Wesley, midwife, which is now on file with the records of this Office.

    There is herewith enclosed blank for proof of birth, which has been filled out. You are requested to have said Lucy Wesley appear before a notary public and swear to same, and when sworn to, the same should be returned to this Office in the enclosed envelope. In case the said Lucy Wesley is unable to write and her signature is by mark, the same must be attested by two disinterested witnesses. Be careful to see that the notary public before whom the affidavit is sworn to, attaches his name and seal to the affidavit.

                            Respectfully,
JYM-10-1
Env   Acting Commissioner.

Applications for Enrollment of Creek Newborn
Act of 1905 Volume VIII

BIRTH AFFIDAVIT.

DEPARTMENT OF THE INTERIOR.
COMMISSION TO THE FIVE CIVILIZED TRIBES.

IN RE APPLICATION FOR ENROLLMENT, as a citizen of the Creek Nation, of Lecus Beaver, born on the 7 day of February, 1905

Name of Father: Poyer[sic] Beaver   a citizen of the   Creek   Nation.
Okfuske Town
Name of Mother: Mulsie Beaver   a citizen of the   Creek   Nation.
Eufaula Canadian Town
                 Postoffice   Eufaula, Ind. Ter.

Child present.

AFFIDAVIT OF MOTHER.

UNITED STATES OF AMERICA, Indian Territory,
     Western   DISTRICT.

     I, Mulsie Beaver, on oath state that I am about 30 years of age and a citizen by blood, of the Creek Nation; that I am the lawful wife of Poyer[sic] Beaver, who is a citizen, by blood of the Creek Nation; that a male child was born to me on 7 day of February, 1905, that said child has been named Lecus Beaver, and was living March 4, 1905.

                                     Mulsie Beaver

Witnesses To Mark:

     Subscribed and sworn to before me this 4 day of April, 1905.

                                       Drennan C Skaggs
                                         Notary Public.

AFFIDAVIT OF ATTENDING PHYSICIAN OR MID-WIFE.

UNITED STATES OF AMERICA, Indian Territory,
     Western   DISTRICT.

     I, Cinthia[sic] Corsar[sic], a mid-wife, on oath state that I attended on Mrs. Mulsie Beaver, wife of Poyer[sic] Beaver on or about the 7 day of February, 1905; that there was born to her on said date a male child; that said child was living March 4, 1905, and is said to have been named Lecus Beaver

                                     Cynthia Cosar

Applications for Enrollment of Creek Newborn
Act of 1905   Volume VIII

Witnesses To Mark:
{

Subscribed and sworn to before me this 4 day of April, 1905.

        Drennan C Skaggs
        Notary Public.

BIRTH AFFIDAVIT.

DEPARTMENT OF THE INTERIOR.
COMMISSION TO THE FIVE CIVILIZED TRIBES.

IN RE APPLICATION FOR ENROLLMENT, as a citizen of the Creek Nation, of Walter Beaver, born on the 6 day of June, 1902

Name of Father: Poyer[sic] Beaver a citizen of the Creek Nation.
Okfuske Town
Name of Mother: Mulsie Beaver a citizen of the Creek Nation.
Eufaula Canadian.

      Postoffice Eufaula, Ind.Terr.

       Child present.
AFFIDAVIT OF MOTHER.

UNITED STATES OF AMERICA, Indian Territory,
 Western   **DISTRICT.**

I, Mulsie Beaver, on oath state that I am about 30 years of age and a citizen by blood, of the Creek Nation; that I am the lawful wife of Poyer[sic] Beaver, who is a citizen, by blood of the Creek Nation; that a male child was born to me on 6 day of June, 1902, that said child has been named Walter Beaver, and was living March 4, 1905.

        Mulsie Beaver

Witnesses To Mark:
{

Subscribed and sworn to before me this 4 day of April, 1905.

        Drennan C Skaggs
        Notary Public.

Applications for Enrollment of Creek Newborn
Act of 1905   Volume VIII

AFFIDAVIT OF ATTENDING PHYSICIAN OR MID-WIFE.

UNITED STATES OF AMERICA, Indian Territory, } Western DISTRICT.

I, Lucy Wesley , a mid-wife , on oath state that I attended on Mrs. Mulsie Beaver , wife of Poyer Beaver ~~on the (blank) day of (blank) , 1~~ ; that there was born to her on said date a male child; that said child was living March 4, 1905, and is said to have been named Walter Beaver

                                            her
                                   Lucy x Beaver

Witnesses To Mark: mark
  { DC Skaggs
    L.G. McIntosh

Subscribed and sworn to before me this 4 day of April , 1905.

                             Drennan C Skaggs
                             Notary Public.

BIRTH AFFIDAVIT.

DEPARTMENT OF THE INTERIOR.
COMMISSION TO THE FIVE CIVILIZED TRIBES.

IN RE APPLICATION FOR ENROLLMENT, as a citizen of the Creek Nation, of Walter Beaver, born on the 6th day of June , 1902

Name of Father: Byer Beaver	a citizen of the	Creek Nation.
Name of Mother: Mulsie Beaver	a citizen of the	Creek Nation.

                         Postoffice   Eufaula, I.T.

AFFIDAVIT OF ATTENDING PHYSICIAN OR MID-WIFE.

UNITED STATES OF AMERICA, Indian Territory, } Western DISTRICT.

I, Lucy Wesley , a mid-wife , on oath state that I attended on Mrs. Mulsie Beaver , wife of Byer Beaver on the 6th day of June , 1902 ; that there was born to her on said date a male child; that said child was living March 4, 1905, and is said to have been named Walter Beaver

                                            her
                                   Lucy x Beaver

Witnesses To Mark: mark
  { DC Skaggs
    Alex Posey

Applications for Enrollment of Creek Newborn
Act of 1905   Volume VIII

Subscribed and sworn to before me this 16 day of Sept, 1905.

Drennan C Skaggs
Notary Public.

NC-614

Muskogee, Indian Territory, August 10, 1905.

Daniel Hawkins,
    Stidham, Indian Territory.

Dear Sir:

    In the matter of the application for the enrollment of your minor children, Kate Hawkins, born September 1, 1902 and Melissa Hawkins, born February 6, 1904, as citizens by blood of the Creek Nation, it will be necessary for you to furnish this Office with the affidavits of the attending midwife at the birth of said children, and two blanks for that purpose are enclosed herewith.

    However, if the attending midwife at the birth of said children still refuses to execute affidavits relative to their birth, you may furnish, in lieu of her affidavits as to the birth of said children, the affidavits of two disinterested persons. Said affidavits must set forth the names of said children, the dates of their birth, the names of their parents, and whether or not they were living on March 4, 1905.

    This matter should have your prompt attention.

Respectfully,

Acting Commissioner.

2 B C
Env

Applications for Enrollment of Creek Newborn
Act of 1905   Volume VIII

BIRTH AFFIDAVIT.

DEPARTMENT OF THE INTERIOR.
COMMISSION TO THE FIVE CIVILIZED TRIBES.

IN RE APPLICATION FOR ENROLLMENT, as a citizen of the Creek Nation, of Kate Hawkins, born on the 1 day of Sept, 1902

Name of Father: Daniel Hawkins   a citizen of the   Creek   Nation.
Ketchopatcky Town
Name of Mother: Rhoda Hawkins (nee Beaver)   a citizen of the   Creek   Nation.
Hickory Ground Town
                      Postoffice   Stidham, Ind. Ter.

AFFIDAVIT OF MOTHER.

UNITED STATES OF AMERICA, Indian Territory,
   Western   DISTRICT.   Child is present

I, Rhoda Hawkins , on oath state that I am 23 years of age and a citizen by blood , of the Creek Nation; that I am the lawful wife of Daniel Hawkins , who is a citizen, by blood of the Creek Nation; that a female child was born to me on 1 day of September , 1902 , that said child has been named Kate Hawkins , and was living March 4, 1905. That the midwife, Jennie McGilbra, who attended on me at the birth of the child refuses to execute an affidavit.
                           Rhoda Hawkins
Witnesses To Mark:
   {

Subscribed and sworn to before me this 4 day of April , 1905.

                           Drennan C Skaggs
                              Notary Public.

BIRTH AFFIDAVIT.

DEPARTMENT OF THE INTERIOR.
COMMISSION TO THE FIVE CIVILIZED TRIBES.

IN RE APPLICATION FOR ENROLLMENT, as a citizen of the *(blank)* Nation, of Kate Hawkins, born on the 1 day of September, 1902

Name of Father: Daniel Hawkins   a citizen of the   Creek   Nation.
Name of Mother: Rhoda Hawkins (nee Beaver)   a citizen of the   Creek   Nation.

Applications for Enrollment of Creek Newborn
Act of 1905   Volume VIII

Postoffice   Stidham

AFFIDAVIT OF MOTHER.

UNITED STATES OF AMERICA, Indian Territory, }
   Western   DISTRICT.

    I, Rhoda Hawkins , on oath state that I am 23 years of age and a citizen by Blood , of the Creek Nation; that I am the lawful wife of Daniel Hawkins , who is a citizen, by Blood of the Creek Nation; that a female child was born to me on first day of September , 1902 , that said child has been named Kate Hawkins , and was living March 4, 1905.

                                  Rhoda Hawkins

Witnesses To Mark:
{

    Subscribed and sworn to before me this 16 day of August , 1905.

My Commission   Preston Janway
Expires May 19 1908   Notary Public.

AFFIDAVIT OF ATTENDING PHYSICIAN OR MID-WIFE.

UNITED STATES OF AMERICA, Indian Territory, }
   Western   DISTRICT.

                                   know

    I, Edward H Walker , a citizen , on oath state that I ~~attended on~~ Mrs. Rhoda Hawkins , wife of Daniel Hawkins on the first day of September , 1902 ; that there was born to her on said date a female child; that said child was living March 4, 1905, and is said to have been named Kate Hawkins   I know this by seeing her just before and just after the child was borned[sic]

                                Edward H Walker

Witnesses To Mark:
{

    Subscribed and sworn to before me this 16 day of August , 1905.

My Commission   Preston Janway
Expires May 19 1908   Notary Public.

Applications for Enrollment of Creek Newborn
Act of 1905   Volume VIII

BIRTH AFFIDAVIT.

DEPARTMENT OF THE INTERIOR.
COMMISSION TO THE FIVE CIVILIZED TRIBES.

IN RE APPLICATION FOR ENROLLMENT, as a citizen of the Creek Nation, of Melissa Hawkins, born on the 6 day of Feb., 1904

Name of Father: Daniel Hawkins   a citizen of the   Creek   Nation. Ketchopatcky Town
Name of Mother: Rhoda Hawkins (nee Beaver) a citizen of the   Creek   Nation. Hickory Ground Town

                        Postoffice   Stidham, Ind. Ter.

AFFIDAVIT OF MOTHER.

UNITED STATES OF AMERICA, Indian Territory,
    Western   DISTRICT.   Child is present

    I, Rhoda Hawkins , on oath state that I am 23   years of age and a citizen by blood , of the Creek   Nation; that I am the lawful wife of Daniel Hawkins , who is a citizen, by blood of the Creek Nation; that a female   child was born to me on 6 day of February , 1904 , that said child has been named Melissa Hawkins , and was living March 4, 1905.

                                      Rhoda Hawkins
Witnesses To Mark:

{

    Subscribed and sworn to before me this 4 day of April , 1905.

                                      Drennan C Skaggs
                                      Notary Public.

AFFIDAVIT OF ATTENDING PHYSICIAN OR MID-WIFE.

UNITED STATES OF AMERICA, Indian Territory,
    Western   DISTRICT.

                                                  my wife
    I, Daniel Hawkins   , a (blank) , on oath state that I attended on ^ Mrs. Rhoda Hawkins , wife of (blank)   on the 6 day of Feb , 1904 ; that there was born to her on said date a   female   child; that said child was living March 4, 1905, and is said to have been named Melissa Hawkins

                                      Daniel Hawkins
Witnesses To Mark:

{

Applications for Enrollment of Creek Newborn
Act of 1905   Volume VIII

Subscribed and sworn to before me this 4 day of April, 1905.

                                      Drennan C Skaggs
                                      Notary Public.

BIRTH AFFIDAVIT.

DEPARTMENT OF THE INTERIOR.
COMMISSION TO THE FIVE CIVILIZED TRIBES.

IN RE APPLICATION FOR ENROLLMENT, as a citizen of the *(blank)* Nation, of Melissa Hawkins, born on the 6 day of February[sic] ,1904

Name of Father:	Daniel Hawkins	a citizen of the	Creek	Nation.
Name of Mother:	Rhoda Hawkins	a citizen of the	Creek	Nation.

                         Postoffice   Stidham

AFFIDAVIT OF MOTHER.

UNITED STATES OF AMERICA, Indian Territory,
     Western   **DISTRICT.**

I, Rhoda Hawkins , on oath state that I am 23 years of age and a citizen by Blood , of the Creek Nation; that I am the lawful wife of Daniel Hawkins , who is a citizen, by Blood of the Creek Nation; that a female child was born to me on 6 day of February , 1904 , that said child has been named Melissa Hawkins , and was living March 4, 1905.

                                      Rhoda Hawkins

Witnesses To Mark:

Subscribed and sworn to before me this 16 day of August , 1905.

My Commission   Preston Janway
Expires May 19 1908   Notary Public.

AFFIDAVIT OF ATTENDING PHYSICIAN OR MID-WIFE.

UNITED STATES OF AMERICA, Indian Territory,
     Western   **DISTRICT.**

                                                know

I, Edward H Walker , a citizen , on oath state that I ~~attended on~~ Mrs. Rhoda Hawkins , wife of Daniel Hawkins on the 6 day of february[sic] , 1904 ; that there

Applications for Enrollment of Creek Newborn
Act of 1905   Volume VIII

was born to her on said date a female child; that said child was living March 4, 1905, and is said to have been named Melissa Hawkins   I know this by seeing her just before and just after the child was borned[sic]

Edward H Walker

Witnesses To Mark:
{

Subscribed and sworn to before me this 16 day of August , 1905.

My Commission   Preston Janway
Expires May 19 1908   Notary Public.

BIRTH AFFIDAVIT.

See duplicate application

DEPARTMENT OF THE INTERIOR.
COMMISSION TO THE FIVE CIVILIZED TRIBES.

IN RE APPLICATION FOR ENROLLMENT, as a citizen of the Creek Nation, of Floyd Lee Stewart , born on the 31 day of Aug, 1903

Name of Father: William Stewart   a citizen of the   U.S.   Nation.
Name of Mother: America Stewart (nee Self)   a citizen of the   Creek   Nation.
(Broken Arrow)
                                                Postoffice   Mounds

AFFIDAVIT OF MOTHER.

UNITED STATES OF AMERICA, Indian Territory, }
     Western   DISTRICT.   Child present

I, America Stewart , on oath state that I am 40 years of age and a citizen by blood , of the Creek   Nation; that I am the lawful wife of William Stewart , who is a citizen, by *(blank)* of the U.S. Nation; that a male child was born to me on 31 day of August , 1903 , that said child has been named Floyd Lee Stewart , and was living March 4, 1905.

America Stewart

Witnesses To Mark:
{

Applications for Enrollment of Creek Newborn
Act of 1905   Volume VIII

Subscribed and sworn to before me this 25 day of April , 1905.
(Seal)   Edw C Griesel
                                                  Notary Public.

BIRTH AFFIDAVIT.

DEPARTMENT OF THE INTERIOR.
COMMISSION TO THE FIVE CIVILIZED TRIBES.

IN RE APPLICATION FOR ENROLLMENT, as a citizen of the Creek Nation, of Floyd Lee Stewart , born on the 31st day of August , 1903

Name of Father: William Stewart   a non-citizen of the   Creek   Nation.
Name of Mother: America Stewart (nee Self)   a citizen of the   Creek   Nation.

                              Postoffice   Mounds, Indian Territory.

AFFIDAVIT OF MOTHER.

UNITED STATES OF AMERICA, Indian Territory,
       Western   DISTRICT.   Child present

I, America Stewart , on oath state that I am forty years of age and a citizen by blood , of the Creek Nation; that I am the lawful wife of William Stewart , who is a non- citizen, by *(blank)* of the Creek Nation; that a male   child was born to me on 31st day of August , 1903 , that said child has been named Floyd Lee Stewart , and was living March 4, 1905.

                                        America Stewart
Witnesses To Mark:
{

Subscribed and sworn to before me this 27th day of March , 1905.

                                        DJ Red
                                               Notary Public.

AFFIDAVIT OF ATTENDING PHYSICIAN OR MID-WIFE.

UNITED STATES OF AMERICA, Indian Territory,
       Western   DISTRICT.

I, M. D. Taylor , a physician , on oath state that I attended on Mrs. America Stewart , wife of William H. Stewart on the 31st day of August , 1903 ; that there

Applications for Enrollment of Creek Newborn
Act of 1905 Volume VIII

was born to her on said date a male child; that said child was living March 4, 1905, and is said to have been named Floyd Lee Stewart

M.D. Taylor, M.D.

Witnesses To Mark:
{

Subscribed and sworn to before me this 27th day of March, 1905.

DJ Red
Notary Public.

NC-616

Muskogee, Indian Territory, August 10, 1905.

Mahala Johnson,
    Okomah[sic], Indian Territory.

Dear Madam:

In the matter of the application for the enrollment of your minor child, Ulter Johnson, as a citizen by blood of the Creek Nation, it will be necessary for you to furnish this Office with the affidavit of the attending midwife at the birth of said child relative to his birth.

For that purpose, there is herewith enclosed a blank for proof of birth, which has been filled out. You are requested to have the midwife appear before a notary public, and wear[sic] to same; and when sworn to, return it to this Office in the enclosed envelope.

The affidavit of said midwife which is now on file is defective, inasmuch as the notary public before whom it was sworn to neglected to affix his seal to said affidavit.

Please give this matter your immediate attention.

Respectfully,

JYM-10-2
Env

Acting Commissioner.

Applications for Enrollment of Creek Newborn
Act of 1905   Volume VIII

BIRTH AFFIDAVIT.

DEPARTMENT OF THE INTERIOR.
COMMISSION TO THE FIVE CIVILIZED TRIBES.

IN RE APPLICATION FOR ENROLLMENT, as a citizen of the Creek Nation, of Ulter Johnson, born on the 1st day of May, 1902

Name of Father: Cullie Johnson	a citizen of the Creek	Nation.
Name of Mother: Mahala Johnson	a citizen of the Creek	Nation.

Postoffice   Okemah, Indian Territory.

AFFIDAVIT OF ATTENDING PHYSICIAN OR MID-WIFE.

UNITED STATES OF AMERICA, Indian Territory,
Western   DISTRICT.

I, Annie West, a mid-wife, on oath state that I attended on Mrs. Mahala Johnson, wife of Cullie Johnson on the 1st day of May, 1902 ; that there was born to her on said date a male child; that said child was living March 4, 1905, and is said to have been named Ulter Johnson

Mrs Annie West

Witnesses To Mark:
{ L.P. Caldwell Okemah, I.T.
{ Tupper Dunn   Okemah, I.T.

Subscribed and sworn to before me this 5 day of Sept, 1905.

My Commission Expires July 8" 1906   W.H. Dill
Notary Public.

BIRTH AFFIDAVIT.

DEPARTMENT OF THE INTERIOR.
COMMISSION TO THE FIVE CIVILIZED TRIBES.

IN RE APPLICATION FOR ENROLLMENT, as a citizen of the Creek Nation, of Ulter Johnson, born on the 1st day of May, 1902

Name of Father: Cully Johnson	a citizen of the Blood[sic]	Nation.
Name of Mother: Mahala Johnson	a citizen of the Blood[sic]	Nation.

Postoffice   Okemah, I.T.

Applications for Enrollment of Creek Newborn
Act of 1905 Volume VIII

AFFIDAVIT OF MOTHER.

UNITED STATES OF AMERICA, Indian Territory,
Western Judicial   DISTRICT.

I, Mahala Johnson , on oath state that I am 30 years of age and a citizen by Blood , of the Muskokee[sic] or Creek Nation; that I am the lawful wife of Cully Johnson , who is a citizen, by Blood of the Muskokee[sic] or Creek Nation; that a male child was born to me on 1st day of May , 1902 , that said child has been named Ulter Johnson , and was living March 4, 1905.

Mahala Johnson

Witnesses To Mark:

Subscribed and sworn to before me this 18th day of March , 1905.

My Commission Expires Sept 6th 1906

John H. Phillips
Notary Public.

AFFIDAVIT OF ATTENDING PHYSICIAN OR MID-WIFE.

UNITED STATES OF AMERICA, Indian Territory,
Western Judicial   DISTRICT.

I, Annie West , a Mid- Wife , on oath state that I attended on Mrs. Mahala Johnson , wife of Cully Johnson on the 1st day of May , 1902 ; that there was born to her on said date a Male child; that said child was living March 4, 1905, and is said to have been named Ulter Johnson

Annie West

Witnesses To Mark:

Subscribed and sworn to before me this 27th day of March, 1905.

John H. Phillips
Notary Public.

BIRTH AFFIDAVIT.

DEPARTMENT OF THE INTERIOR.
COMMISSION TO THE FIVE CIVILIZED TRIBES.

IN RE APPLICATION FOR ENROLLMENT, as a citizen of the Creek Nation, of Bessie Johnson, born on the 5th day of February , 1904

Applications for Enrollment of Creek Newborn
Act of 1905 Volume VIII

Name of Father: Cully Johnson   a citizen of the   Creek   Nation.
Name of Mother: Mahala Johnson   a citizen of the   Creek   Nation.

Postoffice   Okemah, I.T.

AFFIDAVIT OF MOTHER.

UNITED STATES OF AMERICA, Indian Territory,
(blank)   DISTRICT.

I, Mahala Johnson , on oath state that I am 30 years of age and a citizen by Blood , of the Muskokee[sic] or Creek Nation; that I am the lawful wife of Cully Johnson , who is a citizen, by Blood of the Muskokee[sic] or Creek Nation; that a Female child was born to me on 5th day of February , 1904 , that said child has been named Bessie Johnson , and was living March 4, 1905.

                        Mahala Johnson

Witnesses To Mark:

Subscribed and sworn to before me this 18th day of March , 1905.

My Commission Expires Sept 6th 1906   John H. Phillips
                                         Notary Public.

AFFIDAVIT OF ATTENDING PHYSICIAN OR MID-WIFE.

UNITED STATES OF AMERICA, Indian Territory,
Western Judicial   DISTRICT.

I, Jennie Johnson , a Mid- Wife , on oath state that I attended on Mrs. Mahala Johnson , wife of Cully Johnson on the 5th day of May[sic] , 1904 ; that there was born to her on said date a Male[sic] child; that said child was living March 4, 1905, and is said to have been named Bessie Johnson   her
                                          Jennie Johnson x
Witnesses To Mark: mark
   T.W. Morton
   John H. Phillips

Subscribed and sworn to before me this 18th day of March , 1905.

My Commission Expires Sept 6th 1906   John H. Phillips
                                         Notary Public.

Applications for Enrollment of Creek Newborn
Act of 1905 Volume VIII

BIRTH AFFIDAVIT.

DEPARTMENT OF THE INTERIOR.
COMMISSION TO THE FIVE CIVILIZED TRIBES.

IN RE APPLICATION FOR ENROLLMENT, as a citizen of the Creek Nation, of George McGirt, born on the 18 day of March, 1904

Name of Father: Billy McGirt   a citizen of the Creek Nation.
Tuckabatche Town
Name of Mother: Emma McGirt   a citizen of the Creek Nation.
Tuckabatche Town

Postoffice   Holdenville, I.T.

AFFIDAVIT OF MOTHER.

Child present.

UNITED STATES OF AMERICA, Indian Territory,
    Western   DISTRICT.

I, Emma McGirt, on oath state that I am about 30 years of age and a citizen by blood, of the Creek Nation; that I am the lawful wife of Billy McGirt, who is a citizen, by blood of the Creek Nation; that a male child was born to me on 18 day of March, 1904, that said child has been named George McGirt, and was living March 4, 1905.

Emma McGirt

Witnesses To Mark:
{

Subscribed and sworn to before me this 27 day of March, 1905.

Drennan C Skaggs
Notary Public.

AFFIDAVIT OF ATTENDING PHYSICIAN OR MID-WIFE.

UNITED STATES OF AMERICA, Indian Territory,
    Western   DISTRICT.

my wife
I, Billy McGirt, a *(blank)*, on oath state that I attended on ^ Mrs. Emma McGirt, ~~wife of~~ *(blank)* on the 18 day of March, 1904; that there was born to her on said date a male child; that said child was living March 4, 1905, and is said to have been named George McGirt   his

Applications for Enrollment of Creek Newborn
Act of 1905   Volume VIII

Witnesses To Mark:
{

Billy x McGirt
        mark

Subscribed and sworn to before me this 27 day of March, 1905.

Drennan C Skaggs
Notary Public.

AFFIDAVIT.

Wardley Goat   a Creek citizen and 34 years of age states upon oath that he is well acquainted with Emma McGirt (Nee Smith) the mother of Nora Watson who was born on the 1st day of June 1901, and said child is now liveing[sic],
and on the 18th day of march[sic], 1904, a male child was born to Emma McGirt (Nee Smith) which said child was named George McGirt, and said child died on the 16th day of September 1905,
the said Emma McGirt was enrolled as Emma Smith, her father,s[sic] name is John Smith, and her Mothers[sic] Nane[sic] was Louisa Smith,
her roll number is _____ as per her deeds.
I make this statement as a disinterested party, and have no claim whatever in this only as a friend and a member of the creek[sic] Nation. to all of which I make oath to.

(Deeds misplaced)

Wardley Goat

Subscribed and sworn to before me this the 23rd day of October 1905

Chas Rider
Notary Public.

Commission Expires July 11th, 1906

AFFIDAVIT.

J W Todd   a Creek citizen and 34 years of age states upon oath that he is well acquainted with Emma McGirt (Nee Smith) the mother of Nora Watson who was born on the 1st day of June 1901, and said child is now liveing[sic],
and on the 18th day of march[sic], 1904, a male child was born to Emma McGirt (Nee Smith) which said child was named George McGirt, and said child died on the 16th day of September 1905,
the said Emma McGirt was enrolled as Emma Smith, her father,s[sic] name is John Smith, and her Mothers[sic] Nane[sic] was Louisa Smith,
her roll number is _____ as per her deeds.

Applications for Enrollment of Creek Newborn
Act of 1905   Volume VIII

I make this statement as a disinterested party, and have no claim whatever in this only as a friend and a member of the creek[sic] Nation. to all of which I make oath to.

    (Deeds misplaced)   J. W. Todd

Subscribed and sworn to before me this the 23rd day of October 1905

                                      Chas Rider
                                      Notary Public.

Commission Expires July 11th, 1906

United States of America
)
Indian Territory   )SS.
)
Western Judicial District)

       Personall[sic] appeared before me   Mollie Palmer and upon oath deposes and says that   he[sic]   is well acquainted with Emma McGirt nee Smith mother of George McGirt, and that on the 18th day of march[sic] 1904 their[sic] was born to her a male child who was named George McGirt,
and said George McGirt died on the 16th day of September, 1905.
Billy McGirt was the father of the said child, and is now dead. The roll number is 8086 as per deed, Enrolled as Emma Smith
That they are all Creek Citizens by birth, her mothers[sic] name was Louisa Smith, and her fathers[sic] name was John Smith,
I further state that I have no claim in this matter and make this statement as a disinterested person.   her
Witness to mark   Mollie Palmer x
Alfred F. Goat   mark
E.R. Nix
Subscribed and sworn to before me this the 9th day of October, 1905

                                      Chas Rider
                                      Notary Public.

My Commission expires July 11th, 1906.

United States of America
)
Indian Territory   )SS.
)
Western Judicial District)

Applications for Enrollment of Creek Newborn
Act of 1905   Volume VIII

Personall[sic] appeared before me   Palmer Mickey   and upon oath deposes and says that   he[sic]   is well acquainted with Emma McGirt nee Smith mother of George McGirt, and that on the 18th day of march[sic] 1904 their[sic] was born to her a male child who was named George McGirt,
and said George McGirt died on the 16th day of September, 1905.
Billy McGirt was the father of the said child, and is now dead. The roll number is   8086 as per deed, Enrolled as Emma Smith
That they are all Creek Citizens by birth, her mothers[sic] name was Louisa Smith, and her fathers[sic] name was John Smith,
I further state that I have no claim in this matter and make this statement as a disinterested person.

Witness to mark	his Palmer Mickey x mark
E.R. Nax	
Alfred F. Goat	

Subscribed and sworn to before me this the 9th day of October, 1905

            Chas Rider
              Notary Public.
My Commission expires July 11th, 1906.

NC-617

         Muskogee, Indian Territory, August 10, 1905.

Billy McGirt,
  Holdenville, Indian Territory.

Dear Sir:

  In the matter of the application for the enrollment of your minor son, George McGirt, born March 18, 1904, as a citizen by blood of the Creek Nation, it will be necessary for you to furnish this Office with the affidavits of two disinterested persons relative to the birth of said child. Said affidavits must set forth said child's name, the date of his birth, the names of his parents, and whether or not he was living on March 4, 1905.

  From the evidence now on file, this Office is unable to identify Emma McGirt, the mother of said child, upon the final roll of citizens by blood of the Creek Nation. It is necessary that she be so identified before the rights of said child can be finally determined. You are therefore requested to state the name under which said Emma McGirt was finally enrolled, the names of her parents and other members of her family, and her final roll number as the same appears upon her allotment certificates and deeds.

           Respectfully,

              Acting Commissioner.

Applications for Enrollment of Creek Newborn
Act of 1905   Volume VIII

NC-617

Muskogee, Indian Territory, October 17, 1905.

Billy McGirt,
    Holdenville, Indian Territory.

Dear Sir:

    In the matter of the application for the enrollment of your minor son, George McGirt, born March 18, 1904, as a citizen by blood of the Creek Nation, it will be necessary for you to furnish this office with the affidavits of two disinterested persons relative to the birth of said child. Said affidavits must set forth said child's name, the date of his birth, the names of his parents, and whether or not he was living on March 4, 1905.

    From the evidence now on file, this Office is unable to identify Emma McGirt, the mother of said child, upon the final roll of citizens by blood of the Creek Nation. It is necessary that she be so identified before the rights of said child can be finally determined.

    You are therefore requested to state the name under which Emma McGirt was finally enrolled, the names of her parents and other members of her family, and her final roll number as the same appears upon her allotment certificate and deeds.

                             Respectfully,

                                     Commissioner.

NC-618

Muskogee, Indian Territory, August 10, 1905.

John Bright,
    Mellette, Indian Territory.

Dear Sir:

    In the matter of the application for the enrollment of your minor children, Reubin Bright, born March 31, 1902, and Lafa Bright, born December 28, 1903, as citizens by blood of the Creek Nation, it will be necessary for you to furnish this office with the affidavits of two disinterested persons as to the birth of said children. Said affidavits must set forth said names of said children, the dates of their birth, the names of their parents, and whether or not they were living on March 4, 1905.

    Please give this matter your immediate attention.

Applications for Enrollment of Creek Newborn
Act of 1905 Volume VIII

Respectfully,

Acting Commissioner.

AFFIDAVIT.

United States of America,)
Western District,) ss
Indian Territory.)

We, Will Cook and Tom Crews, non citizens of the Creek Nation, on oath state that we are personally acquainted with John and Rhoda Bright, citizens by blood of the Creek Nation; and that here was born to them a male child on or about the 28th of December 1903; and that said child has been named Lafa Bright and is now living.

Will Cook

Tom Crews

Subscribed and sworn to before me this 30 day of Sept. 1905.

SM Gold
MY COMMISSION EXPIRES FEB. 19, 1908.   Notary Public.

BIRTH AFFIDAVIT.

DEPARTMENT OF THE INTERIOR.
COMMISSION TO THE FIVE CIVILIZED TRIBES.

IN RE APPLICATION FOR ENROLLMENT, as a citizen of the Creek Nation, of Lafa Bright, born on the 28 day of December, 1903

Name of Father: John Bright   a citizen of the   Creek   Nation.
Name of Mother: Rhody Bright   a citizen of the   Creek   Nation.

Postoffice   Mellette I.T.

Applications for Enrollment of Creek Newborn
Act of 1905 Volume VIII

AFFIDAVIT OF MOTHER.

UNITED STATES OF AMERICA, Indian Territory,
Western DISTRICT.

I, Simon Blake , on oath state that I ~~am~~ that ~~years of age and a citizen by~~ I know John & Rhody Bright, of the citizens of the Creek Nation; ~~that I am the lawful wife of~~ that a male child was born unto them ~~who is a citizen, by~~ name ~~of the~~ Lafa Bright ~~Nation~~; that a male child was born to me on 28 day of December , 1903 , that said child has been named Lafa Bright , and was living March 4, 1905.

                                        Simon Blake his x mark

Witnesses To Mark:
{ Lena Bright

Subscribed and sworn to before me this 30 day of August , 1905.

                                        L.G. McIntosh
                                        Notary Public.

AFFIDAVIT OF ATTENDING PHYSICIAN OR MID-WIFE.

UNITED STATES OF AMERICA, Indian Territory,
Western DISTRICT.

I, Jim Asbury , a *(blank)* , on oath state that I ~~attended on Mrs.~~ that I know John & Rhody Bright , ~~wife of~~ *(blank)* on the 31 day of March[sic] , 1903 ; that there was born to her on said date a male child; that said child was living March 4, 1905, and is said to have been named Lafa Bright

                                        Jim Asbury his x mark

Witnesses To Mark:
{ Lena Bright

Subscribed and sworn to before me this 30 day of August , 1905.

                                          L.G. McIntosh
                                        Notary Public.

Applications for Enrollment of Creek Newborn
Act of 1905   Volume VIII

BIRTH AFFIDAVIT.

DEPARTMENT OF THE INTERIOR.
COMMISSION TO THE FIVE CIVILIZED TRIBES.

IN RE APPLICATION FOR ENROLLMENT, as a citizen of the Creek Nation, of Lafa Bright, born on the ~~31~~ 28 day of ~~March~~ December, 1903

Name of Father: John Bright   a citizen of the   Creek   Nation.
Name of Mother: Rhody Bright   a citizen of the   Creek   Nation.

Postoffice   Mellette I.T.

AFFIDAVIT OF MOTHER.

UNITED STATES OF AMERICA, Indian Territory,
Western   DISTRICT.

I, Rhody Bright, on oath state that I am 25 years of age and a citizen by blood, of the Creek Nation; that I am the lawful wife of John Bright, who is a citizen, by blood of the Creek Nation; that a male child was born to me on ~~31~~ 28 day of ~~March~~ December, 1903, that said child has been named Lafa Bright, and was living March 4, 1905.

Rhody Bright

Witnesses To Mark:
{

Subscribed and sworn to before me this 30 day of Aug, 1905.

L.G. McIntosh
Notary Public.

AFFIDAVIT OF ATTENDING PHYSICIAN OR MID-WIFE.

UNITED STATES OF AMERICA, Indian Territory,
Western   DISTRICT.

I, John Bright, a state[sic], on oath state that I attended on Mrs. Rhody Bright, ~~wife of~~ my wife on the 28 day of December, 1903; that there was born to her on said date a male child; that said child was living March 4, 1905, and is said to have been named Lafa Bright

John Bright

Witnesses To Mark:
{

Applications for Enrollment of Creek Newborn
Act of 1905   Volume VIII

Subscribed and sworn to before me this 30 day of Aug, 1905.

         L.G. McIntosh
          Notary Public.

BIRTH AFFIDAVIT.

DEPARTMENT OF THE INTERIOR.
COMMISSION TO THE FIVE CIVILIZED TRIBES.

IN RE APPLICATION FOR ENROLLMENT, as a citizen of the Creek Nation, of Lafa Bright, born on the 28 day of December, 1903

Name of Father: John Bright   a citizen of the Creek Nation.
(Illegible) Town
Name of Mother: Rhoda Bright   a citizen of the Creek Nation.
Eufaula Canadian
        Postoffice Mellette, Ind. Terr.

AFFIDAVIT OF MOTHER.

              Child present

UNITED STATES OF AMERICA, Indian Territory,
  Western   DISTRICT.

  I, Rhoda Bright, on oath state that I am 25 years of age and a citizen by blood, of the Creek Nation; that I am the lawful wife of John Bright, who is a citizen, by blood of the Creek Nation; that a male child was born to me on 28 day of December, 1903, that said child has been named Lafa Bright, and was living March 4, 1905.

         Rhody Bright

Witnesses To Mark:

  Subscribed and sworn to before me this 4 day of April, 1905.

         Drennan C Skaggs
          Notary Public.

Applications for Enrollment of Creek Newborn
Act of 1905   Volume VIII

father
AFFIDAVIT OF <s>ATTENDING PHYSICIAN OR MID-WIFE.</s>

UNITED STATES OF AMERICA, Indian Territory, }
Western   DISTRICT.

                                                                    my wife

I, John Bright , a *(blank)* , on oath state that I attended on ^ Mrs. Rhoda Bright, <s>wife of (blank)</s> on the 28 day of December , 1903 ; that there was born to her on said date a male child; that said child was living March 4, 1905, and is said to have been named Lafa Bright

                                              John Bright

Witnesses To Mark:
{

Subscribed and sworn to before me this 4 day of April , 1905.

                                              Drennan C Skaggs
                                              Notary Public.

AFFIDAVIT.

United States of America,)
)
      Western District,)   SS
)
Indian Territory.   )

We, Will Cook and Tom Crews, non citizens of the Creek Nation, on oath state that we are personally acquainted with John and Rhoda Bright, citizens by blood of the Creek Nation; and that here was born to them a male child on or about the 31 of March 1902; and that said child has been named Reubin Bright and is now living.

                                              Will Cook

                                              Tom Crews

Subscribed and sworn to before me this 30 day of Sept. 1905.

                                              SM Gold
MY COMMISSION EXPIRES FEB. 19, 1908.   Notary Public.

Applications for Enrollment of Creek Newborn
Act of 1905   Volume VIII

BIRTH AFFIDAVIT.

DEPARTMENT OF THE INTERIOR.
COMMISSION TO THE FIVE CIVILIZED TRIBES.

IN RE APPLICATION FOR ENROLLMENT, as a citizen of the Creek Nation, of Rheubin[sic] Bright, born on the 31 day of March ~~Creek~~ , 1902

Name of Father: John Bright   a citizen of the   Creek   Nation.
Name of Mother: Rhoda Bright   a citizen of the   Creek   Nation.

Postoffice   Mellette, I.T.

AFFIDAVIT OF MOTHER.

UNITED STATES OF AMERICA, Indian Territory,
Western   DISTRICT.

I, Rhody Bright , on oath state that I am 25 years of age and a citizen by blood, of the Creek Nation; that I am the lawful wife of John Bright , who is a citizen, by blood of the Creek Nation; that a male child was born to me on 31 day of March , 1902 , that said child has been named Rheubin Bright , and was living March 4, 1905.

Rhody Bright

Witnesses To Mark:
{

Subscribed and sworn to before me this 30 day of Aug , 1905.

L.G. McIntosh
Notary Public.

AFFIDAVIT OF ATTENDING PHYSICIAN OR MID-WIFE.

UNITED STATES OF AMERICA, Indian Territory,
Western   DISTRICT.

my wife
I, John Bright , a *(blank)* , on oath state that I attended on ^ Mrs. Rhoda Bright , ~~wife of~~ my wife on the 31 day of March , 1902 ; that there was born to her on said date a male child; that said child was living March 4, 1905, and is said to have been named Rhebin[sic] Bright

John Bright

Witnesses To Mark:
{

Applications for Enrollment of Creek Newborn
Act of 1905   Volume VIII

Subscribed and sworn to before me this 30 day of Aug, 1905.

                                   L.G. McIntosh
                                   Notary Public.

BIRTH AFFIDAVIT.

DEPARTMENT OF THE INTERIOR.
COMMISSION TO THE FIVE CIVILIZED TRIBES.

IN RE APPLICATION FOR ENROLLMENT, as a citizen of the Creek Nation, of Rheubin Bright, born on the 31 day of March, 1902

Name of Father: John Bright   a citizen of the   Creek   Nation.
Name of Mother: Rhody Bright   a citizen of the   Creek   Nation.
(Illegible Entry)
                        Postoffice   Eufaula I.T.

AFFIDAVIT OF MOTHER.

UNITED STATES OF AMERICA, Indian Territory, ⎫
    Western   DISTRICT. ⎭

    I, Simon Blake, on oath state that I ~~am~~ that ~~years of age and a citizen by~~ I know John & Rhody Bright, ~~of the~~ *(blank)* Nation; ~~that I am the lawful wife of~~ that they [sic] citizens of the Creek Nation, ~~who is a citizen, by~~ that one child was born ~~Nation~~; ~~that a~~ to them ~~child was born to me on~~ on March 31 -1902 ~~day of~~ A ~~fe~~male child ; ~~that said child has been~~ named He called Rheubin Bright and was living March 4, 1905.

                                Simon Blake his x mark

Witnesses To Mark:
  { Lena Bright
    L.G. McIntosh

Subscribed and sworn to before me this 30 day of August, 1905.

                                   L.G. McIntosh
                                   Notary Public.

Applications for Enrollment of Creek Newborn
Act of 1905 Volume VIII

AFFIDAVIT OF ATTENDING PHYSICIAN OR MID-WIFE.

UNITED STATES OF AMERICA, Indian Territory,
   (blank)   DISTRICT.

    I, Jim Asbury , a *(blank)* , on oath state that I ~~attended on Mrs.~~ that I know John & Rhody Bright , ~~wife of~~ that on the March ~~day of~~ 31 , 1902 ; that there was born to ~~her~~ them on said date a male child; that said child was living March 4, 1905, and is said to have been named Rheubin Bright

                                                           Jim Asbury his x mark

Witnesses To Mark:
    Lena Bright
    L.G. McIntosh

    Subscribed and sworn to before me this 30 day of August , 1905.

                                                     L.G. McIntosh
                                                     Notary Public.

BIRTH AFFIDAVIT.

Department of the Interior,
COMMISSION TO THE FIVE CIVILIZED TRIBES.

    IN RE APPLICATION FOR ENROLLMENT, as a citizen of the Creek Nation, of Reubin Bright , born on the 31 day of March , 190 2

Name of Father: John Bright Tuladega	a citizen of the Creek	Nation.
Name of Mother: Rhoda Bright Eufaula Canadian	a citizen of the Creek	Nation.

                           Post-Office: Melete[sic][sic I.T.

AFFIDAVIT OF MOTHER.

                                                 Child present

UNITED STATES OF AMERICA,
    INDIAN TERRITORY,
    Western   District.

    I, Rhoda Bright , on oath state that I am 25 years of age and a citizen by blood , of the Creek   Nation; that I am the lawful wife of John Bright , who is a citizen, by blood of the Creek   Nation; that a male   child was born to me on 31 day of March , 1902 , that said child has been named Reubin Bright , and is ~~now living~~. on 4 day of March 1905

                                                   Rhoda Bright

Applications for Enrollment of Creek Newborn
Act of 1905   Volume VIII

WITNESSES TO MARK:
{

Subscribed and sworn to before me this 4 *day of* Apr, 1905.

L.G. McIntosh
Notary Public.

---

father
AFFIDAVIT OF ~~ATTENDING PHYSICIAN OR MID-WIFE~~.

UNITED STATES OF AMERICA,
INDIAN TERRITORY,
Western   District.

I, John Bright , a citizen , on oath state that I attended on Mrs. Rhody Bright , wife of mine on the 31 day of March , 1902 ; that there was born to her on said date a male child; that said child is ~~now~~ was living on March 4, 1905 and is said to have been named Reubin Bright

John Bright

WITNESSES TO MARK:
{ Sander Bright
  Cooper *(Illegible)*

Subscribed and sworn to before me this 18 *day of* March, 1905.

L.G. McIntosh
Notary Public.

NC-619

Muskogee, Indian Territory, August 10, 1905.

Mary Ansiel,
    Eufaula, Indian Territory.

Dear Madam:

In the matter of the application for the enrollment of your minor children, William F. Ansiel and Robert Leroy Ansiel, as citizens by blood of the Creek Nation, it will be necessary for you to file with this Office either the original or a certified copy of the marriage license, showing the marriage between you and Charlie Ansiel, the father of said children.

Respectfully,

Acting Commissioner.

Applications for Enrollment of Creek Newborn
Act of 1905 Volume VIII

BIRTH AFFIDAVIT.

DEPARTMENT OF THE INTERIOR.
COMMISSION TO THE FIVE CIVILIZED TRIBES.

IN RE APPLICATION FOR ENROLLMENT, as a citizen of the Creek Nation, of Robert Leroy Ansiel , born on the 25 day of January , 1905

Name of Father: Charlie Ansiel a citizen of the Creek Nation. Hitchitee Town
Name of Mother: Mary Ansiel a citizen of the United States Nation.

Postoffice Eufaula, Ind. Ter.

Child present

AFFIDAVIT OF MOTHER.

UNITED STATES OF AMERICA, Indian Territory, }
     Western   DISTRICT.

I, Mary Ansiel , on oath state that I am 20 years of age and a citizen by *(blank)*, of the United States Nation; that I am the lawful wife of Charlie Ansiel , who is a citizen, by blood of the Creek Nation; that a male child was born to me on 25 day of January , 1905 , that said child has been named Robert Leroy Ansiel , and was living March 4, 1905.

Mary Ansiel

Witnesses To Mark:
{

Subscribed and sworn to before me this 4 day of April , 1905.

Drennan C Skaggs
Notary Public.

AFFIDAVIT OF ATTENDING PHYSICIAN OR MID-WIFE.

UNITED STATES OF AMERICA, Indian Territory, }
     Western   DISTRICT.

I, Jane Tiger , a mid wife , on oath state that I attended on Mrs. Mary Ansiel , wife of Charlie Ansiel on the 25 day of January , 1905 ; that there was born to her on said date a male child; that said child was living March 4, 1905, and is said to have been named Robert Leroy Ansiel

Jane Tiger

Witnesses To Mark:
{

Applications for Enrollment of Creek Newborn
Act of 1905   Volume VIII

Subscribed and sworn to before me this 4 day of April, 1905.

          Drennan C Skaggs
          Notary Public.

BIRTH AFFIDAVIT.

DEPARTMENT OF THE INTERIOR.
COMMISSION TO THE FIVE CIVILIZED TRIBES.

IN RE APPLICATION FOR ENROLLMENT, as a citizen of the Creek Nation, of William F. Ansiel, born on the 26 day of August, 1902

Name of Father: Charlie Ansiel   a citizen of the Creek Nation.
Hitchitee Town
Name of Mother: Mary Ansiel   a citizen of the United States Nation.

     Postoffice   Eufaula, Ind. Ter.

         Child present

AFFIDAVIT OF MOTHER.

UNITED STATES OF AMERICA, Indian Territory, ⎫
  Western   DISTRICT.   ⎬

I, Mary Ansiel, on oath state that I am 20 years of age and a citizen by *(blank)*, of the United States Nation; that I am the lawful wife of Charlie Ansiel, who is a citizen, by blood of the Creek Nation; that a male child was born to me on 26 day of August, 1902, that said child has been named William F Ansiel, and was living March 4, 1905.

         Mary Ansiel

Witnesses To Mark:

Subscribed and sworn to before me this 4 day of April, 1905.

         Drennan C Skaggs
         Notary Public.

Applications for Enrollment of Creek Newborn
Act of 1905   Volume VIII

AFFIDAVIT OF ATTENDING PHYSICIAN OR MID-WIFE.

UNITED STATES OF AMERICA, Indian Territory, ⎱
    Western   DISTRICT.   ⎰

    I, W. A. Tolleson , a Physician , on oath state that I attended on Mrs. Mary Ansiel , wife of Charlie Ansiel on the 26 day of August , 1902 ; that there was born to her on said date a male child; that said child was living March 4, 1905, and is said to have been named William F. Ansiel

                                               W.A. Tolleson M.D.

Witnesses To Mark:
⎰
⎱

    Subscribed and sworn to before me this 4 day of April, 1905.

                                            Drennan C Skaggs
                                                Notary Public.

BIRTH AFFIDAVIT.
DEPARTMENT OF THE INTERIOR.
COMMISSION TO THE FIVE CIVILIZED TRIBES.

    IN RE APPLICATION FOR ENROLLMENT, as a citizen of the Creek Nation, of Albert Robert Ansiel , born on the 12 day of September , 1902

Name of Father: Robert Lee Ansiel   a citizen of the   Creek   Nation.
Hitchitee Town
Name of Mother: Statie Ann Ansiel   a citizen of the United States Nation.

                                Postoffice   Eufaula, Ind. Ter.

                                           Child present
                              AFFIDAVIT OF MOTHER.

UNITED STATES OF AMERICA, Indian Territory, ⎱
    Western   DISTRICT.   ⎰

    I, Statie Ann Ansiel , on oath state that I am 24 years of age and a citizen ~~by (blank)~~ , of the United States ~~Nation~~; that I am the lawful wife of Robert Lee Ansiel , who is a citizen, by blood of the Creek Nation; that a male child was born to me on

Applications for Enrollment of Creek Newborn
Act of 1905 Volume VIII

12 day of September, 1902, that said child has been named Albert Robert Ansiel, and was living March 4, 1905.

Witnesses To Mark:
{ Alex Posey

          her
       Statie Ann x Ansiel
          mark

Subscribed and sworn to before me this 4 day of April, 1905.

         Drennan C Skaggs
         Notary Public.

AFFIDAVIT OF ATTENDING PHYSICIAN OR MID-WIFE.

UNITED STATES OF AMERICA, Indian Territory,
  Western DISTRICT.

I, Jane Tiger, a mid-wife, on oath state that I attended on Mrs. Statie Ann Ansiel, wife of Robert Lee Ansiel on the 12 day of September, 1902; that there was born to her on said date a male child; that said child was living March 4, 1905, and is said to have been named Albert Robert Ansiel

         Jane Tiger

Witnesses To Mark:
{

Subscribed and sworn to before me this 4 day of April, 1905.

         Drennan C Skaggs
         Notary Public.

BIRTH AFFIDAVIT.

DEPARTMENT OF THE INTERIOR.
COMMISSION TO THE FIVE CIVILIZED TRIBES.

IN RE APPLICATION FOR ENROLLMENT, as a citizen of the Creek Nation, of Edna Smith, born on the 8 day of May, 1903

Name of Father: Wade Smith   a citizen of the United States Nation.
Name of Mother: Martha Smith a citizen of the Creek Nation.
Thlewathle Town.

       Postoffice Eufaula, Ind. Ter.

Applications for Enrollment of Creek Newborn
Act of 1905 Volume VIII

AFFIDAVIT OF MOTHER.

UNITED STATES OF AMERICA, Indian Territory, }   Child is present
   Western   DISTRICT.

I, Martha Smith , on oath state that I am 31 years of age and a citizen by blood, of the Creek Nation; that I am the lawful wife of Wade Smith , who is a citizen, ~~by (blank)~~ of the United States Nation; that a female child was born to me on 8 day of May, 1903 , that said child has been named Edna Smith , and was living March 4, 1905.

                                    Martha Smith

Witnesses To Mark:
{

Subscribed and sworn to before me this 4 day of April , 1905.

                                      Drennan C Skaggs
                                      Notary Public.

AFFIDAVIT OF ATTENDING PHYSICIAN OR MID-WIFE.

UNITED STATES OF AMERICA, Indian Territory, }
   Western   DISTRICT.

I, Adeline Grayson, a midwife , on oath state that I attended on Mrs. Martha Smith , wife of Wade Smith on the 8 day of May , 1903 ; that there was born to her on said date a female child; that said child was living March 4, 1905, and is said to have been named Edna Smith   her

                                    Adeline x Grayson

Witnesses To Mark: mark
{ Alex Posey
  DC Skaggs

Subscribed and sworn to before me this 4 day of April, 1905.

                                      Drennan C Skaggs
                                      Notary Public.

Applications for Enrollment of Creek Newborn
Act of 1905   Volume VIII

NC-622

DEPARTMENT OF THE INTERIOR,
COMMISSIONER TO THE FIVE CIVILIZED TRIBES.

Muskogee, Indian Territory, December 16, 1905.

In the matter of the application for the enrollment of Martin Gambler as a citizen by blood of the Creek Nation.

Hepsey McGilbray being sworn, testified as follows (through Jesse McDermott, Official Interpreter):

EXAMINATION BY THE COMMISSION:
Q What is your name? A Hepsey McGilbray.
Q How old are you? A I don't know that.

Witness appears to be about 19 or 20 years of age.

Q What is your postoffice? A Mellette.
Q You gave your postoffice as Eufaula when you made application for the enrollment of this child. You want it changed to Mellette? A Yes sir.
Q What is the name of your father? A His name was Daniel McGilbray; he is dead.
Q The name of your mother? A Lizzie McGilbray.

The witness is identified as Hepsey McGilbray, on Creek Indian card, Field No. 428, and her name if contained in the partial list of citizens by blood of the Creek Nation approved by the Secretary of the Interior March 13, 1902, Roll No. 1399.

Q Are you the mother of Martin ~~McGilbray?~~ Gambler? A Yes sir.
Q Who is the father of that child? A John ~~McGilbray.~~ Gambler.
Q You were not married to John, were you? A No.
Q You know the name of John Gambler's father? A Billy Gambler was his name.

John Gambler is identified on Creek Indian card, Field No. 5459, and his name is contained in the partial list of citizens by blood of the Creek Nation approved by the Secretary of the Interior March 28, 1902, opposite Roll No. 8595.

INDIAN TERRITORY, Western District.
I, J. Y. Miller, a stenographer to the Commissioner to the Five Civilized Tribes, do hereby certify that the above and foregoing is a true and complete translation of my notes as same appear in my stenographic report of this case.

JY Miller

Applications for Enrollment of Creek Newborn
Act of 1905   Volume VIII

Sworn to and subscribed before me
this the 20th day of December,
1905.   J McDermott
                                                    Notary Public.

NC-622

Muskogee, Indian Territory, September 8, 1905.

Hepsey McGilbray,
    Eufaula, Indian Territory.

Dear Madam:

In the matter of the application for the enrollment of your minor son Martin Gambler, as a citizen by blood of the Creek Nation, there are on file the affidavit of Hepsey Gambler and the affidavit of Lizzie McGilbra relative to the birth of said child. It is stated in the affidavit of said Hepsey Gambler that she is not the lawful wife of John Gambler. It is apparent that said Hepsey Gambler is identical with yourself and that the name Hepsey Gambler as it appears in said affidavit is erroneous and should read Hepsey McGilbray, inasmuch as you are not the lawful wife of the said John Gambler.

For the purpose of correcting the discrepancy above noted there is inclosed herewith blank for proof of birth which has been filled out. You are requested to have the same properly executed and when so executed return it to this office in the inclosed envelope. Be careful to see that the affiants sign their names as the same appear in the body of the affidavits and that the notary public, before whom the affidavits are sworn to, attaches his name and seal to each affidavit. In case any signature is by mark the same must be attested by two disinterested witnesses.

                              Respectfully,

                                                    Acting Commissioner.
CTD-2.
Env.

N.C. 622

Muskogee, Indian Territory, September 15, 1905.

Hepsie McGilbra,
    Care John Gambler,
        Eufaula, Indian Territory.

Dear Madam:

Applications for Enrollment of Creek Newborn
Act of 1905   Volume VIII

In the matter of the application for the enrollment of your minor children, Emanuel Sarty and Martin Gambler, as citizens of the Creek Nation, you are advised that you will be allowed fifteen days from date hereof within which to appear before the office of the Commissioner to the Five Civilized Tribes in Muskogee, Indian Territory, for the purpose of being examined under oath.

This matter should receive your prompt attention.

Respectfully,

Acting Commissioner.

N.C. 622

Muskogee, Indian Territory, October 2, 1905.

Hepsie McGilbra,
Eufaula, Indian Territory.

Dear Madam:

In the matter of the application for the enrollment of your minor child, Martin Gambler, as a citizen of the Creek Nation, you are advised that you will be allowed fifteen days from date hereof within which to appear before the office of the Commissioner to the Five Civilized Tribes at Muskogee, Indian Territory, for the purpose of being examined under oath.

Respectfully,

Commissioner.

BIRTH AFFIDAVIT.

DEPARTMENT OF THE INTERIOR.
COMMISSION TO THE FIVE CIVILIZED TRIBES.

IN RE APPLICATION FOR ENROLLMENT, as a citizen of the Creek Nation, of Martin Gambler, born on the 16" day of Oct, 1902

Name of Father: John Gambler   a citizen of the   Creek   Nation.
Name of Mother: Hepsey McGilbray   a citizen of the   Creek   Nation.

Postoffice   Mellette, I.T.

Applications for Enrollment of Creek Newborn
Act of 1905   Volume VIII

AFFIDAVIT OF MOTHER.

UNITED STATES OF AMERICA, Indian Territory, }
Western   DISTRICT.

I, Hepsey McGilbray, on oath state that I am about 20 years of age and a citizen by blood, of the Creek Nation; that I am not the lawful wife of John Gambler, who is a citizen, by blood of the Creek Nation; that a male child was born to me on 16" day of October, 1902, that said child has been named Martin Gambler, and is now living.

                                                             her
Witnesses To Mark: Hepsey x McGilbray
{ H.G. Hains   mark
{ Jesse McDermott

Subscribed and sworn to before me this 16" day of December, 1905.

                                          Jesse McDermott
My Commission expires July 25th, 1907   Notary Public.

BIRTH AFFIDAVIT.

DEPARTMENT OF THE INTERIOR.
COMMISSION TO THE FIVE CIVILIZED TRIBES.

IN RE APPLICATION FOR ENROLLMENT, as a citizen of the Creek Nation, of Martin Gambler, born on the 16 day of October, 1903

Name of Father: John Gambler   a citizen of the   Creek   Nation.
Tuckabatchee Town
Name of Mother: Hepsey McGilbra   a citizen of the   Creek   Nation.

                            Postoffice   Eufaula, Ind. Ter.

AFFIDAVIT OF MOTHER.

UNITED STATES OF AMERICA, Indian Territory, }   <u>Child</u> is <u>present</u>
Western   DISTRICT.

I, Hepsey Gambler, on oath state that I am about 20 years of age and a citizen by blood, of the Creek Nation; that I am not the lawful wife of John Gambler, who is a citizen, by blood of the Creek Nation; that a male child was born to me on 16 day of October, 1903, that said child has been named Martin Gambler, and was living March 4, 1905.

Applications for Enrollment of Creek Newborn
Act of 1905   Volume VIII

                     her
               Hepsey x Gambler
                    mark

Witnesses To Mark:
{ Alex Posey
{ DC Skaggs

Subscribed and sworn to before me this 4 day of April, 1905.

               Drennan C Skaggs
               Notary Public.

AFFIDAVIT OF ATTENDING PHYSICIAN OR MID-WIFE.

UNITED STATES OF AMERICA, Indian Territory, }
     Western   DISTRICT.

I, Lizzie McGilbra, a midwife, on oath state that I attended on ~~Mrs.~~ Hepsey McGilbra, not the lawful wife of John Gambler on the 16 day of October, 1903 ; that there was born to her on said date a male child; that said child was living March 4, 1905, and is said to have been named Martin Gambler

                    her
               Lizzie x McGilbra
Witnesses To Mark: mark
{ Alex Posey
{ DC Skaggs

Subscribed and sworn to before me this 4 day of April, 1905.

               Drennan C Skaggs
               Notary Public.

N.C. 623.

       DEPARTMENT OF THE INTERIOR,
  COMMISSIONER TO THE FIVE CIVILIZED TRIBES.
          Lenna, I.T., September 6, 1905.

In the matter of the application for the enrollment of Tootie and Leah Riley as citizens by blood of the Creek Nation.

     EMMA WILLINGHAM, being duly sworn, testified as follows:

Through Alex Posey Official Interpreter:

Applications for Enrollment of Creek Newborn
Act of 1905   Volume VIII

BY COMMISSIONER:
Q What is your name? A Emma Willingham.
Q How old are you? A Twenty-two.
Q What is your post office address? A Lenna.
Q Are you a citizen of the Creek Nation? A Yes, sir.
Q To what town do you belong? A Coweta.
Q Have you two children named Tootie and Leah Riley? A Yes, sir.
Q Who is the father of these two children? A Thomas Riley.
Q Are you and Thomas Riley living together now as man and wife? A No, sir.
Q Have you seperated[sic] ? A Yes, sir.
Q Was Thomas Riley your lawful husband at the time these two children were born? A Yes, sir.
Q What caused the seperation[sic] between you and Thomas Riley? A He deserted me and failed to support me.
Q Have you married again? A Yes, sir.
Q To whom? A To Dock Willingham?[sic]
Q How long have you been married to Dock Willingham? A We have been married about two months.
Q You are now known as Emma Willingham? A Yes, sir.
Q What was your maiden name? A Emma Deresaw.
Q There are on file with the Commissioner two affidavits executed April 4, 1905, by Thomas Riley, relative to the births of these two children. In the one concerning Tootie Riley, the date of birth is given as February 24, 1902. In your affidavit you state that the child was born April 24, 1902. Which of the two dates is correct? A Thomas Riley is mistaken. The child was born April 24, 1902.
Q Have you a record of the birth of the child? A No, sir.
Q Who attended on you as mid-wife? A My grandmother, Polly Deresaw, who is now dead.
Q Was Polly Deresaw present when your child, Leah, was born? A No, sir, she was dead at that time. This woman here, Mary Murrell, attended on me when Leah was born.
Q Was Sissie Barnett in attendance on you at the birth of Tootie? A No, sir, there was no one present but Polly Deresaw.

---oooOOOooo---

I, D. C. Skaggs, on oath state that the above and foregoing is a full and true transcript of my stenographic notes as taken in said cause on said date.

DC Skaggs

Subscribed and sworn to before me this 16 day of October 1905.

Edw C Griesel
Notary Public.

Applications for Enrollment of Creek Newborn
Act of 1905 Volume VIII

N.C. 623.

DEPARTMENT OF THE INTERIOR,
COMMISSIONER TO THE FIVE CIVILIZED TRIBES.
Lenna, I.T., September 7, 1905.

SUPPLEMENTAL TESTIMONY in the matter of the application for the enrollment of Tootie and Leah Riley as citizens by blood of the Creek Nation.

THOMAS RILEY, being duly sworn, testified as follows:

Through Alex Posey Official Interpreter:

BY COMMISSIONER:
Q What is your name? A Thomas Riley.
Q How old are you? A Twenty-six.
Q What is your post office address? A Lenna.
Q Are you a citizen of the Creek Nation?
Q To what town do you belong? A Quasarte No. 1.
Q Do you know Emma Willingham? A Yes, sir.
Q Was she formerly your wife and known as Emma Riley? A Yes, sir.
[sic] You have seperated[sic] from her have you? A Yes, sir.
Q Did you and Emma have two children named Tootie and Leah Riley? A Yes, sir.
Q You appeared before the Commission and made application for them, did you not? A Yes, sir.
Q In the affidavit executed by you April 4, 1905, relative to the birth of Tootie Riley, you state that she was born February 24, 1902. The mother of the child swears that it was born April 24, 1902? A I must have been in error. The mother should know the exact date. I was not present when the child was born.
Q Then you did not know the exact date of the birth of the child at the time you executed the affidavit? A No, sir. I had made a record of the child's birth but had lost it at the time I executed the affidavit and the date as given was from memory.
Q The mother has the custody of these children has she not? A Yes, sir.

---oooOOOooo---

I, D. C. Skaggs, on oath state that the above and foregoing is a full and true transcript of my stenographic notes as taken in said cause on said date.

DC Skaggs

Subscribed and sworn to before me this 16 day of October 1905.

Edw C Griesel
Notary Public.

Applications for Enrollment of Creek Newborn
Act of 1905   Volume VIII

NC-623

Muskogee, Indian Territory, August 11, 1905.

Thomas Riley,
   Lenna, Indian Territory.

Dear Sir:

In the matter of the application for the enrollment of your minor children, Tootie Riley, born February 24, 1902, and Leah Riley, born February 19, 1905, as citizens by blood of the Creek Nation, it will be necessary for you to file with this office the affidavits of the mother of said children and of the attending physician or midwife relative to their birth. For that purpose, there are enclosed herewith the blanks for proof of birth. In having same executed, be careful to see that all blank spaces are properly filled, all names written in full and that the notary public before whom the affidavits are sworn to attaches his name and seal to each of the affidavits. In case any signature is by mark, the same must be attested by two disinterested witnesses.

Please give this matter your prompt attention.

Respectfully,

Env

Acting Commissioner.

BIRTH AFFIDAVIT.

DEPARTMENT OF THE INTERIOR.
COMMISSION TO THE FIVE CIVILIZED TRIBES.

IN RE APPLICATION FOR ENROLLMENT, as a citizen of the Creek Nation, of Tootie Riley, born on the 24 day of Feb., 1902

Name of Father: Thomas Riley   a citizen of the   Creek   Nation.
Quasarte No. 1
Name of Mother: Emma Riley (nee Deresaw)   a citizen of the   Creek   Nation.
Coweta Town
                          Postoffice   Lenna, Ind. Ter.

Applications for Enrollment of Creek Newborn
Act of 1905 Volume VIII

AFFIDAVIT OF ~~MOTHER~~. Father

UNITED STATES OF AMERICA, Indian Territory, }
Western DISTRICT.

Child is not present

I, Thomas Riley , on oath state that I am 25 years of age and a citizen by blood , of the Creek Nation; that I am the lawful ~~wife~~ husband of Emma Riley, who is a citizen, by blood of the Creek Nation; that a female child was born to ~~me~~ her on 24 day of February , 1902 , that said child has been named Tootie Riley , and was living March 4, 1905. That the mother refused to make application for the enrollment of the child; the midwife Sissy Barnett also refuses to make affidavit.

Thomas Riley

Witnesses To Mark:
{

Subscribed and sworn to before me this 4 day of April, 1905.

Drennan C Skaggs
Notary Public.

BIRTH AFFIDAVIT.

DEPARTMENT OF THE INTERIOR.
COMMISSION TO THE FIVE CIVILIZED TRIBES.

IN RE APPLICATION FOR ENROLLMENT, as a citizen of the Creek Nation, of Tootie Riley , born on the 24 day of April , 1902

Name of Father: Thomas Riley a citizen of the Creek Nation.
Quasarte No. 1 Willingham
Name of Mother: Emma ~~Riley~~ (nee Deresaw) a citizen of the Creek Nation.
Coweta Town
Postoffice Lenna, I.T.

AFFIDAVIT OF MOTHER. Child present.

UNITED STATES OF AMERICA, Indian Territory, }
Western DISTRICT.

I, Emma Willingham , on oath state that I am 22 years of age and a citizen by blood , of the Creek Nation; that I ~~am~~ was formerly the lawful wife of Thomas Riley , who is a citizen, by blood of the Creek Nation; that a female child was born to me on 24 day of April , 1902 , that said child has been named Tootie Riley , and was living March 4, 1905. The mid-wife who attended on me at the child's birth is now dead.

Applications for Enrollment of Creek Newborn
Act of 1905   Volume VIII

                                      her
                          Emma x Willingham

Witnesses To Mark: mark
{ DC Skaggs
  Alex Posey

Subscribed and sworn to before me this 6 day of September, 1905.

                                  Drennan C Skaggs
                                    Notary Public.

AFFIDAVIT OF ATTENDING PHYSICIAN OR MID-WIFE.

UNITED STATES OF AMERICA, Indian Territory,
    Western   DISTRICT.

                                    we are well acquainted with
~~I~~, We the undersigned, ~~a (blank)~~, on oath state that ~~I attended on~~ Mrs. Emma Willingham, former wife of Thomas Riley ~~on the (blank) day of (blank), 1~~; that there was born to her on or about the 24 day of April 1902 said date a female child; that said child was living March 4, 1905, and is said to have been named Tootie Riley

                                  Louis Collins
                                    his
                                Limbo x Carr

Witnesses To Mark: mark
{ DC Skaggs
  Alex Posey

Subscribed and sworn to before me this 6 day of September, 1905.

                                  Drennan C Skaggs
                                  Notary Public.

Applications for Enrollment of Creek Newborn
Act of 1905   Volume VIII

BIRTH AFFIDAVIT.

DEPARTMENT OF THE INTERIOR.
COMMISSION TO THE FIVE CIVILIZED TRIBES.

IN RE APPLICATION FOR ENROLLMENT, as a citizen of the Creek Nation, of Leah Riley, born on the 19 day of Feb, 1905

Name of Father: Thomas Riley   a citizen of the   Creek   Nation.
Quasarte No. 1
Name of Mother: Emma Riley (Nee Deerisaw[sic]) a citizen of the   Creek   Nation.
Coweta Town
                        Postoffice   Lenna, Ind. Ter.

AFFIDAVIT OF MOTHER.

UNITED STATES OF AMERICA, Indian Territory,   }   Child is not present
        Western   DISTRICT.

I, Thomas Riley, on oath state that I am 25 years of age and a citizen by blood, of the Creek Nation; that I am the lawful ~~wife~~ husband of Emma Riley, who is a citizen, by blood of the Creek Nation; that a female child was born to me on 19 day of February, 1905, that said child has been named Leah Riley, and was living March 4, 1905. That the mother refuses to make application for the enrollment of the child; that the midwife, Polly Deerisaw[sic], who attended on the mother at the time this child was born is now dead.

                                         Thomas Riley
Witnesses To Mark:
{

Subscribed and sworn to before me this 4 day of April, 1905.

                                  Drennan C Skaggs
                                     Notary Public.

Applications for Enrollment of Creek Newborn
Act of 1905   Volume VIII

BIRTH AFFIDAVIT.

DEPARTMENT OF THE INTERIOR.
COMMISSION TO THE FIVE CIVILIZED TRIBES.

IN RE APPLICATION FOR ENROLLMENT, as a citizen of the Creek Nation, of Leah Riley, born on the 19 day of February, 1905

Name of Father: Thomas Riley   a citizen of the   Creek   Nation.
   Quasarte No. 1.   (nee Deresaw)
Name of Mother: Emma Willingham   a citizen of the   Creek   Nation.
   Coweta Town
                        Postoffice   Lenna, I.T.

AFFIDAVIT OF MOTHER.

UNITED STATES OF AMERICA, Indian Territory, ⎫
   Western   DISTRICT.   ⎭

   I, Emma Willingham, on oath state that I am 22 years of age and a citizen by blood, of the Creek Nation; that I ~~am~~ was formerly the lawful wife of Thomas Riley, who is a citizen, by blood of the Creek Nation; that a female child was born to me on 19 day of February, 1905, that said child has been named Leah Riley, and was living March 4, 1905.
                                     her
                              Emma x Willingham
Witnesses To Mark: mark
  ⎧ DC Skaggs
  ⎩ Alex Posey

   Subscribed and sworn to before me this 6 day of September, 1905.

                                 Drennan C Skaggs
                                 Notary Public.

AFFIDAVIT OF ATTENDING PHYSICIAN OR MID-WIFE.

UNITED STATES OF AMERICA, Indian Territory, ⎫
   Western   DISTRICT.   ⎭

   I, Mary Murrell, a mid-wife, on oath state that I attended on Mrs. Emma Willingham, the former wife of Thomas Riley on the 19 day of February, 1905; that there was born to her on said date a female child; that said child was living March 4, 1905, and is said to have been named Leah Riley   her
                                 Mary x Murrell
                                 mark

Applications for Enrollment of Creek Newborn
Act of 1905   Volume VIII

Witnesses To Mark:
{ DC Skaggs
  Alex Posey

Subscribed and sworn to before me this 6 day of September, 1905.

Drennan C Skaggs
Notary Public.

BIRTH AFFIDAVIT.

DEPARTMENT OF THE INTERIOR.
COMMISSION TO THE FIVE CIVILIZED TRIBES.

IN RE APPLICATION FOR ENROLLMENT, as a citizen of the Creek Nation, of Susie Francis, born on the ~~(blank)~~ day of April, 1902

Name of Father: Mitchell Francis   a citizen of the   Creek   Nation. Hickory Ground Town
Name of Mother: Menaffie Francis   a citizen of the   Creek   Nation. Tulmachusse

Postoffice   Eufaula, I.T.

AFFIDAVIT OF MOTHER.

UNITED STATES OF AMERICA, Indian Territory,
    Western   DISTRICT.

I, Menaffie Francis, on oath state that I am about 30 years of age and a citizen by blood, of the Creek Nation; that I am the lawful wife of Mitchell Francis, who is a citizen, by blood of the Creek Nation; that a female child was born to me on ---- day of April, 1902, that said child has been named Susie Francis, and was living March 4, 1905.

                                  her
                        Menaffie x Francis
Witnesses To Mark: mark
{ Alex Posey

Subscribed and sworn to before me this 4 day of April, 1905.

Drennan C Skaggs
Notary Public.

Applications for Enrollment of Creek Newborn
Act of 1905   Volume VIII

AFFIDAVIT OF ATTENDING PHYSICIAN OR MID-WIFE.

UNITED STATES OF AMERICA, Indian Territory, }
Western   DISTRICT.

I, Lizzie McGilbra , a mid-wife , on oath state that I attended on Mrs. Mennaffa[sic] Francis , wife of Mitchell Francis ~~on the~~ in the early part day of April , 1902 ; that there was born to her on said date a female child; that said child was living March 4, 1905, and is said to have been named Susie Francis

             her
          Lizzie x McGilbra
Witnesses To Mark: mark
 { DC Skaggs
   Alex Posey

Subscribed and sworn to before me this 4 day of April, 1905.

         Drennan C Skaggs
           Notary Public.

NC-627

        Muskogee, Indian Territory, July 20, 1905.

Susanna McIntosh,
  Eufaula, Indian Territory.

Dear Madam:

  In the matter of the application for the enrollment of application for the enrollment of your minor child, Ida McIntosh, as a citizen of the Creek Nation, you are advised that without further information this office cannot identify Dick McIntosh, the father of said child, as a citizen of said nation.

  You are requested state the names of Dick McIntosh's parents, the Creek Nation to which he belongs, his age, and if possible, the roll number as same appears on his deeds to land in the Creek Nation.

         Respectfully,

            Commissioner.

Applications for Enrollment of Creek Newborn
Act of 1905   Volume VIII

NC-627

Muskogee, Indian Territory, September 8, 1905

Rosanna[sic] McIntosh,
  Eufaula, Indian Territory.

Dear Madam:

In the matter of the application for the enrollment of your minor daughter, Ida McIntosh, as a citizen by blood of the Creek Nation there are on file with the records of this office your affidavit and the affidavit of Sophia Herrod relative to the birth of said children, in which affidavits your name appears as Susanna McIntosh (nee Herrod). You have been identified upon the final roll of citizens by blood of the Creek Nation as Rosanna Herrod.

For the purpose of correcting the discrepancy above noted there is inclosed herewith for your execution an affidavit as to the birth of your said daughter in which your name appears as Rosanna McIntosh. You are requested to appear before a notary public swear to the same and when sworn to return same to this office in the inclosed envelope.

Respectfully,

Acting Commissioner.

CTD-1
Env.

DEPARTMENT OF THE INTERIOR,
COMMISSIONER TO THE FIVE CIVILIZED TRIBES.

REFER IN REPLY TO THE FOLLOWING:
NC-540

Muskogee, Indian Territory, Oc**tober 5, 1905.**

Susanna McIntosh,
  Eufaula, Indian Territory.

Dear Madam:

You are hereby advised that on **September 27, 1905** , the Secretary of the Interior approved the enrollment of your minor child, **Ida McIntosh** , as a citizen by blood of the **Creek** Nation, and that the name of said child appears upon the roll of new born citizens of the **Creek** Nation as Number **540** .

The child is now entitled to an allotment, and application therefor should be made without delay at the Land Office for the Nation in which the prospective allotment is located.

Applications for Enrollment of Creek Newborn
Act of 1905   Volume VIII

An entire allotment for said child must be selected at the time of the original application.

      Respectively,

          Tams Bixby
          Commissioner.

REFER IN REPLY TO THE FOLLOWING:
NC 627.

**DEPARTMENT OF THE INTERIOR,
COMMISSIONER TO THE FIVE CIVILIZED TRIBES.**

Muskogee, Indian Territory, July 11, 1906.

Susanna McIntosh,
  Fame, Indian Territory.

Dear Madam:

  You are again advised that the name of your minor child, Ida McIntosh, is contained in the partial list of citizens by blood of the Creek Nation, approved by the Secretary of the Interior September 27, 1905, and that a selection of land in the Creek Nation may now be made for said child at the Creek Land Office in Muskogee, Indian Territory.

      Respectfully,

         Wm. O. Beall
         Acting Commissioner.

BIRTH AFFIDAVIT.

**DEPARTMENT OF THE INTERIOR.
COMMISSION TO THE FIVE CIVILIZED TRIBES.**

  IN RE APPLICATION FOR ENROLLMENT, as a citizen of the Creek Nation, of Ida McIntosh, born on the 12 day of April, 1902

Name of Father: Dick McIntosh   a citizen of the Creek Nation. Hillabee Town
Name of Mother: Susanna McIntosh (nee Herrod)a citizen of the Creek Nation. Quasarte No.

      Postoffice Eufaula, Ind. Terr.

Applications for Enrollment of Creek Newborn
Act of 1905   Volume VIII

AFFIDAVIT OF MOTHER.

UNITED STATES OF AMERICA, Indian Territory,
Western DISTRICT.

Child is present

I, Susanna McIntosh (nee Herrod), on oath state that I am 28 years of age and a citizen by blood, of the Creek Nation; that I ~~am~~ was formerly the lawful wife of Dick McIntosh, who is a citizen, by blood of the Creek Nation; that a female child was born to me on 12" day of April, 1902, that said child has been named Ida McIntosh, and was living March 4, 1905.

                her
Susanna x McIntosh
       mark

Witnesses To Mark:
{ Alex Posey
  DC Skaggs

Subscribed and sworn to before me this 4 day of April, 1905.

Drennan C Skaggs
Notary Public.

AFFIDAVIT OF ATTENDING PHYSICIAN OR MID-WIFE.

UNITED STATES OF AMERICA, Indian Territory,
Western DISTRICT.

I, Sophia Herrod, a midwife, on oath state that I attended on Mrs. Susanna McIntosh (nee Herrod), formerly wife of Dick McIntosh on the 12 day of April, 1902; that there was born to her on said date a female child; that said child was living March 4, 1905, and is said to have been named Ida McIntosh

        her
Sophia x McIntosh
   mark

Witnesses To Mark:
{ Alex Posey
  DC Skaggs

Subscribed and sworn to before me this 4 day of April, 1905.

Drennan C Skaggs
Notary Public.

Applications for Enrollment of Creek Newborn
Act of 1905 Volume VIII

BIRTH AFFIDAVIT.

DEPARTMENT OF THE INTERIOR.
COMMISSION TO THE FIVE CIVILIZED TRIBES.

IN RE APPLICATION FOR ENROLLMENT, as a citizen of the Creek Nation, of Ferdinand Wilber Crosby, born on the 21st day of February, 1904

Name of Father: Charles E. Crosby   a citizen of the   Creek   Nation.
Name of Mother: Elizabeth A. Crosby   a citizen of the   Creek   Nation.

Postoffice   Bixby, Ind. Ter

AFFIDAVIT OF MOTHER.

UNITED STATES OF AMERICA, Indian Territory,
Western   DISTRICT.

I, Elizabeth A. Crosby, on oath state that I am thirty four years of age and a citizen by blood, of the Creek Nation; that I am the lawful wife of Charles E. Crosby, who is a citizen, by blood of the Creek Nation; that a male child was born to me on twenty-first day of February, 1904, that said child has been named Ferdinand Wilber Crosby, and was living March 4, 1905.

Elizabeth A Crosby

Witnesses To Mark:
  Mrs. Tillie Hodges   Bixby I.T.

Subscribed and sworn to before me this fourth day of April, 1905.

Francis R. Brennan
Notary Public.

AFFIDAVIT OF ATTENDING PHYSICIAN OR MID-WIFE.

UNITED STATES OF AMERICA, Indian Territory,
Western   DISTRICT.

I, William A Funk, a Physician, on oath state that I attended on Mrs. Elizabeth A Crosby, wife of Charles E. Crosby on the 21st day of February, 1904; that there was born to her on said date a male child; that said child was living March 4, 1905, and is said to have been named Ferdinand Wilber Crosby

William Adam Funk

Applications for Enrollment of Creek Newborn
Act of 1905   Volume VIII

Witnesses To Mark:
- Marion F. Young Bixby IT.
- Jason L. Best Bixby I.T.

Subscribed and sworn to before me this fourth day of April, 1905.

Francis R. Brennan
Notary Public.

BIRTH AFFIDAVIT.

DEPARTMENT OF THE INTERIOR.
COMMISSION TO THE FIVE CIVILIZED TRIBES.

IN RE APPLICATION FOR ENROLLMENT, as a citizen of the Creek Nation, of Berry Martin Crosby, born on the 27th day of December, 1901

Name of Father: Charles E. Crosby   a citizen of the Creek   Nation.
Name of Mother: Elizabeth A. Crosby   a citizen of the Creek   Nation.

Postoffice   Bixby, Ind. Ter

AFFIDAVIT OF MOTHER.

UNITED STATES OF AMERICA, Indian Territory,
Western   DISTRICT.

I, Elizabeth A. Crosby, on oath state that I am thirty four years of age and a citizen by blood, of the Creek Nation; that I am the lawful wife of Charles E. Crosby, who is a citizen, by blood of the Creek Nation; that a male child was born to me on 27th day of December, 1901, that said child has been named Berry Martin Crosby, and was living March 4, 1905.

Elizabeth A Crosby

Witnesses To Mark:
- Mrs. Tillie Hodges   Bixby I.T.

Subscribed and sworn to before me this fourth day of April, 1905.

Francis R. Brennan
Notary Public.

Applications for Enrollment of Creek Newborn
Act of 1905   Volume VIII

AFFIDAVIT OF ATTENDING PHYSICIAN OR MID-WIFE.

UNITED STATES OF AMERICA, Indian Territory,
Western   DISTRICT. }

I, Mary Ann Crosby, a mid-wife, on oath state that I attended on Mrs. Elizabeth A Crosby, wife of Charles E. Crosby on the 27th day of December, 1901; that there was born to her on said date a male child; that said child was living March 4, 1905, and is said to have been named Berry Martin Crosby

              Mary Ann Crosby

Witnesses To Mark:
{ Marion F. Young   Bixby Ind Ter.
 Jason L. Best Bixby I.T.

Subscribed and sworn to before me this fourth day of April, 1905.

             Francis R. Brennan
             Notary Public.

BIRTH AFFIDAVIT.

DEPARTMENT OF THE INTERIOR.
COMMISSION TO THE FIVE CIVILIZED TRIBES.

IN RE APPLICATION FOR ENROLLMENT, as a citizen of the Creek Nation, of Melissa McGilbra, born on the 27 day of December, 1903

Name of Father: Jackson McGilbra a citizen of the   Creek   Nation.
Kialagee Town
Name of Mother: Cinda McGilbra (nee Tiger)   a citizen of the   Creek   Nation.
Kialagee Town
         Postoffice Eufaula, Ind. Ter.

         Child present.
AFFIDAVIT OF MOTHER.

UNITED STATES OF AMERICA, Indian Territory,
Western   DISTRICT. }

I, Cinda McGilbra, on oath state that I am 24 years of age and a citizen by blood, of the Creek Nation; that I am the lawful wife of Jackson McGilbra, who is

Applications for Enrollment of Creek Newborn
Act of 1905   Volume VIII

a citizen, by blood of the Creek Nation; that a female child was born to me on 27 day of December, 1903, that said child has been named Melissa McGilbra, and was living March 4, 1905.   (Lucinda McGilbra)

Cinda x McGilbra

Witnesses To Mark:
{ DC Skaggs
{ Alex Posey

Subscribed and sworn to before me this 4 day of April, 1905.

Drennan C Skaggs
Notary Public.

AFFIDAVIT OF ATTENDING PHYSICIAN OR MID-WIFE.

UNITED STATES OF AMERICA, Indian Territory,
   Western   DISTRICT.

I, Sallie Tiger, a mid-wife, on oath state that I attended on Mrs. Cinda McGilbra, wife of Jackson McGilbra on the 27 day of December, 1903; that there was born to her on said date a female child; that said child was living March 4, 1905, and is said to have been named Melissa McGilbra

her
Sallie x Tiger
mark

Witnesses To Mark:
{ DC Skaggs
{ Alex Posey

Subscribed and sworn to before me this 4 day of April, 1905.

Drennan C Skaggs
Notary Public.

Applications for Enrollment of Creek Newborn
Act of 1905 Volume VIII

BIRTH AFFIDAVIT.

DEPARTMENT OF THE INTERIOR.
COMMISSION TO THE FIVE CIVILIZED TRIBES.

IN RE APPLICATION FOR ENROLLMENT, as a citizen of the Creek Nation, of Arthur E. Postoak, born on the 25th day of October, 1901

Name of Father: Lincoln Postoak	a citizen of the	Creek Nation.
Name of Mother: Lillie Postoak	a citizen of the	Creek Nation.

Postoffice   Red Fork, Ind. Ter.

AFFIDAVIT OF MOTHER.

UNITED STATES OF AMERICA, Indian Territory,
Western   DISTRICT.

I, Lillie Postoak, on oath state that I am 35 years of age and a citizen by blood, of the Creek Nation; that I am the lawful wife of Lincoln Postoak, who is a citizen, by blood of the Creek Nation; that a male child was born to me on 25th day of October, 1901, that said child has been named Arthur E. Postoak, and is now living.

Lillie Postoak

Witnesses To Mark:

Subscribed and sworn to before me this 12th day of April, 1905.

My Commission expires Oct. 19, 1907.   Allen Henry
Notary Public.

AFFIDAVIT OF ATTENDING PHYSICIAN OR MID-WIFE.

UNITED STATES OF AMERICA, Indian Territory,
Western   DISTRICT.

I, Sarah Berryhill, a mid-wife, on oath state that I attended on Mrs. Lillie Postoak, wife of Lincoln Postoak on the 25th day of October, 1901; that there was born to her on said date a male child; that said child is now living and is said to have been named Arthur E. Postoak

Sarah Berryhill

Witnesses To Mark:

Applications for Enrollment of Creek Newborn
Act of 1905   Volume VIII

Subscribed and sworn to before me this 12th day of April, 1905.

My Commission expires *(blank)*   Allen Henry
                                  Notary Public.

BIRTH AFFIDAVIT.

DEPARTMENT OF THE INTERIOR.
COMMISSION TO THE FIVE CIVILIZED TRIBES.

IN RE APPLICATION FOR ENROLLMENT, as a citizen of the Creek Nation, of Hattie L. Postoak, born on the 7th day of October, 1903

Name of Father: Lincoln Postoak   a citizen of the   Creek   Nation.
Name of Mother: Lillie Postoak   a citizen of the   Creek   Nation.

Postoffice   Red Fork, Ind. Ter.

AFFIDAVIT OF ATTENDING PHYSICIAN OR MID-WIFE.

UNITED STATES OF AMERICA, Indian Territory,
   Western   DISTRICT.

I, Sarah Berryhill, a mid-wife, on oath state that I attended on Mrs. Lillie Postoak, wife of Lincoln Postoak on the 7th day of October, 1903; that there was born to her on said date a Female child; that said child is now living and is said to have been named Hattie L. Postoak

                                  Sarah Berryhill
Witnesses To Mark:
{

Subscribed and sworn to before me this 12th day of April, 1905.

My Commission expires Oct. 19, 1907.   Allen Henry
                                       Notary Public.

BIRTH AFFIDAVIT.

DEPARTMENT OF THE INTERIOR.
COMMISSION TO THE FIVE CIVILIZED TRIBES.

IN RE APPLICATION FOR ENROLLMENT, as a citizen of the CREEK Nation, of Hattie L. Postoak, born on the 7 day of Oct, 1903

Applications for Enrollment of Creek Newborn
Act of 1905 Volume VIII

Name of Father: Lincoln Postoak   a citizen of the   Creek   Nation.
Name of Mother: Lillie   "   a citizen of the   "   Nation.

Postoffice   Red~~bird~~ fork

(Child present)

AFFIDAVIT OF MOTHER.

UNITED STATES OF AMERICA, Indian Territory, ⎫
    Western   DISTRICT.   ⎬

    I, Lilly Postoak, on oath state that I am 35 years of age and a citizen by blood, of the Creek Nation; that I am the lawful wife of Lincoln Postoak, who is a citizen, by blood of the Creek Nation; that a female child was born to me on 7th day of Oct., 1903, that said child has been named Hattie L. Postoak, and is now living.

                                Lillie Postoak

Witnesses To Mark:
{

    Subscribed and sworn to before me this 6" day of April, 1905.

                                Edw C Griesel
                                     Notary Public.

BIRTH AFFIDAVIT.

DEPARTMENT OF THE INTERIOR.
COMMISSION TO THE FIVE CIVILIZED TRIBES.

    IN RE APPLICATION FOR ENROLLMENT, as a citizen of the Creek Nation, of Arthur E. Postoak, born on the 25" day of Oct., 1901

Name of Father: Lincoln Postoak   a citizen of the   Creek   Nation.
Name of Mother: Lillie   "   a citizen of the   "   Nation.

Postoffice   Redfork

(Child present)

AFFIDAVIT OF MOTHER.

UNITED STATES OF AMERICA, Indian Territory, ⎫
    Western   DISTRICT.   ⎬

    I, Lilly Postoak, on oath state that I am 35 years of age and a citizen by blood, of the Creek Nation; that I am the lawful wife of Lincoln Postoak, who is a citizen,

Applications for Enrollment of Creek Newborn
Act of 1905 Volume VIII

by blood of the Creek Nation; that a male child was born to me on 25" day of Oct. , 1901 , that said child has been named Arthur E. Postoak , and is now living.

                                        Lillie Postoak

Witnesses To Mark:
{

   Subscribed and sworn to before me this 6" day of April , 1905.

                                          Edw C Griesel
                                          Notary Public.

NC-631

                                 Muskogee, Indian Territory, August 10, 1905.

Maggie J. Clarkston,
    Redbird, Indian Territory.

Dear Madam:

   In the matter of the application for the enrollment of your minor son, Raymond Clarkston, as a citizen by blood of the Creek Nation, it will be necessary for you to furnish this office with the affidavit of Maggie A. Girdner, midwife, relative to the birth of said child, and for that purpose there is enclosed herewith a blank for proof of birth, which has been filled out.

   The affidavit of the said Maggie A. Girdner as to the birth of said child, which is now on file, is defective, inasmuch as the notary public before whom the same was sworn to neglected to affix his signature to said affidavit.

                                         Respectfully,

                                                          Acting Commissioner.

JYM-10-3
Env

Applications for Enrollment of Creek Newborn
Act of 1905 Volume VIII

BIRTH AFFIDAVIT.

DEPARTMENT OF THE INTERIOR.
COMMISSION TO THE FIVE CIVILIZED TRIBES.

IN RE APPLICATION FOR ENROLLMENT, as a citizen of the Creek Nation, of Raymond Clarkston , born on the 12th day of June , 1902

Name of Father: Alex Clarkston   a citizen of the United States Nation.
Name of Mother: Maggie J. Clarkston   a citizen of the   Creek   Nation.

Postoffice   Red Bird, I.T.

AFFIDAVIT OF ATTENDING PHYSICIAN OR MID-WIFE.

UNITED STATES OF AMERICA, Indian Territory,
     Western   DISTRICT.

I, Maggie A. Girdner , a mid-wife , on oath state that I attended on Mrs. Maggie J. Clarkston , wife of Alex Clarkston on the 12th day of June , 1902 ; that there was born to her on said date a male child; that said child was living March 4, 1905, and is said to have been named Raymond Clarkston

                             Maggie A Girdner

Witnesses To Mark:
    { Mollie Clarkston
    { J.F. Funk

Subscribed and sworn to before me this 15 day of Aug, 1905.

                             J W Hensley
                                    Notary Public.
                    My Com Ex[6/29-1908

BIRTH AFFIDAVIT.

DEPARTMENT OF THE INTERIOR.
COMMISSION TO THE FIVE CIVILIZED TRIBES.

IN RE APPLICATION FOR ENROLLMENT, as a citizen of the Creek (Muskogee) Nation, of Raymond Clarkston, born on the 12th day of June , 1902

Name of Father: Alex Clarkston   a citizen of the ——(blank)——Nation.
Name of Mother: Maggie J Clarkston   a citizen of the Creek (Muskogee)Nation.

Applications for Enrollment of Creek Newborn
Act of 1905   Volume VIII

Postoffice   Red Bird, Ind. Ter.

AFFIDAVIT OF MOTHER.

UNITED STATES OF AMERICA, Indian Territory,
Western   DISTRICT.

  I, Maggie J. Clarkston, on oath state that I am 23 years of age and a citizen by birth, of the Creek (Muskogee) Nation; that I am the lawful wife of Alex Clarkston, who is a citizen, by —— of the —— Nation; that a male child was born to me on 12th day of June, 1902, that said child has been named Raymond Clarkston, and was living March 4, 1905.

            Maggie J Clarkston

Witnesses To Mark:

  Subscribed and sworn to before me this 27th day of March, 1905.

            Lawrence Wright
            Notary Public.

AFFIDAVIT OF ATTENDING PHYSICIAN OR MID-WIFE.

UNITED STATES OF AMERICA, Indian Territory,
Western   DISTRICT.

  I, Maggie J. Girdner, a midwife, on oath state that I attended on Mrs. Maggie J Clarkston, wife of Alex Clarkston on the 12th day of June, 1902 ; that there was born to her on said date a male child; that said child was living March 4, 1905, and is said to have been named Raymond Clarkston

Witnesses To Mark:

  Subscribed and sworn to before me this 27th day of March, 1905.

            (No signature given)
            Notary Public.

Applications for Enrollment of Creek Newborn
Act of 1905 Volume VIII

DEPARTMENT OF THE INTERIOR,
COMMISSION TO THE FIVE CIVILIZED TRIBES.
Eufaula, I. T., April 3, 1905.

In the matter of the application for the enrollment of Edmund and Hammer Barnett as citizens by blood of the Creek Nation.

LIZA BARNETT, being duly sworn, testified as follows:

Through Alex Posey Official Interpreter:

BY COMMISSION:
Q What is your name? A Liza Barnett.
Q How old are you? A About thirty.
Q What is your post office address? A Eufaula.
Q Are you a citizen of the Creek Nation? A ~~Yes~~, No, sir, I am a Seminole.
Q Do you make application for the enrollment of your two minor children, Edmund and Hammer Barnett, as citizens by blood of the Creek Nation? A Yes, sir.
Q What is the name of the father of these two children? A Austin Barnett.
Q Is he your lawful husband? A Yes, sir.
Q If it should be found that these two children are entitled to be enrolled in either the Creek or Seminole Nations, in which nation do you elect to have them enrolled? A In the Creek Nation.

---oooOOOooo---

I, D. C. Skaggs, on oath state that the above and foregoing is a full and true transcript of my stenographic notes as taken in said cause on said date.

DC Skaggs

Subscribed and sworn to before me this 21 day of July, 1905.

J McDermott
Notary Public.

Applications for Enrollment of Creek Newborn
Act of 1905   Volume VIII

BIRTH AFFIDAVIT.

DEPARTMENT OF THE INTERIOR.
COMMISSION TO THE FIVE CIVILIZED TRIBES.

IN RE APPLICATION FOR ENROLLMENT, as a citizen of the Creek Nation, of Hammer Barnett, born on the 13 day of June, 1904

Name of Father: Austin Barnett   a citizen of the   Creek   Nation.
Okchiye Town
Name of Mother: Liza Barnett (nee Hawkins)   a citizen of the   Seminole Nation.

Postoffice   Eufaula, Ind. Ter.

AFFIDAVIT OF MOTHER.

UNITED STATES OF AMERICA, Indian Territory, }
    Western   DISTRICT.   Child is present

I, Liza Barnett, on oath state that I am about 30 years of age and a citizen by blood, of the Seminole Nation; that I am the lawful wife of Austin Barnett, who is a citizen, by blood of the Creek Nation; that a male child was born to me on 13 day of June, 1904, that said child has been named Hammer Barnett, and was living March 4, 1905.
                                         her
                                Liza x Barnett
Witnesses To Mark: mark
 { Alex Posey
 { DC Skaggs

Subscribed and sworn to before me this 3 day of April, 1905.

Drennan C Skaggs
Notary Public.

Father
AFFIDAVIT OF ~~ATTENDING PHYSICIAN OR MID-WIFE~~.

UNITED STATES OF AMERICA, Indian Territory, }
    Western   DISTRICT.

                                                    my wife
I, Austin Barnett, ~~a~~ *(blank)*, on oath state that I attended on ^ Mrs. Liza Barnett, ~~wife of~~ *(blank)* on the 13 day of June, 1904; that there was born to her on said date a male child; that said child was living March 4, 1905, and is said to have been named Hammer Barnett
                                       his
                              Austin x Barnett
                                      mark

Applications for Enrollment of Creek Newborn
Act of 1905 Volume VIII

Witnesses To Mark:
{

    Subscribed and sworn to before me this 4 day of April, 1905.

                            Drennan C Skaggs
                            Notary Public.

BIRTH AFFIDAVIT.

DEPARTMENT OF THE INTERIOR.
COMMISSION TO THE FIVE CIVILIZED TRIBES.

IN RE APPLICATION FOR ENROLLMENT, as a citizen of the Creek Nation, of Hammer Barnett, born on the 13 day of June, 1904

Name of Father: Austin Barnett   a citizen of the   Creek   Nation. Okchiye Town
Name of Mother: Liza Barnett (nee Hawkins)   a citizen of the   Seminole   Nation.

                    Postoffice   Eufaula, Ind. Ter.

AFFIDAVIT OF ATTENDING PHYSICIAN OR MID-WIFE.

UNITED STATES OF AMERICA, Indian Territory,
       Western   **DISTRICT.**

                                  we are personally acquainted with
   I, We the undersigned, a *(blank)*, on oath state that I attended on Mrs. Liza Barnett, wife of Austin Barnett on the *(blank)* day of *(blank)*, 1; that there was born to her on said date June 13, 1904 a male child; that said child was living March 4, 1905, and is said to have been named Hammer Barnett

                                W M Sullivan
Witnesses To Mark: her
 { DC Skaggs   Hagie x Sullivan
   Alex Posey   mark

    Subscribed and sworn to before me this 21 day of Sept, 1905.

                            Drennan C Skaggs
                            Notary Public.

Applications for Enrollment of Creek Newborn
Act of 1905   Volume VIII

BIRTH AFFIDAVIT.

DEPARTMENT OF THE INTERIOR.
COMMISSION TO THE FIVE CIVILIZED TRIBES.

IN RE APPLICATION FOR ENROLLMENT, as a citizen of the Creek Nation, of Edmund Barnett, born on the 12 day of June, 1901

Name of Father: Austin Barnett   a citizen of the   Creek   Nation.
Okchiye Town
Name of Mother: Liza Barnett (nee Hawkins)   a citizen of the   Seminole   Nation.

Postoffice   Eufaula, Ind. Ter.

AFFIDAVIT OF MOTHER.

UNITED STATES OF AMERICA, Indian Territory, }
    Western   DISTRICT.   }   Child is present

I, Liza Barnett, on oath state that I am about 30 years of age and a citizen by blood, of the Seminole Nation; that I am the lawful wife of Austin Barnett, who is a citizen, by blood of the Creek Nation; that a male child was born to me on 12 day of June, 1901, that said child has been named Edmund Barnett, and was living March 4, 1905.
                                          her
                              Liza x Barnett
Witnesses To Mark: mark
{ Alex Posey
{ DC Skaggs

Subscribed and sworn to before me this 3 day of April, 1905.

                              Drennan C Skaggs
                                Notary Public.

Father
AFFIDAVIT OF ~~ATTENDING PHYSICIAN OR MID-WIFE~~.

UNITED STATES OF AMERICA, Indian Territory, }
    Western   DISTRICT.   }
                                                    my wife
I, Austin Barnett, ~~a~~ *(blank)*, on oath state that I attended on ^ Mrs. Liza Barnett, ~~wife of~~ *(blank)* on the 12 day of June, 1901; that there was born to her on said date a male child; that said child was living March 4, 1905, and is said to have been named Edmund Barnett   his
                              Austin x Barnett
                                mark

Applications for Enrollment of Creek Newborn
Act of 1905   Volume VIII

Witnesses To Mark:
{ Alex Posey
{ DC Skaggs

    Subscribed and sworn to before me this 3 day of April, 1905.

                                     Drennan C Skaggs
                                      Notary Public.

BIRTH AFFIDAVIT.

DEPARTMENT OF THE INTERIOR.
COMMISSION TO THE FIVE CIVILIZED TRIBES.

    IN RE APPLICATION FOR ENROLLMENT, as a citizen of the Creek Nation, of Edmund Barnett, born on the 12 day of June, 1901

Name of Father: Austin Barnett   a citizen of the   Creek   Nation. Okchiye Town
Name of Mother: Liza Barnett (nee Hawkins)   a citizen of the   Seminole   Nation.

                        Postoffice   Eufaula, Ind. Ter.

AFFIDAVIT OF ATTENDING PHYSICIAN OR MID-WIFE.

UNITED STATES OF AMERICA, Indian Territory, }
    Western   DISTRICT.   }

                                        we are personally acquainted with
    ~~I~~, We the undersigned, ~~a~~ *(blank)*, on oath state that ~~I attended on~~ Mrs. Liza Barnett, wife of Austin Barnett ~~on the (blank) day of (blank), 1~~; that there was born to her on ~~said date~~ June 12, 1901 a male child; that said child was living March 4, 1905, and is said to have been named Edmund Barnett

                                    W M Sullivan
Witnesses To Mark: her
{ DC Skaggs   Hagie x Sullivan
{ Alex Posey   mark

    Subscribed and sworn to before me this 21 day of Sept, 1905.

                                      Drennan C Skaggs
                                      Notary Public.

Applications for Enrollment of Creek Newborn
Act of 1905 Volume VIII

NC. 632.

Muskogee, Indian Territory, July 15, 1905.

Chief Clerk,
    Seminole Enrollment Division,
        Muskogee, Indian Territory.

Dear Sir:

    April 6, 1905, application was made to the Commission to the Five Civilized Tribes for the enrollment of Edmund Barnett, born June 12, 1901, and Hannah[sic] Barnett, born June 13, 1904, as citizens by blood of the Creek Nation. It is stated in said application that the father of said children is Austin Barnett, a citizen of the Creek Nation, and that the mother is Lizanna Barnett, a citizen of the Seminole Nation.

    You are requested to inform the Creek Enrollment Division as to whether application has been made for the enrollment of said children as citizens of the Seminole Nation, and if so, what disposition has been made of the same.

        Respectfully,

                Commissioner.

NC-632

Muskogee, Indian Territory, August 10, 1905.

Austin Barnett,
    Eufaula, Indian Territory.

Dear Sir:

    In the matter of the application for the enrollment of your minor children, Edmund Barnett, born June 12, 1901, and Hammer Barnett, born June 13, 1904, as citizens by blood of the Creek Nation, it will be necessary for you to furnish this Office with the affidavits of two disinterested persons as to the birth of said children. Said affidavits must set forth the names of said children, the date of their birth, the names of their parents, and whether or not they were living on March 4, 1905.

        Respectfully,

                Acting Commissioner.

Applications for Enrollment of Creek Newborn
Act of 1905   Volume VIII

W.F.

REFER IN REPLY TO THE FOLLOWING:

DEPARTMENT OF THE INTERIOR,
COMMISSIONER TO THE FIVE CIVILIZED TRIBES.

Muskogee, Indian Territory, August 11, 1905.

Clerk in Charge,
    Creek Enrollment Division.

Dear Sir:

    In reply to your verbal inquiry of this date as to whether application was ever made to the Commission to the Five Civilized Tribes for the enrollment of Edmund Barnett, born June 12, 1901, and Hammer Barnett, born June 13, 1904, children of Austin Barnett, a citizen of the Creek Nation, and Liza Barnett, a citizen of the Seminole Nation, you are advised that it does not appear from an examination of the records of this office that any application was ever made for the enrollment of the said Edmund Barnett and Hammer Barnett as citizens of the Seminole Nation.

                   Respectfully,

                            Wm. O. Beall
                            Acting Commissioner.

NC 632

Muskogee, Indian Territory, November 12, 1906.

Chief Clerk,
    Seminole Enrollment Division,
        General Office.

Dear Sir:

    You are hereby advised that the names of Edmund and Hammer Barnett, children of Austin Barnett, a citizen by blood of the Creek Nation and Liza Barnett, an alleged citizen of the Seminole Nation, are contained in schedule of minor citizens by blood of the Creek Nation, approved by the Secretary of the Interior, September 27, 1905, opposite Roll numbers 724 and 725.

                   Respectfully,

                            Commissioner.

Applications for Enrollment of Creek Newborn
Act of 1905   Volume VIII

STATE OF INDIANA, COUNTY OF PORTER, SCT:

I, C. S. PEIRCE, Clerk of the Circuit Court within and for the County and State aforesaid (the same being a Court of Record), do hereby certify that   Kate Corboy   whose name is subscribed to the   Birth Affidavit   , the annexed instrument, was at the date of taking such   affidavit   , an acting   Notary Public   within and for the County aforesaid duly commissioned and qualified, and authorized to take the same.

~~And further, that I am acquainted with the handwriting of said Kate Corboy, and that the said signature purporting to be his, is true and genuine and the said instrument executed in accordance with the laws of the State of Indiana.~~

In Testimony Whereof, I have hereunto set my hand and affixed the seal of said Court, this 21   day of   April   1905

                                              CS Peirce   Clerk.

NC-635

                        Muskogee, Indian Territory, August 11, 1905.

Osborn A Morton
    559 S. E. Street,
        Valparaiso, Indiana.

Dear Sir:

    In the matter of the application for the enrollment of your minor son, Leo Britt Morton, as a citizen by blood of the Creek Nation, it will be necessary for you to furnish this office with the original or a certified copy of the marriage license and certificate, showing marriage between you and Mittie B. Morton, the non-citizen mother of said child.

                    Respectfully,

                                          Acting Commissioner.

STATE OF INDIAN[sic])
COUNTY OF PORTER) S.S.

    Osborn A. Morton of lawful age, being first duly sworn, deposes and says that he has in his possession, Marriage License, No. 1341, which was regularly and lawfully issued out of the office of the Clerk of the United States Court for the Northern District, of the Indian Territory, on the 23, day of September, 1898, and that the attached instrument is a true copy of the same, together with certificate of Marriage and the certificate of Record.

                                      Osborn A. Morton

Applications for Enrollment of Creek Newborn
Act of 1905   Volume VIII

Subscribed and sworn to before me this the 14th day of Aug. 1905.

    And I further certify that the original license No. 1341, issued out of the office of the clerk for the United States Court for the Northern District of Indian Territory, was this day exhibited to me by the said Osborn A. Morton, and that the same bears the signature of James A. Winston, as clerk of the United States Court for the Northern District of the Indian Territory, also the Official seal of the said Court; And that the certificate of Marriage is signed by M. O. Keller as a Minister of the Gospel;

    And I further certify that the attached instrumrnet[sic] is a true copy of the said Original Marriage License No. 1341, as well as ~~the~~ of[sic] the Certificate of Marriage and certificate of Record.

    In witness whereof I have hereunto affixed my name and Notarial Seal, this the 14th day of Aug. 1905.

                                       Kate Corboy
My commission expires, _July 11, 1908._   Notary Public.

COPY.

MARRIAGE LICENSE.

UNITED STATES OF AMERICA)
       INDIAN TERRITORY) S.S.   NO. 1341.
       NORTHERN DISTRICT)
                     by law
TO ANY PERSON AUTHORIZED ^ TO SOLEMNIZE MARRIAGE,---GREETING:

    YOU ARE HEREBY COMMANDED to solemnize the right and publish the Banns of Matrimony between Mr. Osborn A. Morton of Sapulpa, in the Indian Territory, aged 28 years, and Miss Mittie B. Britt of Sapulpa, in the Indian Territory, aged 26 years, according to law, and do you officially sign and return this License to the parties therein named.   and

        WITNESS my hand ^ official seal at Muskogee, Indian Territory, this 23 day of September, A. D. 1898.

                                              James A. Winston
                    (SEAL)   Clerk of the U.S. Court.
By _____Deputy

Applications for Enrollment of Creek Newborn
Act of 1905   Volume VIII

CERTIFICATE OF MARRIAGE.

UNITED STATES OF AMERICA)
INDIAN TERRITORY) S.S.
NORTHERN DISTRICT)

I, H.[sic]O. Keller, a Minister of the Gospel, DO Hereby Certify, that on the 24th day of September, A.D. 1898, I did duly and according to law, as commanded in the foregoing license, solemnize the right and publish the Banns of Matrimony between the parties therein named.
WITNESS my hand this 24th day of September, A. D. 1898.
My credentials are recorded in the office of the Clerk of the United States Court, Indian Territory, Northern District, Book B, Page 173.

H.O. Keller
A Minister of the Gospel.

Note-- This license and certificate of marriage must be returned to the office of the clerk of the U.S. Court in the Northern District, Indian Territory, from whence it was issued, within sixty days from the date thereof, or the party to whom the license was issued will be liable in the sum of One Hundred Dollard - ($100.00). -

----

CERTIFICATE OF RECORD.

UNITED STATES OF AMERICA)
INDIAN TERRITORY) S.S.
NORTHERN DISTRICT)

I, James A. Winston, Clerk of the United States Court in the Northern District, Indian Territory, do hereby certify that the instrument hereto attached was filed for record in my office the 24th day of September, 1898, at -----., and duly recorded in Book --G--, Marriage Record, Page 153.
WITNESS my hand and seal of said Court at Muskogee, in said Territory this 26th day of September A.D. 1898.

Jas. A. Winston
By)))))))))))))))))))))))-Deputy,   Clerk.

Applications for Enrollment of Creek Newborn
Act of 1905 Volume VIII

Valparaiso, Ind.   Apr. 28th, 1905.
Hon. Commission to the Five Civilized Tribes,
          Muskogee, I.T.

Gentlemen: I hand you herewith enclosed certificate of appointment of Kate Corboy as a Notary Public, you will notice she is the Notary Public before whom the witnesses appeared and made oath to the Birth affidavits filed in the matter of the application of Leo Britt Morton, for enrollment as a citizen of the Creek Nation, under recent act of Congress.
       Please consider this certificate in connection with the said application.

                     Very truly,

                              O.A. Morton
                              559 S.E. Street
                              Valparaiso Ind.

                 DEPARTMENT OF THE INTERIOR,
                 Commission to the Five Civilized Tribes.

      IN RE Application for the enrollment of Leo Britt Morton as a citizen of the Creek Nation.

                 __Affidavit of attending Physician.__

State of Indiana ⎤
               ⎬ ss
County of Porter, ⎦

      I, Simon J. Young, a practicing Physician, on oath state that I attended on Mrs. Mittie B. Morton, wife of Osborn A. Morton, on the 18th day of February, 1905;

      That there was born to her on said date a male child;

      That said child was living March 4, 1905, and is said to have been named Leo Britt Morton.
                                  S.J. Young

Subscribed and sworn to before me this 25 day of March, 1905.

                          Franklin T. Fetting
My com. expires *(blank)*.   ~~Notary Public.~~
                          Judge of the City court of Valparaiso Ind.

Applications for Enrollment of Creek Newborn
Act of 1905   Volume VIII

BIRTH AFFIDAVIT.

DEPARTMENT OF THE INTERIOR.
COMMISSION TO THE FIVE CIVILIZED TRIBES.

IN RE APPLICATION FOR ENROLLMENT, as a citizen of the Creek Nation, of Leo Britt Morton, born on the 18th day of February, 1905

Name of Father: Osborn A. Morton   a citizen of the   Creek   Nation.
Name of Mother: Mittie B. Morton, an inter-married a citizen of the   Creek   Nation.

Postoffice   Valparaiso, Ind.

AFFIDAVIT OF MOTHER.

UNITED STATES OF AMERICA, Indian Territory,   State of Indiana
　　　　　　　　　　　　　　　　DISTRICT.   County of Porter   S.S.

I, Mittie B. Morton, on oath state that I am 33 years of age and a citizen by marriage, of the Creek Nation; that I am the lawful wife of Osborn A. Morton, who is a citizen, by blood of the Creek Nation; that a male child was born to me on 18th day of February, 1905, that said child has been named Leo Britt Morton, and was living March 4, 1905.

　　　　　　　　　　　　　　　　Mittie B. Morton

Witnesses To Mark:
{

Subscribed and sworn to before me this 25th day of March, 1905.

My commission expires July 11, 1905[sic].   Kate Corboy
　　　　　　　　　　　　　　　　　　　　　Notary Public.

AFFIDAVIT OF ATTENDING PHYSICIAN OR MID-WIFE.

UNITED STATES OF AMERICA, Indian Territory,   State of Indiana
　　　　　　　　　　　　　　　　DISTRICT.   County of Porter   S.S.

I, Lydia Curtis, a mid-wife, on oath state that I attended on Mrs. Mittie B. Morton, wife of Osborn A. Morton on the 18th day of February, 1905; that there was born to her on said date a male child; that said child was living March 4, 1905, and is said to have been named Leo Britt Morton

　　　　　　　　　　　　　　　　Lydia Curtis

Witnesses To Mark:
{

Applications for Enrollment of Creek Newborn
Act of 1905   Volume VIII

Subscribed and sworn to before me this 25th day of March , 1905.

My commission expires July 11, 1905[sic].   Kate Corboy
                                                                        Notary Public.

BIRTH AFFIDAVIT.

DEPARTMENT OF THE INTERIOR.
COMMISSION TO THE FIVE CIVILIZED TRIBES.

    IN RE APPLICATION FOR ENROLLMENT, as a citizen of the Creek Nation, of Jesse Wind , born on the 26th day of March , 1903

Name of Father: George Wind	a citizen of the Creek	Nation.
Name of Mother: Millie Wind	a citizen of the Creek	Nation.

                    Postoffice   Okemah, I.T.

AFFIDAVIT OF MOTHER.

UNITED STATES OF AMERICA, Indian Territory,
      Western Judicial   DISTRICT.

    I, Millie Wind , on oath state that I am 24 years of age and a citizen by Blood , of the Muskogee or Creek Nation; that I am the lawful wife of George Wind , who is a citizen, by Blood of the Muskogee or Creek   Nation; that a Male   child was born to me on 26th day of March , 1903 , that said child has been named Jesse Wind , and was living March 4, 1905.

                                Millie Wind

Witnesses To Mark:

{

    Subscribed and sworn to before me this 27th day of March , 1905

My Commission Expires Sept 6th 1906.   John H. Phillips
                                                                     Notary Public.

Applications for Enrollment of Creek Newborn
Act of 1905   Volume VIII

AFFIDAVIT OF ATTENDING PHYSICIAN OR MID-WIFE.

UNITED STATES OF AMERICA, Indian Territory, }
Western Judicial   DISTRICT.

I, Malinda Knight, a Mid-Wife, on oath state that I attended on Mrs. Millie Wind, wife of George Wind on the 26th day of March, 1903; that there was born to her on said date a Male child; that said child was living March 4, 1905, and is said to have been named Jesse Wind

                                              her
                                     Malinda x Knight
Witnesses To Mark: mark
  { L.E. Dunson
    J.H. Phillips

Subscribed and sworn to before me this 27th day of March, 1905

My Commission Expires Sept 6th 1906.   John H. Phillips
                                                            Notary Public.

NC. 635.

Muskogee, Indian Territory, July 15, 1905.

Chief Clerk,
    Seminole Enrollment Division,
        Muskogee, Indian Territory.

Dear Sir:

    April 6, 1905, application was made to the Commission to the Five Civilized Tribes for the enrollment of Ruth Brown, born March 17, 1902, and John William Brown, born June 5, 1904, as citizens by blood of the Creek Nation. It is stated in said application that the father of said child[sic] is Clarence William Brown, a citizen of the Creek Nation, and that the mother is Rebecca Brown, a citizen of the Seminole Nation.

    You are requested to inform the Creek Enrollment Division as to whether application has been made for the enrollment of said children as citizens of the Seminole Nation, and if so, what disposition has been made of the same.

                                        Respectfully,

                                                             Commissioner.

Applications for Enrollment of Creek Newborn
Act of 1905   Volume VIII

W.F.

DEPARTMENT OF THE INTERIOR.
COMMISSION TO THE FIVE CIVILIZED TRIBES.

Muskogee, Indian Territory, July 19, 1905.

Chief Clerk,
    Creek Enrollment Division.

Dear Sir:

    Receipt is acknowledged of your letter of July 15, 1905 (NC-635) stating that application was made to the Commission to the Five Civilized Tribes for the enrollment of Ruth Brown, born March 17, 1902, and John William Brown, born June 5, 1904, children of Clarence William Brown, a citizen of the Creek Nation, and Rebeca Brown, a citizen of the Seminole Nation, as citizens by blood of the Creek Nation and requesting to be informed as to whether application was made for the enrollment of said children as citizens of the Seminole Nation.

    In reply to your letter you are informed that it does not appear from an examination of the records of this office that any application was made for the enrollment of the said Ruth Brown and John William Brown as citizens of the Seminole Nation.

Respectfully,

Tams Bixby   Commissioner.

NC-635.

Muskogee, Indian Territory, August 12, 1905.

Rebecca Brown,
    c/o Clarence W. Brown,
        Wewoka, Indian Territory.

Dear Madam:

    In the matter of the application for the enrollment of your minor children, Ruth Brown and John William Brown, as citizens by blood of the Creek Nation, it will be necessary for you to furnish this office with either the original or a certified copy of the marriage license and certificate showing marriage between you and Clarence William Brown, the father of said children.

Applications for Enrollment of Creek Newborn
Act of 1905 Volume VIII

You are also requested to furnish this office, as to the birth of said children, the affidavits of the said Clarence William Brown and for that purpose two blanks for proof of birth, which have [sic] filled out, are inclosed herewith.

It is also essential for you to furnish this office the joint affidavit of yourself and husband electing whether you will have your said children enrolled as citizens by blood of the Creek Nation or of the Seminole Nation.

You should give the matters herein referred to your immediate attention.

Respectfully,

CTD-12 Env.   Acting Commissioner.

NC 635

Muskogee, Indian Territory, November 13, 1906

Chief Clerk,
    Seminole Enrollment Division,
        General Office.

Dear Sir:

You are hereby advised that the names of Ruth and John William Brown, children of Clarence W. Brown, a citizen of the Creek Nation and Rebecca Brown an alleged citizen of the Seminole Nation, is contained in schedule of minor citizens by blood of the Creek Nation, approved by the Secretary of the Interior, September 27, 1905, opposite Roll numbers 604 and 605.

Respectfully,

Commissioner.

BIRTH AFFIDAVIT.

DEPARTMENT OF THE INTERIOR.
COMMISSION TO THE FIVE CIVILIZED TRIBES.

IN RE APPLICATION FOR ENROLLMENT, as a citizen of the Creek Nation, of Ruth Brown, born on the 17th day of March, 1902

Name of Father: Clarence W. Brown   a citizen of the   Creek   Nation.
Name of Mother: Rebecca Brown   a citizen of the   Seminole Nation.

Postoffice   Wewoka, I.T.

Applications for Enrollment of Creek Newborn
Act of 1905   Volume VIII

AFFIDAVIT OF ~~MOTHER~~. Father

UNITED STATES OF AMERICA, Indian Territory, }
    Western   DISTRICT.

    I, Clarence W. Brown, on oath state that I am 25 years of age and a citizen by blood, of the Creek Nation; that I am the lawful ~~wife of~~ husband of Rebecca Brown, who is a citizen, by blood of the Seminole Nation; that a female child was born to ~~me~~ us on 17th day of March, 1902, that said child has been named Ruth Brown, and was living March 4, 1905.

                                      Clarence W. Brown

Witnesses To Mark:
{

    Subscribed and sworn to before me this 16 day of August, 1905.

                                    Arthur M. Seran
                                          Notary Public.
         My commission expires May 11th 1909

BIRTH AFFIDAVIT.

DEPARTMENT OF THE INTERIOR.
COMMISSION TO THE FIVE CIVILIZED TRIBES.

    IN RE APPLICATION FOR ENROLLMENT, as a citizen of the Creek Nation, of Ruth Brown, born on the 17" day of March, 1902

Name of Father: Clarence William Brown   a citizen of the   Creek   Nation.
Name of Mother: Rebecca Brown   a citizen of the   Seminole   Nation.

                       Postoffice   Wewoka, I.T.

AFFIDAVIT OF MOTHER.

UNITED STATES OF AMERICA, Indian Territory, }
    Western Judicial   DISTRICT.

    I, Rebecca Brown, on oath state that I am 24 years of age and a citizen by birth, of the Seminole Nation; that I am the lawful wife of Clarence William Brown, who is a citizen, by blood of the Creek Nation; that a Female child was born to me on 17" day of March, 1902, that said child has been named Ruth Brown, and was living March 4, 1905.

Applications for Enrollment of Creek Newborn
Act of 1905   Volume VIII

Rebecca Brown

Witnesses To Mark:
{

Subscribed and sworn to before me this 1st day of April, 1905.

WJ Ryan
Notary Public.

AFFIDAVIT OF ATTENDING PHYSICIAN OR MID-WIFE.

UNITED STATES OF AMERICA, Indian Territory, }
Western Judicial   DISTRICT.

I, Charles P. Linn, a Physician, on oath state that I attended on Mrs. Rebecca Brown, wife of CW Brown on the 17th day of March, 1902; that there was born to her on said date a Female child; that said child was living March 4, 1905, and is said to have been named Ruth

Charles P. Linn

Witnesses To Mark:
{ Irene E Bruce

Subscribed and sworn to before me this 1st day of April, 1905.

My commission expires   WJ Ryan
Sept 1st 1906   Notary Public.

BIRTH AFFIDAVIT.

DEPARTMENT OF THE INTERIOR.
COMMISSION TO THE FIVE CIVILIZED TRIBES.

IN RE APPLICATION FOR ENROLLMENT, as a citizen of the Creek Nation, of John William Brown, born on the 5th day of June, 1904

Name of Father: Clarence W. Brown   a citizen of the   Creek   Nation.
Name of Mother: Rebecca Brown   a citizen of the   Seminole Nation.

Postoffice   Wewoka, I.T.

Applications for Enrollment of Creek Newborn
Act of 1905   Volume VIII

AFFIDAVIT OF ~~MOTHER~~. Father

UNITED STATES OF AMERICA, Indian Territory, }
Western   DISTRICT.

I, Clarence W. Brown, on oath state that I am 25 years of age and a citizen by blood, of the Creek Nation; that I am the lawful ~~wife of~~ husband of Rebecca Brown, who is a citizen, by blood of the Seminole Nation; that a male child was born to ~~me~~ us on 5th day of June, 1904, that said child has been named John William Brown, and was living March 4, 1905.

Clarence W. Brown

Witnesses To Mark:
{

Subscribed and sworn to before me this 16 day of August, 1905.

Arthur M. Seran
Notary Public.
My commission expires May 11th 1909

BIRTH AFFIDAVIT.

DEPARTMENT OF THE INTERIOR.
COMMISSION TO THE FIVE CIVILIZED TRIBES.

IN RE APPLICATION FOR ENROLLMENT, as a citizen of the Creek Nation, of John William Brown, born on the 5 day of June, 1904

Name of Father: Clarence William Brown   a citizen of the   Creek   Nation.
                 Hickory Ground
Name of Mother: Rebecca Brown   a citizen of the   Seminole Nation.

Postoffice   Wewoka, I.T.

AFFIDAVIT OF MOTHER.

UNITED STATES OF AMERICA, Indian Territory, }
Western Judicial   DISTRICT.

I, Rebecca Brown, on oath state that I am 24 years of age and a citizen by birth, of the Seminole Nation; that I am the lawful wife of Clarence William Brown, who is a citizen, by birth of the Creek Nation; that a male child was born to me on 5" day of June, 1904, that said child has been named John William Brown, and was living March 4, 1905.

Rebecca Brown

Applications for Enrollment of Creek Newborn
Act of 1905   Volume VIII

Witnesses To Mark:
{

   Subscribed and sworn to before me this 1ˢᵗ day of April, 1905.

   WJ Ryan
   Notary Public.

AFFIDAVIT OF ATTENDING PHYSICIAN OR MID-WIFE.

UNITED STATES OF AMERICA, Indian Territory, }
   Western Judicial   DISTRICT.

I, OG Cranston, a Physician, on oath state that I attended on Mrs. Rebecca Brown, wife of Clarence William Brown on the 5 day of June, 1904; that there was born to her on said date a male child; that said child was living March 4, 1905, and is said to have been named John William Brown

O.G. Cranston

Witnesses To Mark:
{

   Subscribed and sworn to before me this 1ˢᵗ day of April, 1905.

   WJ Ryan
   Notary Public.

CERTIFICATE OF RECORD.

United States of America, }
   INDIAN TERRITORY,   } ss.
   Northern District.

I, JAMES A. WINSTON, Clerk of the United States Court in the Northern District, Indian Territory, do hereby certify that the instrument hereto attached was filed for record in my office the 24 day of Mch 1898 at *(blank)* M., and duly recorded in Book 2, Marriage Record, Page 389

   WITNESS my hand and seal of said Court at Muscogee, in said Territory, this 28 day of Mch A. D. 1898

   Jas. A. Winston   Clerk.
   By   Deputy.

Applications for Enrollment of Creek Newborn
Act of 1905 Volume VIII

MARRIAGE LICENSE

United States of America,
   INDIAN TERRITORY, } ss.
   Northern District.

No. 1057

To Any Person Authorized by Law to Solemnize Marriage---Greeting:

You are Hereby Commanded to Solemnize the Rite and publish the Banns of Matrimony between Mr.   Clarence W. Brown   of   Wewoka , in the Indian Territory, aged   18   years and Miss Rebecca Bell   of   Wewoka   in the Indian Territory aged   17   years according to law, and do you officially sign and return this License to the parties therein named.

    WITNESS my hand and official seal at Muscogee Indian Territory this   18   day of   March   A.D. 1898

                             James A. Muston
                                  Clerk of the U.S. Court

By   N. S. Young   Deputy

CERTIFICATE OF MARRIAGE.

United States of America,
   INDIAN TERRITORY, } ss.
   Northern District.

    I,   Wm. P. Blake   , a Minister of the Gospel, DO HEREBY CERTIFY that on the 20   day of   March   A. D. 1898, I did duly and according to law as commanded in the foregoing License, solemnize the Rite and publish the Banns of Matrimony between the parties therein named.

    WITNESS my hand this   20   day of   March   A. D. 1898

    My credentials are recorded in the office of the Clerk of the United States Court, Indian Territory, Northern District, Book   A   , Page   120   .

                                  Wm. P. Blake
                                  A Minister of the Gospel

Applications for Enrollment of Creek Newborn
Act of 1905 Volume VIII

Note—This License and Certificate of Marriage must be returned to the Office of the Clerk of the United States Court in the Northern District, Indian Territory, from whence it was issued, within sixty days from the date thereof, or the party to whom the license was issued will be liable in the amount of the One Hundred Dollars ($100.00)

United States of America,)
)
Indian Territory,   ) ss
)
Western Judicial District.)

    We, Rebecca Brown and Clarence W. Brown, mother and father respectively of their monor[sic] children, Ruth Brown and John William Brown, being duly sworn upon oath state that they elect to have their minor children enrolled as citizens by blood of the Creek Nation.

    Given under our hands this 16th day of August, A.D. 1905.

                              Rebecca Brown
                              Clarence W Brown

Subscribed and sworn to before me this 16th day of August, 1905.

                              Harry H. Rogers
                              Notary Public.
My commission expires April 26, 2909.

(The below letter typed as given.)

                    C O P Y.

              Coal Creek Indian Territory Nov 11th 1905.

Commissioner
        Muskogee Indian T.

Dear Sir:

    I received your kind and welcome letter a few days ago and I will tell you that I am the Creek Nation, and are family is Creek Nation and the Emma is family is Creek Nation, and I will tell you that about my father named is Harbey Vann and the Emma is father named is Gobey Kelley. Yes we are fullblood of Creek Nation and the Lydia Vann is fullblood of Creek Nation.

Applications for Enrollment of Creek Newborn
Act of 1905 Volume VIII

oblige yours truly

Watlie Vann,

Address to Coweta Indian Territory.

NC-636.

Muskogee, Indian Territory, October 17, 1905.

Emma Vann,
    c/o Watlie Vann,
        Coweta, Indian Territory.

Dear Madam:

In the matter of the application for the enrollment of your daughter Lydia Vann as a citizen by blood of the Creek Nation this office is unable to identify you upon the final roll of citizens by blood of the Creek Nation.

It is necessary that you be so identified before the rights of said child can be finally determined. You are therefore requested to state the name under which you were finally enrolled, the names of your parents and other members of your family, the Creek Indian town to which you belong, your final roll number as the same appears upon your allotment certificate and deeds and any other information that will enable this office to identify you upon the final roll of citizens by blood of the Creek Nation,

Respectfully,

Commissioner.

NC-636.

Muskogee, Indian Territory, August 12, 1905.

Emma Vann,
    Coweta, Indian Territory.

Dear Madam:

In the matter of the application for the enrollment of your daughter Lydia Vann as a citizen by blood of the Creek Nation this office is unable to identify you upon the final roll of citizens by blood of the Creek Nation. It is necessary that you be identified before the rights of said child can be finally determined.

Applications for Enrollment of Creek Newborn
Act of 1905   Volume VIII

You are, therefore, requested to state the name under which you are finally enrolled, the names of your parents and other members of your family, the Creek Indian town to which you belong, your final roll number as the same appears upon your allotment certificate and deeds and any other information which you think will enable this office to identify you upon the final roll of citizens by blood of the Creek Nation.

                    Respectfully,

                    Acting Commissioner.

BIRTH AFFIDAVIT.

DEPARTMENT OF THE INTERIOR.
COMMISSION TO THE FIVE CIVILIZED TRIBES.

IN RE APPLICATION FOR ENROLLMENT, as a citizen of the Creek Nation, of Lydia Vann, born on the 18th day of December, 1903

Name of Father: Wadley Vann	a citizen of the Creek	Nation.
Name of Mother: Emma Vann	a citizen of the Creek	Nation.

                Postoffice   Coweta, Ind. Ter.

AFFIDAVIT OF MOTHER.

UNITED STATES OF AMERICA, Indian Territory,
    Western   **DISTRICT.**

I, Emma Vann, on oath state that I am Twenty (20) years of age and a citizen by blood[sic], of the Creek Nation; that I am the lawful wife of Wadley Vann, who is a citizen, by blood of the Creek Nation; that a female child was born to me on 18th day of December, 1903, that said child has been named Lydia Vann, and was living March 4, 1905.

                          her
                    Emma x Vann
Witnesses To Mark: mark
   { Jas Tiger
   { Ned Kelley

Subscribed and sworn to before me this 27th day of March, 1905.

                  B.J. Beavers
My commission expires Dec 19, 1908   Notary Public.

Applications for Enrollment of Creek Newborn
Act of 1905 Volume VIII

AFFIDAVIT OF ATTENDING PHYSICIAN OR MID-WIFE.

UNITED STATES OF AMERICA, Indian Territory,
    Western   DISTRICT.

    I, Susan Fulotka , a Midwife , on oath state that I attended on Mrs. Emma Vann , wife of Wadley Vann on the 18th day of December , 1903 ; that there was born to her on said date a female child; that said child was living March 4, 1905, and is said to have been named Lydia Vann

                                                           her
                                                  Susan x Fulotka

Witnesses To Mark: mark
    { Jas Tiger
      Ned Kelley

    Subscribed and sworn to before me this 27th day of March, 1905.

                                                B.J. Beaver
                                                            Notary Public.

BIRTH AFFIDAVIT.

Department of the Interior,
COMMISSION TO THE FIVE CIVILIZED TRIBES.

    IN RE APPLICATION FOR ENROLLMENT, as a citizen of the Creek Nation, of Ethel Luler Dixon , born on the 24 day of July, 1901

Name of Father: Sam Dixon   a citizen of the United States Nation.
Name of Mother: Della Dixon (nee Self)   a citizen of the Creek Nation.
Broken Arrow Town

                           Post-Office: Eufaula, Ind. Ter.

                                    AFFIDAVIT OF MOTHER.

UNITED STATES OF AMERICA,
    INDIAN TERRITORY,
      Western   District.

    I, Della Dixon , on oath state that I am 20 years of age and a citizen by blood , of the Creek Nation; that I am the lawful wife of Sam Dixon , who is a citizen, by *(blank)* of the United States ~~Nation~~; that a female child was born to me on 24 day of July , 1901 , that said child has been named Ethel Luler Dixon , and ~~is now~~ was living. on March 4, 1905

                                                Della Dixon

Applications for Enrollment of Creek Newborn
Act of 1905 Volume VIII

WITNESSES TO MARK:

{

    Subscribed and sworn to before me this 3 *day of* April, *1905*.

                          Drennan C Skaggs
                              Notary Public.

AFFIDAVIT OF ATTENDING PHYSICIAN OR MID-WIFE.

UNITED STATES OF AMERICA,
  INDIAN TERRITORY,
    Western   District.

    I, W.A. Tolleson , a physician , on oath state that I attended on Mrs. Della Dixon , wife of Sam Dixon on the 24 day of July , 1901; that there was born to her on said date a female child; that said child ~~is now~~ was living on March 4, 1905 and is said to have been named Ethel Luler Dixon

                           W A Tolleson MD

WITNESSES TO MARK:

{

    Subscribed and sworn to before me this 3 *day of* April, *1905*.

                             Drennan C Skaggs
                              Notary Public.

BIRTH AFFIDAVIT.

Department of the Interior,
COMMISSION TO THE FIVE CIVILIZED TRIBES.

    IN RE APPLICATION FOR ENROLLMENT, as a citizen of the Creek Nation, of Henry Jefferson Dixon , born on the 15 day of December, 1903

Name of Father: Sam Dixon   a citizen of the United States Nation.
Name of Mother: Della Dixon (nee Self)   a citizen of the   Creek   Nation.
Broken Arrow Town
                      Post-Office: Eufaula, Ind. Ter.

Applications for Enrollment of Creek Newborn
Act of 1905   Volume VIII

AFFIDAVIT OF MOTHER.

UNITED STATES OF AMERICA,
   INDIAN TERRITORY,
  Western   District.

I, Della Dixon , on oath state that I am 20 years of age and a citizen by blood , of the Creek Nation; that I am the lawful wife of Sam Dixon , who is a citizen, by *(blank)* of the United States Nation; that a male child was born to me on 15 day of December , 1903 , that said child has been named Henry Jefferson Dixon , and is now was living. on March 4, 1905

Della Dixon

WITNESSES TO MARK:

{

Subscribed and sworn to before me this 3 day of April, 1905.

Drennan C Skaggs
Notary Public.

AFFIDAVIT OF ATTENDING PHYSICIAN OR MID-WIFE.

UNITED STATES OF AMERICA,
   INDIAN TERRITORY,
  Western   District.

I, W.A. Tolleson , a physician , on oath state that I attended on Mrs. Della Dixon , wife of Sam Dixon on the 15 day of December , 1903; that there was born to her on said date a male child; that said child is now was living on March 4, 1905 and is said to have been named Henry Jefferson Dixon

W A Tolleson MD

WITNESSES TO MARK:

{

Subscribed and sworn to before me this 3 day of April, 1905.

Drennan C Skaggs
Notary Public.

Applications for Enrollment of Creek Newborn
Act of 1905   Volume VIII

NC-638.

Muskogee, Indian Territory, [sic] 12, 1905.

John Lewis,
    Eufaula, Indian Territory.

Dear Sir:

In the matter of the application for the enrollment of your minor daughter Lulu Lewis, born May 21, 1903, as a citizen by blood of the Creek Nation it will be necessary for you to furnish this office the affidavits of two disinterested persons to the birth of said child. Said affidavits must set forth said child's name, the date of her birth, the names of her parents, and whether or not she was living on March 4, 1905.

Please give this matter your prompt attention.

                Respectfully,

                Acting Commissioner.

BIRTH AFFIDAVIT.

DEPARTMENT OF THE INTERIOR.
COMMISSION TO THE FIVE CIVILIZED TRIBES.

IN RE APPLICATION FOR ENROLLMENT, as a citizen of the Creek Nation, of Lulu Lewis, born on the 21st day of May, 1903

Name of Father: Johnson Lewis   a citizen of the Creek Nation.
Name of Mother: Lucinda Lewis   a citizen of the Creek Nation.

           Postoffice   Eufaula, Indian Territory.

AFFIDAVIT OF MOTHER.

UNITED STATES OF AMERICA, Indian Territory, ⎫
    Western   DISTRICT.   ⎬

I, Lucinda Lewis, on oath state that I am thirty-five years of age and a citizen by blood, of the Creek Nation; that I am the lawful wife of Johnson Lewis, who is a citizen, by blood of the Creek Nation; that a female child was born to me on 21st day of May, 1903, that said child has been named Lulu Lewis, and was living March 4, 1905.

Applications for Enrollment of Creek Newborn
Act of 1905   Volume VIII

                                              her
                                   Lucinda Lewis x
Witnesses To Mark: mark
  { C.E. Wilcox
    William C. *(Illegible)*

Subscribed and sworn to before me this 30th day of August, 1905.

                                        W.T. *(Illegible)*
                                            Notary Public.

AFFIDAVIT OF ATTENDING PHYSICIAN OR MID-WIFE.

UNITED STATES OF AMERICA, Indian Territory, }
    Western   DISTRICT.

    I, Sallie Johnson, a mid-wife, on oath state that I attended on Mrs. Lucinda Lewis, wife of Johnson Lewis on the 21st day of May, 1903 ; that there was born to her on said date a female child; that said child was living March 4, 1905, and is said to have been named Lulu Lewis   her
                                      Sallie Johnson x
Witnesses To Mark: mark
  { B.L. *(Illegible)*
    Daniel Lewis
      Aug 1-1906.

Subscribed and sworn to before me this 31st day of August, 1905.

                                        Thomas F. *(Illegible)*
                                            Notary Public.

BIRTH AFFIDAVIT.

Department of the Interior,
COMMISSION TO THE FIVE CIVILIZED TRIBES.

    IN RE APPLICATION FOR ENROLLMENT, as a citizen of the Creek Nation, of Lulu Lewis, born on the 21 day of May, 1903

Name of Father: Johnson Lewis   a citizen of the   Creek   Nation.
Eufaula Canadian Town
Name of Mother: Cinda Lewis   a citizen of the   Creek   Nation.
Okfusky[sic] Canadian Town
                                Post-Office: Eufaula, Ind. Ter.

Applications for Enrollment of Creek Newborn
Act of 1905 Volume VIII

AFFIDAVIT OF MOTHER.

UNITED STATES OF AMERICA,
INDIAN TERRITORY,
Western District.

Child is present

I, Cinda Lewis, on oath state that I am about 35 years of age and a citizen by blood, of the Creek Nation; that I am the lawful wife of Johnson Lewis, who is a citizen, by blood of the Creek Nation; that a female child was born to me on 21 day of May, 1903, that said child has been named Lulu Lewis, and ~~is now~~ was living. on March 4, 1905

                                          her
                                 Cinda x Lewis
WITNESSES TO MARK: mark
   Alex Posey
   DC Skaggs

Subscribed and sworn to before me this 3 *day of* April, *1905.*

                                     Drennan C Skaggs
                                         Notary Public.

AFFIDAVIT OF ATTENDING PHYSICIAN OR MID-WIFE.

UNITED STATES OF AMERICA,
INDIAN TERRITORY,
Western District.

                                                     my wife

I, Johnson Lewis, ~~a (blank)~~, on oath state that I attended on ^ Mrs. Cinda Lewis, ~~wife of (blank)~~ on the 21 day of May, 1903; that there was born to her on said date a female child; that said child ~~is now~~ was living on March 4, 1905 and ~~is said to have~~ has been named Lulu Lewis

                                     Johnson Lewis
WITNESSES TO MARK:

Subscribed and sworn to before me this 3 *day of* April, *1905.*

                                     Drennan C Skaggs
                                         Notary Public.

Applications for Enrollment of Creek Newborn
Act of 1905   Volume VIII

NC-639.

Muskogee, Indian Territory, August 12, 1905.

Bunnie McIntosh,
    Eufaula, Indian Territory.

Dear Sir:

    In the matter of the application for the enrollment of your minor daughter Jeanetta McIntosh, born March 19, 1902, as a citizen by blood of the Creek Nation, it will be necessary for you to furnish this office the affidavits of two disinterested persons as to the birth of said child. Said affidavits must set forth said child's name, the date of her birth, the names of her parents, and whether or not she was living March 4, 1905.

    Please give this matter your prompt attention.

                Respectfully,

                          Acting Commissioner.

B.C. 639.

Muskogee, Indian Territory, August 18, 1905.

Bunnie McIntosh,
    Eufaula, Indian Territory.

Dear Sir:

    Receipt is acknowledged of your letter of August 16, 1905, in which you state that you made an affidavit as the midwife in the matter of the application for the enrollment of your minor child, Jeanetta McIntosh.

    You are again advised that this office requires the affidavit of two disinterested parties relative to the birth of said child.

    This matter should receive your prompt attention.

                Respectfully,

                          Acting Commissioner.

Applications for Enrollment of Creek Newborn
Act of 1905 Volume VIII

AFFIDAVITS.

United States of America,
Western District, Indian Territory.

Will Shaver   , being duly sworn before me on this   28   day of   August   , 1905, states on oath that   he   is well acquainted with Bunnie McIntosh and Leah McIntosh his wife; that   he has lived near them and have been frequently with their family, and am acquainted with their children and that there was born to the said Bunnie McIntosh and Leah McIntosh, his wife a girl child on or about the 19th day of March, 1902, and that said child was living on the 4th day of March, 1905, and is still living; and that said child was named Jeanetta.

                      Will Shaver

Subscribed and Sworn to before me this   28 day of   August   1905.

                      Frank W. Rushing
                      Notary Public.

AFFIDAVITS.

United States of America,
Western District, Indian Territory.

S. J. Logan   , being duly sworn before me on this   28   day of   August   , 1905, states on oath that   he   is well acquainted with Bunnie McIntosh and Leah McIntosh his wife; that   he has lived near them and have been frequently with their family, and am acquainted with their children and that there was born to the said Bunnie McIntosh and Leah McIntosh, his wife a girl child on or about the 19th day of March, 1902, and that said child was living on the 4th day of March, 1905, and is still living; and that said child was named Jeanetta.

                      S. J. Logan

Subscribed and Sworn to before me this   28 day of   August   1905.

                      Frank W. Rushing
                      Notary Public.

Applications for Enrollment of Creek Newborn
Act of 1905   Volume VIII

BIRTH AFFIDAVIT.

DEPARTMENT OF THE INTERIOR.
COMMISSION TO THE FIVE CIVILIZED TRIBES.

IN RE APPLICATION FOR ENROLLMENT, as a citizen of the Creek Nation, of Jeanetta McIntosh, born on the 19 day of March, 1902

Name of Father: Bunnie McIntosh   a citizen of the   Creek   Nation.
Cheyaha Town
Name of Mother: Leah McIntosh (nee Jacobs)   a citizen of the   Creek   Nation.
Tuckabatche Town
                        Postoffice   Eufaula, Ind. Ter.

AFFIDAVIT OF MOTHER.   Child present.

UNITED STATES OF AMERICA, Indian Territory,
   Western   DISTRICT.

    I, Leah McIntosh, on oath state that I am 39 years of age and a citizen by blood, of the Creek Nation; that I am the lawful wife of Bunnie McIntosh, who is a citizen, by blood of the Creek Nation; that a female child was born to me on 19 day of March, 1902, that said child has been named Jeanetta McIntosh, and was living March 4, 1905. That the whereabouts of the mid-wife who attended on me at the birth of the child are not known.

                                Leah McIntosh
Witnesses To Mark:

    Subscribed and sworn to before me this 3 day of April, 1905.

                                Drennan C Skaggs
                                Notary Public.

                    Father
AFFIDAVIT OF ~~ATTENDING PHYSICIAN OR MID-WIFE~~.

UNITED STATES OF AMERICA, Indian Territory,
   Western   DISTRICT.

                                                               assisted the mid-wife
    I, Bunnie McIntosh, ~~a (blank)~~, on oath state that I attended on my wife Mrs. Leah McIntosh, ~~wife of (blank)~~ on the 19 day of March, 1905; that there was born to her on said date a female child; that said child was living March 4, 1905, and is said to have been named Jeanetta McIntosh

                                Bunnie McIntosh

Applications for Enrollment of Creek Newborn
Act of 1905   Volume VIII

Witnesses To Mark:
{

Subscribed and sworn to before me this 3 day of April, 1905.

Drennan C Skaggs
Notary Public.

BIRTH AFFIDAVIT.

Department of the Interior,
COMMISSION TO THE FIVE CIVILIZED TRIBES.

IN RE APPLICATION FOR ENROLLMENT, as a citizen of the Creek Nation, of Vonnie Pitman, born on the 10 day of July, 1903

Name of Father: Lewis Pitman   a citizen of the   Blood[sic] Nation.
Coweta Town
Name of Mother: Florence Pitman   a citizen of the   Marriage Nation.

Post-Office: stidham ind.ter.[sic]

Father
AFFIDAVIT OF ~~MOTHER.~~

UNITED STATES OF AMERICA,
  INDIAN TERRITORY,
  Western   District.

I, Lewis Pitman, on oath state that I am 23 years of age and a citizen by blood, of the Creek Nation; that I am the lawful ~~wife~~ husband of Florence Pitman, who ~~is~~ was a citizen, ~~by (blank)~~ of the United States ~~Nation~~; that a male child was born to ~~me~~ her on 10 day of July, 1903, that said child has been named Vonnie Pitman, and ~~is now~~ was living. on March 4, 1905, that the mother of the child is now dead

Lewis Pitman

WITNESSES TO MARK:
{

Subscribed and sworn to before me this 3 day of April, 1905.

Drennan C Skaggs
Notary Public.

Applications for Enrollment of Creek Newborn
Act of 1905 Volume VIII

AFFIDAVIT OF ATTENDING PHYSICIAN OR MID-WIFE.

UNITED STATES OF AMERICA,
  INDIAN TERRITORY,
  Western   District.

I, W.C. Gilliam , a Physician , on oath state that I attended on Mrs. Florence Pitman , wife of Lewis Pitman on the tenth day of July , 1903 ; that there was born to her on said date a male child; that said child is now living and is said to have been named Vonnie

W.C. Gilliam

WITNESSES TO MARK:

Subscribed and sworn to before me this 31 day of March, 1905.

Preston Janway
Notary Public.

Commission to the Five Civilized Tribes

In Re Application for enrollment of Lucy May Kite, born May 21st 1902. Name of Father A. L. Kite. Name of Mother Jemima Kite, a citizen by blood of the Creek Nation. Post Office Eufaula, Indian Territory.

Affidavit of mother.

Indian Territory
Western District

Jemima Kite, being duly sworn on oath states that I am 30 years of age, a citizen by blood of the Creek nation; that I am the lawful wife of A. L. Kite; that on 21st. day of May 1902 there was born unto me a female child; that said child is now living and has been named Lucy May Kite.

Jemima Kite

Sworn and subscribed to before me this 6th day of March 1905.

Applications for Enrollment of Creek Newborn
Act of 1905   Volume VIII

                              (Illegible) Simpson
My Commission expires July 8-1906.   Notary Public.

Affidavit of Physician

Indian Territory
Western District

W. A. Tolleson, a physician, being duly sworn on oath states that I attended on Mrs Jemima Kite, wife of A. L. Kite on the 21st day of May 1902; that there was born unto her on the said date a female child that the said child is now living and have been named Lucy May Kite.

                                    WA. Tolleson

Sworn and subscribed to before me this 6th day of March 1905.

                              (Illegible) Simpson
My Commission expires July 8-1906.   Notary Public.

BIRTH AFFIDAVIT.

Department of the Interior,
COMMISSION TO THE FIVE CIVILIZED TRIBES.

IN RE APPLICATION FOR ENROLLMENT, as a citizen of the Creek Nation, of Lucy May Kite, born on the 21 day of May, 1902

Name of Father: A. L. Kite   a citizen of the United States ~~Nation~~.
Name of Mother: Jemima Kite   a citizen of the Creek Nation.
Eufaula Canadian Town

                   Post-Office: Eufaula, Ind. Ter.

AFFIDAVIT OF MOTHER.

UNITED STATES OF AMERICA,
    INDIAN TERRITORY,   Child is present
    Western   District.

I, Jemima Kite, on oath state that I am 28 years of age and a citizen by blood, of the Creek Nation; that I am the lawful wife of A. L. Kite, who is a citizen, ~~by (blank)~~ of the United States Nation; that a female child was born to me on 21 day of May, 1902, that said child has been named Lucy May Kite, and ~~is now~~ was living. on March 4, 1905.

                                Jemima Kite

Applications for Enrollment of Creek Newborn
Act of 1905   Volume VIII

WITNESSES TO MARK:

{

    Subscribed and sworn to before me this (blank) day of (blank), 190(blank).

(No signature given.)
Notary Public.

DEPARTMENT OF THE INTERIOR,
COMMISSION TO THE FIVE CIVILIZED TRIBES.
Eufaula, I. T., July 5th, 1904.

    IN THE MATTER OF THE APPLICATION for the enrollment of LINDY ISAAC MANLEY as a citizen by blood of the Creek Nation.

    ISAAC MANLEY being first duly sworn, testified as follows sworn: Through L. G. McIntosh, official Interpreter.
By the Commission.
Q What is your name? A Isaac Manley.
Q What is your age? A About twenty-eight.
Q What is your post office address? A Mellette.
Q Are you a citizen of the Creek Nation? A Yes sira[sic].
Q Have you a child named Lindy Isaac Manley? A Yes, sir.; Lindy Manley.
Q Has there heretofore been executed an affidavit in the matter of the application for the enrollment of Lindy as a citizen of the Creek Nation? A Yes, sir.; witnesses, everything sworn and signed.
Q Do you desire to have Lindy enrolled as a citizen of the Creek Nation? A That is the way I made out the affidavit, and I would like for it to go that way.
Q Is Lindy Living? A Yes, sir.
Q What is her mother's name? A Martha.
Q Is Martha your wife? A Yes, sir.
Q Is she living with you now? A Yes, sir.
Q Is Lindy living with you? A Yes, sir.
Q Is Martha a citizen of the Creek Nation? A A Seminole.
Q Has she been enrolled and taken land as a Seminole? A Yes, sir.; been file there.
Q Have you been enrolled and taken your allotment as a citizen of the Creek Nation? A Yes, sir.
Q Can you read and write? A No.
Q Can Martha read and write? A No.
Q Was there any record made of the date of the birth of Lindy? A No, no record of it, only it was made out there at the Seminole--there was an affidavit made, and she was enrolled there, but she gets no land.

Applications for Enrollment of Creek Newborn
Act of 1905   Volume VIII

Q Do you mean to say that an application was made to the Commission for the enrollment of Lindy as a citizen of the Seminole Nation? A No, made no application to have her file there, but to have her file in the Creek Nation. The land is very small there, and if we could get it here, that would be better.
Q How old is Lindy? A A Little over two, pretty near three, somewhere about two and a half years old.
Q Have you any other young children? A Have got one younger. It has land and filed.
Q Do you mean to say that you have a child younger than Lindy who has filed in the Creek Nation? A I didn't intend to state that, but that it was a little older than Lindy, a brother to Lindy.
Q What is its name? A We call him Archie at home, but in the Seminole I think it is recorded as Jacob.
Q He is enrolled as a Seminole then? A Yes, as a Seminole, and filed there. He has been filed there, but they wouldn't allow this younger one in at all, and I wanted to see whether I could get it here in the Creek Nation, is why I made my application.
Q Have you any children younger than Lindy? A No.
Q When was Lindy born? A I don't know exactly now, but there was an affidavit made of it and it is in the office of the Commissioners. I don't know, I can't read or write, and can't keep it in memory.
Q Where did you get the dates that you put in the affidavit? A This man that was right above us would know the dates better than I would. I think the child was born in December, and now dating from that, he is a little over two years old.
Q Is that your best recollection? A Yes, sir.
Q That he is from last December till now over two years old? A Yes, sir.
Q Are you sure that Lindy is not three years old? A Now I don't really know but I am stating to the best of my judgment. I don't know anything about writing or reading, and these others can read and write and they have the record. What I have stated here is to the best of my judgment. I don't know that they will be executed.
Q Who has the record? A William Cully. The record is away there aw[sic] Sasakwa, Indian Territory but I have witnesses here who know it.___

Oliver C. Hinkle, being duly sworn, upon his oath as stenographer for the Commission to the Five Civilized Tribes, states that he reported the proceedings had in the above entitled cause on July 5, 1904, at Eufaula, I.T., and that the above and foregoing is a full, true and correct transcript of his stenographic notes thereof.

Oliver C. Hinkle

Subscribed and sworn to before me this 12th day of July, 1904, at Mellette, Indian Territory.

(Seal)   L. G. McIntosh
                         Notary Public.
My commission expires
Apr. 10 - 1907

Applications for Enrollment of Creek Newborn
Act of 1905   Volume VIII

DEPARTMENT OF THE INTERIOR,
COMMISSION TO THE FIVE CIVILIZED TRIBES.
Okmulgee, I. T., October 11, 1904.

SUPPLEMENTAL TESTIMONY in the matter of the application for the enrollment of Lindy Manley as a citizen by blood of the Creek Nation.

HARLEY THOMAS, being duly sworn, testified as follows:

Through Alex Posey Official Interpreter:

By Commission:
Q What is your name? A Harley Thomas.
Q Are you the Town King of Eufaula Canadian Town? A Yes, sir.
Q Do you know Isaac Manley and his wife, Martha? A Yes, sir.
Q How far do you live from them? A About three miles.
Q Do you know their children? A Yes, sir. I think they had three children.
Q Do you know the name of the oldest one? A I am afraid to give the names for fear I might not give them right but I know that they have been drawing money in the Seminole Nation.
Q About how old is the oldest child? A Perhaps about seven years old.
Q How old do you think the next one is? A Between four and five I think.
Q Do you know whether one of them is called Lindy or not? A The girl is named Lindy I think.
Q About how old is Lindy? A Between four and five years old.
Q Is she living? A Yes, sir., all three are living.

------:O:------

I, D. C. Skaggs, on oath state that the above and foregoing is a full and true transcript of my stenographic notes as taken in said cause on said date.

D C Skaggs

Subscribed and sworn to before me this 4th day of November 1904.

Charles H. Sawyer
Notary Public.

Applications for Enrollment of Creek Newborn
Act of 1905   Volume VIII

En. 626.

DEPARTMENT OF THE INTERIOR,
COMMISSION TO THE FIVE CIVILIZED TRIBES.
Okmulgee, I. T., October 12, 1904.

SUPPLEMENTAL TESTIMONY in the matter of the application for the enrollment of Lindy Manley as a citizen by blood of the Creek Nation.

WILLIAM SULLIVAN, being duly sworn, testified:

Through Alex Posey Official Interpreter:

By Commission:
Q What is your name? A William Sullivan?
Q How old are you? A Forty-seven.
Q What is your post office address? A Eufaula.
Q Do you know Isaac Manley? A Yes, sir.
Q Do you know a child of his named Lindy? A Yes, sir.
Q How old is that child? A A little over three years old.
Q Do you know what month it was born in? A Yes, sir.
Q What month was it? A January.
Q Was that child three years old last January or will it be three next January? Q Will be three years old next January.
Q Is Isaac any kin to you? A Yes, sir.
Q What relation is he to you? A No relation.

No Mr. Posey he has stated that the child is a little over three years old and he again stated that the child will be three years old next January? A I wish you would get from him just what he means as to the age of the child? A (By Mr. Posey) He says the child will be three years old next January.

------:O:------

I, D. C. Skaggs, on oath state that the above and foregoing is a full and true transcript of my stenographic notes as taken in said cause on said date.

DC Skaggs

Subscribed and sworn to before me this 4 day of Nov. 1904.

Charles H Sawyer
Notary Public.

Applications for Enrollment of Creek Newborn
Act of 1905   Volume VIII

En. 626.
DEPARTMENT OF THE INTERIOR,
COMMISSIONER TO THE FIVE CIVILIZED TRIBES.
Melette[sic], I. T., September 12, 1905.

In the matter of the application for the enrollment of Lindy Isaac Manley as a citizen by blood of the Creek Nation.

ISAAC MANLEY, being duly sworn, testified as follows:

Through Alex Posey Official Interpreter:

BY THE COMMISSIONER:
Q What is your name? a Isaac Manley.
Q How old are you? A About twenty-nine.
Q What is your post office address? A Eufaula.
Q Are you a citizen of the Creek Nation? A Yes, sir.
Q To what town do you belong? A Eufaula Canadian.
Q Have you a child named Lindy Isaac Manley? A Yes, sir. The child is here. (indicating a little girl)
Q When was she born? A January 16, 1902.
Q What is the name of her mother? A Martha Manley.
Q Are you positive that the child was born on that date? A Yes, sir., the child will be four years old next January.
Q Did you make a record of the date of the child's birth? A No, sir.
Q Who attended on your wife at the birth of Lindy? A Hagie Sullivan.
Q Is Lindy also known as Lentoce? A Yes, sir.
Q If it should be found that Lindy is entitled to enrollment in both the Creek and Seminole Nations in which nation do you elect to have her enrolled? A In the Creek Nation.

MARTHA MANLEY, being duly sworn, testified as follows:

Through Alex Posey Official Interpreter.

BY THE COMMISSIONER:
Q What is your name? A Martha Manley.
Q How old are you? A Twenty-six.
Q What is your post office address? A Eufaula.
Q Are you a citizen of the Creek Nation? A I am a Seminole.
Q To what band in the Seminole Nation do you belong? A To William Gulley's band.
Q Have you a child named Lindy Isaac Manley? A Yes, sir.
Q When was she born? A January 16, 1902.
Q There are on file with the Commissioner two affidavits executed by you and Hagie Sullivan. In one you state that the child was born on or about May 15, 1900, and in the other you state the child was born January 16, 1903? A Both affidavits are incorrect. I had a lawyer fill out one affidavit at Wewoka. At that time I did not know the exact date

Applications for Enrollment of Creek Newborn
Act of 1905   Volume VIII

of the birth of the child but the lawyer guessed at it. In the second affidavit a mistake was made as to the year.
Q You are positive are you that Lindy was born January 16, 1902? A Yes, sir.
Q If it should be found that your child, Lindy Isaac Manley, is entitled to enrollment in either the Creek or Seminole Nation in which nation do you desire to have her enrolled? A In the Creek Nation.

I, D. C. Skaggs, on oath state that the above and foregoing is a full and true transcript of my stenographic notes as taken in said cause on said date.

DC Skaggs

Subscribed and sworn to before me this 11 day of Oct. 1905.

Edw C Griesel
Notary Public.

N.C. 643.
DEPARTMENT OF THE INTERIOR,
COMMISSIONER TO THE FIVE CIVILIZED TRIBES.
Melette[sic], I.T., September 12, 1905.

In the matter of the application for the enrollment of Melah Manley as a citizen by blood of the Creek Nation.

ISAAC MANLEY, being duly sworn, testified as follows:

Through Alex Posey Official Interpreter:

BY THE COMMISSIONER:
Q What is your name? A Isaac Manley.
Q How old are you? A About twenty-nine.
Q What is your post office address? A Eufaula.
Q Are you a citizen of the Creek Nation? A Yes, sir.
Q To what town do you belong? A Eufaula Canadian.
Q Have you a child named Melah Manley? A Yes, sir. This is the child. (indicating a child in the mother's arms.)
Q What is the name of the mother of that child? A Martha Manley.
Q When was Melah born? A December 4, 1904.
Q Have you made application for the child's enrollment in the Seminole Nation? A No, sir. The town officers of the Seminole Nation made some inquiry about my children but I made no application for the child's enrollment there.
Q It appears that on May 18, 1905, you made application for Melah Manley's enrollment as a Seminole, stating that the child was born January 14, 1905? A That is a mistake and the date of the birth is not correct.

Applications for Enrollment of Creek Newborn
Act of 1905   Volume VIII

Q If it should be found that your child, Melah Manley, is entitled to enrollment in both the Creek and Seminole Nations in which nation do you desire to have her enrolled? A In the Creek Nation.

---oooOOOooo---

I, D. C. Skaggs, on oath state that the above and foregoing is a full and true transcript of my stenographic notes as taken in said cause on said date.

DC Skaggs

Subscribed and sworn to before me this 16 day of Oct 1905.

Edw C Griesel
Notary Public.

En. 526.

DEPARTMENT OF THE INTERIOR,
COMMISSIONER TO THE FIVE CIVILIZED TRIBES.
Melette[sic], I. T., September 12, 1905.

In the matter of the application for the enrollment of Lindy Isaac Manley as a citizen by blood of the Creek Nation.

HAGIE SULLIVAN, being duly sworn, testified as follows:

Through Alex Posey Official Interpreter:

BY THE COMMISSIONER:
Q What is your name? A Hagie Sullivan.
Q How old are you? A Over fifty.
Q What is your post office address? A Eufaula.
Q Are you a citizen of the Creek Nation? A No, sir, I am a Seminole.
Q Do you know Isaac and Martha Manley? A Yes, sir. I am the mother of Martha.
Q Have they a child named Lindy Isaac Manley? A Yes, sir. I attended on the mother at the birth of the child.
Q When was that child born? A The child was born January 16, 1902.
Q You have executed two affidavits about the birth of this child. In one you stat[sic] that the child was born May 15, 1900, and in the other you state that she was born January 16, 1903? A Both affidavits are incorrect. I have investigated the matter and fix the date as January 16, 1902.
Q Are you positive that Lindy was born January 16, 1902? A Yes, sir.
Q Is Lindy sometimes called Lentoce? A Yes, sir.

---oooOOOooo---

Applications for Enrollment of Creek Newborn
Act of 1905 Volume VIII

I, D. C. Skaggs, on oath state that the above and foregoing is a full and true transcript of my stenographic notes as taken in said cause on said date.

DC Skaggs

Subscribed and sworn to before me this 16 day of Oct, 1905.

Edw C Griesel
Notary Public.

DEPARTMENT OF THE INTERIOR,
COMMISSION TO THE FIVE CIVILIZED TRIBES.
Eufaula, I. T., April 3, 1905.

In the matter of the application for the enrollment of Lindy and Melah Manley as citizens by blood of the Creek Nation.

MARTHA MANLEY, being duly sworn, testified as follows:

BY COMMISSION:
Q What is your name? A Martha Manley.
Q What is your age? A Twenty-six.
Q What is your post office address? A Eufaula.
Q Are you a citizen of the Creek Nation? A I am a Seminole.
Q Do you make application for the enrollment of your two minor children, Lindy and Melah Manley, as citizen[sic] by blood of the Creek Nation? A Yesk[sic] sir.
Q What is the name of the father of these children? A Isaac Manley.
Q Is he a citizen of the Creek Nation? A Yes, sir.
Q To what town does he belong? A Eufaula Canadian.
Q If it should be found that your two children, Lindy and Melah Manley, are entitled to be enrolled in either the Creek or Seminole Nations[sic] in which nation do you desire to have them enrolled? A In the Creek Nation.

------:O:------

I, D. C. Skaggs, on oath state that the above and foregoing is a full and true transcript of my stenographic notes as taken in said cause on said date.

DC Skaggs

Subscribed and sworn to before me this 21 day of July, 1905.

J McDermott
Notary Public.

Applications for Enrollment of Creek Newborn
Act of 1905   Volume VIII

Cr. En. 526 and
NC 643.

Muskogee, Indian Territory, June 23, 1905.

Isaac Manley,
    Mellette, Indian Territory.

Dear Sir:

    The Commission desires further evidence in the matter of the application for the enrollment of your minor children, Linda[sic] Isaac (or Lentoce) Manley and Melah Manley, as citizens by blood of the Creek Nation. It appears from the evidence in said case that the mother of said children is a citizen of the Seminole nation.

    You are advised that you will be allowed twenty days from date within which to appear before the Commission at its office in Muskogee, Indian Territory, with the mother of said children and at least one other witness, who knows the exact dates of their birth. It will also be necessary to elect in which Nation you desire said children to be enrolled and receive their allotments of land.

                  Respectfully,

                              Chairman.

COMMISSIONERS:
TAMS BIXBY,
THOMAS B. NEEDLES,
C.R. BRECKINBRIDGE.

WM. O. BEALL
Secretary

DEPARTMENT OF THE INTERIOR,
COMMISSIONER TO THE FIVE CIVILIZED TRIBES.

REFER IN REPLY TO THE FOLLOWING:

Seminole N.B. 66.

ADDRESS ONLY THE
COMMISSION TO THE FIVE CIVILIZED TRIBES.

Muskogee, Indian Territory, June 19, 1905.

Commission to the Five Civilized Tribes,
    Creek Enrollment Division.

Gentlemen:

    On May 18, 1905, application was made to the Commission for the enrollment of Lentoce Manley, born January 16, 1902, and Mela[sic] Manley, born January 4, 1905, as citizens by blood of the Creek Nation. It is stated in said application that the father of said children is Isaac Manley, a citizen by blood of the Creek Nation, and that the mother is Martha Manley, a citizen of the Seminole Nation.

Applications for Enrollment of Creek Newborn
Act of 1905   Volume VIII

You are requested to inform the Seminole Enrollment Division as to whether or not application has been made Commission for the enrollment of said children as citizens of the Creek Nation, and if so what disposition has been made of such applications.

Respectfully,

Tams Bixby Chairman.

NC. 643

Muskogee, Indian Territory, July 15, 1905.

Chief Clerk,
  Seminole Enrollment Division,
    Muskogee, Indian Territory.

Dear Sir:

April 7, 1902[sic], application was made to the Commission to the Five Civilized Tribes for the enrollment of Lindy Manley, born January 16, 1903, and Melah Manley, born December 4, 1904, as citizens by blood of the Creek Nation. It is stated in said application that the father of said children is Isaac Manley, a citizen of the Creek Nation, and that the mother is Martha Manley, a citizen of the Seminole Nation.

You are requested to inform the Creek Enrollment Division as to whether application has been made for the enrollment of said children as citizens of the Seminole Nation, and if so, what disposition has been made of the same.

Respectfully,

Commissioner.

W.F.

Seminole NB-66.
DEPARTMENT OF THE INTERIOR.
COMMISSION TO THE FIVE CIVILIZED TRIBES.

Muskogee, Indian Territory, July 18, 1905.

Chief Clerk,
  Creek Enrollment Division.

Dear Sir:

Applications for Enrollment of Creek Newborn
Act of 1905   Volume VIII

Receipt is hereby acknowledged of your letter of July 15, 1905 (NC-643) in which you state that application was made to the Commission to the Five Civilized Tribes for the enrollment of Linda[sic] Manley and Melah Manley as citizens by blood of the Creek Nation; that the father of said children is Isaac Manley, a citizen by blood of the Creek Nation, and that their mother is Martha Manley, a citizen by blood of the Seminole Nation.

In reply to your letter you are advised that on May 18, 1905 application was made to the Commission to the Five Civilized Tribes for the enrollment of Lentoce Manley, born January 16, 1902 and Mela Manley, born January 4, 1905, children of Isaac Manley, a citizen by blood of the Creek Nation and Martha Manley, a citizen by blood of the Seminole Nation. It is presumed that the Lentoce Manley is identical with Linda Manley of whom you inquire and that Mela Manley is identical with Melah Manley who appears as an applicant for enrollment as a citizen by blood of the Creek Nation.

Respectfully,

Tams Bixby Commissioner.

NC-643.

Muskogee, Indian Territory, October 23, 1905.

Clerk in Charge
   Seminole Enrollment Division.

Dear Sir:

There are herewith inclosed copies of the testimony taken April 3, 1905, and September 12, 1905, in the matter of the application for the enrollment of Linda Isaac Manley and Melah Manely[sic] as citizens by blood of the Creek Nation, in which the parents of said children elect to have them enrolled and allotted as Creeks.

Said Linda Isaac Manley is identified as Lentoce Manley and said Melah Manley is identified as Mela Manley whose names appear on Seminole new born card #66.

Respectfully,

Commissioner.

CTD-15.

Applications for Enrollment of Creek Newborn
Act of 1905 Volume VIII

NC 643

Muskogee, Indian Territory, November 13, 1906.

Chief Clerk,
    Seminole Enrollment Division.
        General Office.

Dear Sir:

    You are hereby advised that the names of Lindy Isaac and Melah Manley, children of Isaac Manly[sic], a citizen by blood of the Creek Nation and Martha Manley a citizen of the Seminole Nation, is contained in schedule of minor citizens by blood of the Creek Nation, approved by the Secretary of the Interior, November 27, 1905, opposite Roll numbers 727 and 728.

                Respectfully,

                          Commissioner.

BIRTH AFFIDAVIT.

DEPARTMENT OF THE INTERIOR.
COMMISSION TO THE FIVE CIVILIZED TRIBES.

IN RE APPLICATION FOR ENROLLMENT, as a citizen of the Creek Nation, of Melah Manley, born on the 4 day of December, 1904

Name of Father: Isaac Manley   a citizen of the Creek Nation.
Eufaula Canadian Town
Name of Mother: Martha Manley   a citizen of the Seminole Nation.

                Postoffice   Eufaula, Ind. Ter.

AFFIDAVIT OF MOTHER.

UNITED STATES OF AMERICA, Indian Territory, } Child is present
    Western   DISTRICT.

    I, Martha Manley, on oath state that I am 26 years of age and a citizen by blood, of the Creek[sic] Nation; that I am the lawful wife of Isaac Manley, who is a citizen, by blood of the Creek Nation; that a female child was born to me on *(blank)* day of December, 1904, that said child has been named Melah Manley, and was living March 4, 1905.

                              her
                      Martha x Manley
                             mark

Applications for Enrollment of Creek Newborn
Act of 1905   Volume VIII

Witnesses To Mark:
{ Alex Posey
{ DC Skaggs

Subscribed and sworn to before me this 3 day of April, 1905.

        Drennan C Skaggs
        Notary Public.

AFFIDAVIT OF ATTENDING PHYSICIAN OR MID-WIFE.

UNITED STATES OF AMERICA, Indian Territory,
 Western DISTRICT.

  I, Hagie Sullivan, a midwife, on oath state that I attended on Mrs. Martha Manley, wife of Isaac Manley on the 4 day of December, 1904; that there was born to her on said date a *(blank)* child; that said child was living March 4, 1905, and is said to have been named Melah Manley
        her
        Hagie x Sullivan
Witnesses To Mark: mark
{ Alex Posey
{ DC Skaggs

Subscribed and sworn to before me this 3 day of April, 1905.

        Drennan C Skaggs
        Notary Public.

BIRTH AFFIDAVIT
DEPARTMENT OF THE INTERIOR,
COMMISSION TO THE FIVE CIVILIZED TRIBES.

  IN RE Application for Enrollment, as a citizen of the Creek Nation, of Lindy Isaac Manley, born on the 15th day of May, 1900

Name of Father: Isaac Manley   a citizen of the Creek Nation.
Name of Mother: Martha *(Blank)*   a citizen of the Seminole Nation.

       Post-office: Eufaula, Indian Territory.

Applications for Enrollment of Creek Newborn
Act of 1905   Volume VIII

AFFIDAVIT OF MOTHER.

UNITED STATES OF AMERICA,
    INDIAN TERRITORY.
Western Judicial District.

    I, Martha Manley , on oath state that I am 26 years of age and a citizen by blood , of the Seminole Nation; that I am the lawful wife of Isaac Manley , who is a citizen, by blood of the Creek Nation; that a female child was born to me on or about the 15th day of May , 1900 , that said child has been named Lindy Isaac Manley , and is now living.

                                                             her
                                        Martha Manley x
WITNESSES TO MARK: mark
    F.C. Owen
    Sam Colbert

Subscribed and sworn to before me this 9 *day of* ~~April~~ May , 1903.

                                        E.I. O'Reilly
                                              NOTARY PUBLIC.

AFFIDAVIT OF ATTENDING PHYSICIAN OR MID-WIFE.

UNITED STATES OF AMERICA,
    INDIAN TERRITORY.
Western Judicial District.

    I, Hagie Sullivan , a Mid-wife , on oath state that I attended on Mrs. Martha Manley , wife of Isaac Manley on or about the 15th day of (May) , 1900 ; that there was born to her on said date a female child; that said child is now living and is said to have been named Lindy Isaac Manley

                                                             her
                                        Hagie Sullivan x
WITNESSES TO MARK: mark
    F.C. Owen
    Sam Colbert

Subscribed and sworn to before me this 9 *day of* ~~April~~ May , 1903.

                                        E.I. O'Reilly
                                              NOTARY PUBLIC.

Applications for Enrollment of Creek Newborn
Act of 1905   Volume VIII

BIRTH AFFIDAVIT.

DEPARTMENT OF THE INTERIOR.
COMMISSION TO THE FIVE CIVILIZED TRIBES.

IN RE APPLICATION FOR ENROLLMENT, as a citizen of the Creek Nation, of Lindy Isaac Manley, born on the 16 day of Jan , 1902

Name of Father: Isaac Manley   a citizen of the   Creek   Nation.
Eufaula Canadian
Name of Mother: Martha Manley   a citizen of the   Seminole   Nation.

Postoffice   Melette[sic], Ind. Ter.

AFFIDAVIT OF MOTHER.

UNITED STATES OF AMERICA, Indian Territory, } Child is present
Western   DISTRICT.

I, Martha Manley , on oath state that I am 26 years of age and a citizen by blood , of the Seminole Nation; that I am the lawful wife of Isaac Manley , who is a citizen, by blood of the Creek Nation; that a female child was born to me on 16" day of January , 1902 , that said child has been named Lindy Isaac Manley , and was living March 4, 1905.
                                    her
                          Martha x Manley
                                    mark
Witnesses To Mark:
 { DC Skaggs
   Alex Posey

Subscribed and sworn to before me this 12" day of September , 1905.

                          Drennan C Skaggs
                              Notary Public.

AFFIDAVIT OF ATTENDING PHYSICIAN OR MID-WIFE.

UNITED STATES OF AMERICA, Indian Territory, }
Western   DISTRICT.

I, Hagie Sullivan , a mid-wife , on oath state that I attended on Mrs. Martha Manley , wife of Isaac Manley on the 16" day of Jan , 1902 ; that there was born to her on said date a female child; that said child was living March 4, 1905, and is said to have been named Lindy Isaac Manley

Applications for Enrollment of Creek Newborn
Act of 1905   Volume VIII

Witnesses To Mark:
{ DC Skaggs
{ Alex Posey

her
Hagie x Sullivan
mark

Subscribed and sworn to before me this 12" day of September, 1905.

Drennan C Skaggs
Notary Public.

BIRTH AFFIDAVIT.

DEPARTMENT OF THE INTERIOR.
COMMISSION TO THE FIVE CIVILIZED TRIBES.

IN RE APPLICATION FOR ENROLLMENT, as a citizen of the Creek Nation, of Lindy Manley, born on the 16 day of January, 1903

Name of Father: Martha[sic] Manley   a citizen of the Seminole Nation.
Name of Mother: Isaac[sic] Manley   a citizen of the Creek Nation.
Eufaula Canadian Town.

Postoffice   Eufaula, Ind. Ter.

AFFIDAVIT OF MOTHER.

UNITED STATES OF AMERICA, Indian Territory,
Western   DISTRICT.   Child is present

I, Martha Manley, on oath state that I am 26 years of age and a citizen by blood, of the Seminole Nation; that I am the lawful wife of Isaac Manley, who is a citizen, by blood of the Creek Nation; that a female child was born to me on 16 day of January, 1903, that said child has been named Lindy Manley, and was living March 4, 1905.

her
Martha x Manley
mark

Witnesses To Mark:
{ DC Skaggs
{ Alex Posey

Subscribed and sworn to before me this 3 day of April, 1905.

Drennan C Skaggs
Notary Public.

Applications for Enrollment of Creek Newborn
Act of 1905   Volume VIII

AFFIDAVIT OF ATTENDING PHYSICIAN OR MID-WIFE.

UNITED STATES OF AMERICA, Indian Territory, ⎫
   Western   DISTRICT.   ⎭

   I, Hagie Sullivan , a midwife , on oath state that I attended on Mrs. Martha Manley , wife of Isaac Manley on the 16 day of January , 1903 ; that there was born to her on said date a *(blank)* child; that said child was living March 4, 1905, and is said to have been named Lindy Manley

                                  her
                        Hagie x Sullivan
Witnesses To Mark: mark
  { Alex Posey
    DC Skaggs

   Subscribed and sworn to before me this 3 day of April, 1905.

                            Drennan C Skaggs
                              Notary Public.

BIRTH AFFIDAVIT.

DEPARTMENT OF THE INTERIOR.
COMMISSION TO THE FIVE CIVILIZED TRIBES.

   IN RE APPLICATION FOR ENROLLMENT, as a citizen of the Creek Nation, of Lizzie Island , born on the 7 day of September , 1903

Name of Father: Napoleon B. Island   a citizen of the   Creek   Nation.
Name of Mother: Maggie Island   a citizen of the   Creek   Nation.

                Postoffice   stidham indian territory[sic]

AFFIDAVIT OF MOTHER.

UNITED STATES OF AMERICA, Indian Territory, ⎫
   Western Dist   DISTRICT.   ⎭

   I, Maggie Island , on oath state that I am 23 years of age and a citizen by marriage , of the Creek Nation; that I am the lawful wife of Napoleon B Island , who is a citizen, by Blood of the Creek Nation; that a Female child was born to me on 7

Applications for Enrollment of Creek Newborn
Act of 1905   Volume VIII

day of September, 1903, that said child has been named Lizzie, and was living March 4, 1905.

                                      Maggie Island

Witnesses To Mark:
{

Subscribed and sworn to before me this 25 day of March, 1905.

                                      Preston Janway
                                            Notary Public.

AFFIDAVIT OF ATTENDING PHYSICIAN OR MID-WIFE.

UNITED STATES OF AMERICA, Indian Territory, }
    Western   DISTRICT.

I, Marry Rich, a midwife, on oath state that I attended on Mrs. Maggie Island, wife of Napoleon b. island[sic] on the 7 day of September, 1903 ; that there was born to her on said date a female child; that said child was living March 4, 1905, and is said to have been named Lizzie
                                            her
                                       Marry x Rich

Witnesses To Mark: mark
{ Preston Janway
  S.C. Cazad

Subscribed and sworn to before me this 25 day of March, 190*(blank)*.

    My commission   Preston Janway
        Expires May 19th 1908   Notary Public.

BIRTH AFFIDAVIT.
                        DEPARTMENT OF THE INTERIOR.
              COMMISSION TO THE FIVE CIVILIZED TRIBES.

    IN RE APPLICATION FOR ENROLLMENT, as a citizen of the Creek Nation, of Yeggues Clarance Island, born on the 3 day of July, 1901

Name of Father: Napoleon B. Island   a citizen of the   Creek   Nation.
Name of Mother: Maggie Island   a citizen of the   Creek   Nation.

                                Postoffice   Stidham Ind Ter

Applications for Enrollment of Creek Newborn
Act of 1905   Volume VIII

AFFIDAVIT OF MOTHER.

UNITED STATES OF AMERICA, Indian Territory,
Western   DISTRICT.

I, Maggie Island, on oath state that I am 23 years of age and a citizen by marriage, of the Creek Nation; that I am the lawful wife of Napoleon B Island, who is a citizen, by Blood of the Creek Nation; that a male child was born to me on 3 day of July, 1901, that said child has been named Yeggues, and was living March 4, 1905.

Maggie Island

Witnesses To Mark:

Subscribed and sworn to before me this 25 day of March, 1905.

Preston Janway
Notary Public.

AFFIDAVIT OF ATTENDING PHYSICIAN OR MID-WIFE.

UNITED STATES OF AMERICA, Indian Territory,
Western   DISTRICT.

I, Susie Island[sic], a midwife, on oath state that I attended on Mrs. Maggie Island, wife of Napoleon B. Island on the 3 day of July, 1901; that there was born to her on said date a male child; that said child was living March 4, 1905, and is said to have been named Yeggues

her
Marry x Rich
mark

Witnesses To Mark:
  Preston Janway
  S.C. Cazad

Subscribed and sworn to before me this 25 day of March, 1905.

My commission   Preston Janway
Expires May 19th 1908   Notary Public.

Applications for Enrollment of Creek Newborn
Act of 1905 Volume VIII

DEPARTMENT OF THE INTERIOR,
COMMISSION TO THE FIVE CIVILIZED TRIBES.

IN RE Application for Enrollment, as a citizen of the Creek (or Muskogee) Nation, of Ida M. McIntosh, born on the 7 day of July, 1901

Name of Father: L. G. McIntosh   a citizen of the   Creek   Nation.
Name of Mother: Leonie McIntosh   a citizen of the   Creek   Nation.

Postoffice   Eufaula I.T.

AFFIDAVIT OF PARENT.
(To be made if child is now living)

UNITED STATES OF AMERICA,
  Indian Territory,
Western   DISTRICT.

I, L.G. McIntosh, on oath state that I am fifty one years of age and a citizen by blood, of the Creek (or Muskogee) Nation; that I am the father of Ida M. McIntosh a female child who was born on the 7 day of July, 1901, that said child is now living.

Witnesses To Mark:
                              L.G. McIntosh
                              Geo$_x$ M$_x$ Jones$_x$[sic]
                              Notary

Subscribed and sworn to before me this 18 *day of* November, *19*02.

                              Geo$_x$ M. Portora
                                  Notary Public.

DEPARTMENT OF THE INTERIOR.

Commission to THE Five Civilized Tribes

In re an application for enrollment as a citizen of the Creek Nation of Ida M. McIntosh, born July seventh 19o1[sic].

Name of Mother Leonie McIntosh, a citizen of the Creek Nation.
Name of Father L. G. McIntosh,   a citizen of the Creek Nation

Post office Eufaula, Indian Territory.

Applications for Enrollment of Creek Newborn
Act of 1905   Volume VIII

Affidavit of Mother.

Indian Territory.
Northern District.

    Leonie M. McIntosh on oath, states, I am, 36 years of age, a citizen by blood of the Creek Nation; that I am the lawful wife of L. G. McIntosh, a citizen by blood of the Creek Nation: that there was born unto me on the 7th day of July 19o1[sic] a female child and that the said child is now living and has been named Ida M. McIntosh.

Leonie McIntosh

Sworn and subscribed to before me this 2 day [sic] August 1901.

RL Simpson
Notary Public
My Commission expires March 19, 1902

Affidavit of Midwife

Indian Territory.
  Northern District.

    Sis Barnett, on oath, states that I attendd[sic] on Mrs Leonie McIntosh wife of L. G. McIntosh on the seventh day of July 19o1 and that there was born unto [sic] on the said date a female child; that the said child is now living and is said to have been named Ida M. McIntosh.

Sis Barnett

Witness

Sworn and subscribed to before me this 2 day [sic] August 19o1.

RL Simpson
Notary Public
My Commission expires March 19, 1902

BIRTH AFFIDAVIT.

Department of the Interior,
COMMISSION TO THE FIVE CIVILIZED TRIBES.

    IN RE APPLICATION FOR ENROLLMENT, as a citizen of the Creek Nation, of Ida M. McIntosh , born on the 7 day of July , 1901

Name of Father: L. G. McIntosh   a citizen of the   Creek   Nation.
Kialigee Town
Name of Mother: Leona McIntosh (deceased)   a citizen of the   Creek   Nation.
Coweta Town

Applications for Enrollment of Creek Newborn
Act of 1905   Volume VIII

Post-Office: Eufaula, Ind. Ter.

AFFIDAVIT OF MOTHER.

UNITED STATES OF AMERICA,
   INDIAN TERRITORY,   } Child is present
Western   District.

I, L. G. McIntosh , on oath state that I am 54 years of age and a citizen by blood , of the Creek Nation; that I am the lawful ~~wife~~ husband of Leona McIntosh , who ~~is a~~ was citizen, by blood of the Creek Nation; that a female child was born to ~~me~~ her on 7 day of July , 1901 , that said child has been named Ida M. McIntosh , and ~~is now~~ was living. on March 4, 1905, that the mother of the child and the midwife who attended on her at the birth of the child are now both dead

L. G. McIntosh

WITNESSES TO MARK:
{

Subscribed and sworn to before me this 3 day of April, 1905.

Drennan C Skaggs
Notary Public.

BIRTH AFFIDAVIT

DEPARTMENT OF THE INTERIOR,
COMMISSION TO THE FIVE CIVILIZED TRIBES.

IN RE Application for Enrollment, as a citizen of the Creek Nation, of Lena Malaney , born on the 16th day of Febey , 1902

Name of Father: Jim Malaney   none ~~a~~ citizen of the   *(blank)* Nation.
Name of Mother: Annie Malaney   a citizen of the   Creek   Nation.

Post-office: Brush Hill I.T.

Applications for Enrollment of Creek Newborn
Act of 1905 Volume VIII

AFFIDAVIT OF MOTHER.

UNITED STATES OF AMERICA,
INDIAN TERRITORY.
Western District.

I, Annie Malaney, on oath state that I am Twenty three years of age and a citizen by blood , of the Creek Nation; that I am the lawful wife of Jim Malaney , who is a non citizen, by *(blank)* of the *(blank)* Nation; that a female child was born to me on 16 day of Feby , 1902 , that said child has been named Lena Malaney , and is now living.

                                        her
                                 Annie x Malaney
WITNESSES TO MARK: mark
{ D.F. Patterson
  S.J. Logan

Subscribed and sworn to before me this 27th day of March , 1905.

                    My Commission expires   Bunnie McIntosh
                         May 16/1908   **NOTARY PUBLIC.**

AFFIDAVIT OF ATTENDING PHYSICIAN OR MID-WIFE.

UNITED STATES OF AMERICA,
INDIAN TERRITORY.
Western District.

I, Louvina Price , a midwife , on oath state that I attended on Mrs. Annie Malaney , wife of Jim Malaney on the 16 day of Feby , 1902 ; that there was born to her on said date a female child; that said child is now living and is said to have been named Lena Malaney   her
                                          Louvina x Price
WITNESSES TO MARK: mark
{ D.F. Patterson
  S.J. Logan

Subscribed and sworn to before me this 27th day of March , 1905.

                    My Commission expires   Bunnie McIntosh
                         May 16/1908   **NOTARY PUBLIC.**

Applications for Enrollment of Creek Newborn
Act of 1905 Volume VIII

BIRTH AFFIDAVIT.

DEPARTMENT OF THE INTERIOR.
COMMISSION TO THE FIVE CIVILIZED TRIBES.

IN RE APPLICATION FOR ENROLLMENT, as a citizen of the Creek Nation, of Edith Walker, born on the 10 day of December, 1904

Name of Father: Edward H. Walker a citizen of the Creek Nation.
Name of Mother: Eula Walker a citizen of the Creek Nation.

Postoffice stidham indian territory[sic]

AFFIDAVIT OF MOTHER.

UNITED STATES OF AMERICA, Indian Territory,
  Western DISTRICT.

I, Eula Walker , on oath state that I am 23 years of age and a citizen by Blood , of the Creek Nation; that I am the lawful wife of Edward H. Walker , who is a citizen, by blood of the Creek Nation; that a female child was born to me on 10 day of December , 1904 , that said child has been named Edith , and was living March 4, 1905.

Eula Walker

Witnesses To Mark:

Subscribed and sworn to before me this 25 day of March , 1905.

Preston Janway
Notary Public.

AFFIDAVIT OF ATTENDING PHYSICIAN OR MID-WIFE.

UNITED STATES OF AMERICA, Indian Territory,
  Western DISTRICT.

I, F. L. Smith , a Physician , on oath state that I attended on Mrs. Eula Walker , wife of Edward H. Walker on the 10 day of Dec , 1904 ; that there was born to her on said date a female child; that said child was living March 4, 1905, and is said to have been named Edith

F.L. Smith

Witnesses To Mark:

Applications for Enrollment of Creek Newborn
Act of 1905   Volume VIII

Subscribed and sworn to before me this 25 day of March , 1905.

Preston Janway
Notary Public.

DEPARTMENT OF THE INTERIOR.
COMMISSION TO THE FIVE CIVILIZED TRIBES.

IN RE APPLICATION FOR ENROLLMENT, as a citizen of the Creek Nation, of George Washington Walker, born on the 31 day of july[sic] , 1902

Name of Father: Edward H. Walker   a citizen of the   Creek   Nation.
Name of Mother: Eula Walker   a citizen of the   Creek   Nation.

Postoffice   stidham[sic] I.T.

AFFIDAVIT OF MOTHER.

UNITED STATES OF AMERICA, Indian Territory,
    Western   DISTRICT.

I, Eula Walker , on oath state that I am 28 years of age and a citizen by blood , of the Creek   Nation; that I am the lawful wife of Edward H. Walker , who is a citizen, by blood of the Creek   Nation; that a male child was born to me on 31st day of july[sic] , 1902 , that said child has been named George Washington , and is now living.

Eula Walker

Witnesses To Mark:
{

Subscribed and sworn to before me this 25 day of March , 1905.

Preston Janway
Notary Public.

AFFIDAVIT OF ATTENDING PHYSICIAN OR MID-WIFE.

UNITED STATES OF AMERICA, Indian Territory,
    Western   DISTRICT.

I, Mary Rich , a mid wife , on oath state that I attended on Mrs. Eula Walker , wife of Edward H Walker on the 31 day of July , 1902 ; that there was born to her on

Applications for Enrollment of Creek Newborn
Act of 1905   Volume VIII

said date a male child; that said child is now living and is said to have been named George Washington

                                                          her
Witnesses To Mark: Mary x Rich
{ *(Name Illegible)*   mark
{ S.C. Cozad

Subscribed and sworn to before me this 25 day of March , 1905.

                                        Preston Janway
                                        Notary Public.

NC-648.

                              Muskogee, Indian Territory, August 12, 1905

James Depriest,
    Eufaula, Indian Territory.

Dear Sir:

    In the matter of the application for the enrollment of your minor child Luther Depriest, born March 1, 1903, as a citizen by blood of the Creek Nation, it will be necessary for you to furnish this office with the affidavit is the attending physician or midwife as to the birth of said child.

    For that purpose there is inclosed herewith a blank for proof of birth. However if there was no attending physician or midwife when said child was born it will be necessary for you to furnish, in lieu of the affidavit of the attending physician or midwife, the affidavits of two disinterested persons relative to the birth of said child, said affidavits to set forth said child's name, the date of his birth, the names of his parents and whether or not he was on living March 4, 1905.

    Please give this matter your immediate attention.

                                    Respectfully,

B C   Acting Commissioner
Env.

Applications for Enrollment of Creek Newborn
Act of 1905   Volume VIII

BIRTH AFFIDAVIT.

DEPARTMENT OF THE INTERIOR.
COMMISSION TO THE FIVE CIVILIZED TRIBES.

IN RE APPLICATION FOR ENROLLMENT, as a citizen of the Creek Nation, of Luther Depriest, born on the first day of March, 1903

Name of Father: James Depriest   a citizen of the   Creek   Nation.
Name of Mother: Emily Depriest   a citizen of the   Creek   Nation.

Postoffice   *(blank)*

AFFIDAVIT OF ATTENDING PHYSICIAN OR MID-WIFE.

UNITED STATES OF AMERICA, Indian Territory,
     (blank)   DISTRICT.

I, *(blank)*, a Physician, on oath state that I attended on Mrs. Emily Depriest, wife of James Depriest on the first day of March, 1903; that there was born to her on said date a male child; that said child was living March 4, 1905, and is said to have been named Luther Depriest

                                       C.E. Coppedge M.D.

Witnesses To Mark:

Subscribed and sworn to before me this 16th day of Sept, 1905.

                                 Chas. M. Sherrill
Com Expires Sep. 4-1906   Notary Public.

BIRTH AFFIDAVIT.

Department of the Interior,
COMMISSION TO THE FIVE CIVILIZED TRIBES.

IN RE APPLICATION FOR ENROLLMENT, as a citizen of the Creek Nation, of Luther Depriest, born on the 1 day of March, 1903

Name of Father: James Depriest   a citizen of the   Creek   Nation.
Artussee Town
Name of Mother: Emily Depriest   a citizen of the   Creek   Nation.
Arbeka Town

                         Post-Office: Eufaula, Ind. Ter.

Applications for Enrollment of Creek Newborn
Act of 1905   Volume VIII

AFFIDAVIT OF MOTHER.

UNITED STATES OF AMERICA,
INDIAN TERRITORY,
Western   District.

Child is present

I, Emily Depriest , on oath state that I am about 30 years of age and a citizen by blood , of the Creek Nation; that I am the lawful wife of James Depriest, who is a citizen, by blood of the Creek Nation; that a male child was born to me on 1 day of March , 1903 , that said child has been named Luther Depriest , and ~~is now~~ was living. on March 4, 1905

WITNESSES TO MARK:

Emily Depriest

Subscribed and sworn to before me this 3 day of April, 1905.

Drennan C Skaggs
Notary Public.

Father
AFFIDAVIT OF ~~ATTENDING PHYSICIAN OR MID-WIFE~~.

UNITED STATES OF AMERICA,
INDIAN TERRITORY,
Western   District.

my wife
I, James Depriest , ~~a (blank)~~ , on oath state that I attended on ^ Mrs. Emily Depriest , ~~wife of (blank)~~ on the 1 day of March , 1903 ; that there was born to her on said date a male child; that said child ~~is now~~ was living on March 4, 1905 and ~~is said to have~~ has been named Luther Depriest

WITNESSES TO MARK:

James Depriest

Subscribed and sworn to before me this 3 day of April, 1905.

Drennan C Skaggs
Notary Public.

Applications for Enrollment of Creek Newborn
Act of 1905   Volume VIII

NC 649.

Muskogee, Indian Territory, August 12, 1905.

Mary Moore,
    c/o Bob Moore,
        Lenna, Indian Territory.

Dear Madam:

    In the matter of the application for the enrollment of your minor daughter Jessie Susan Moore, as a citizen by blood of the Creek Nation You are advised that it will be necessary for you to furnish this office with either the original or a certified copy of the marriage license and certificate showing marriage between you and Bob Moore the father of said child.

    In order that the said Bob Moore may be identified upon the final roll of citizens by blood of the Creek Nation you are requested to state his age, the name of his parents, and other members of his family, the name under which he is finally enrolled and his roll number as the same appears upon his allotment certificate and deeds.

    This matter should have your immediate attention.

        Respectfully,

                Acting Commissioner.

Get marriage certificate.

NC 649.

Muskogee, Indian Territory, October 17, 1905.

Mary Moore,
    c/o Bob Moore,
        Lenna, Indian Territory.

Dear Madam:

    In the matter of the application for the enrollment of your minor daughter, Jessie Susan Moore, as a citizen by blood of the Creek Nation You are advised that it will be necessary for you to furnish this office with either the original or a certified copy of the marriage license and certificate showing marriage between you and Bob Moore, the father of said child.

    In order that the said Bob Moore may be identified upon the final roll of citizens by blood of the Creek Nation you are requested to state his age, the name of his parents,

Applications for Enrollment of Creek Newborn
Act of 1905   Volume VIII

and other members of his family, the name under which he is finally enrolled and his roll number as the same appears upon his allotment certificate and deeds.

    This matter should have your immediate attention.

                Respectfully,

                              Commissioner.

NC 649.

                Muskogee, Indian Territory, January 14, 1907.

Mary Moore,
    c/o Bob Moore,
        Lenna, Indian Territory.

Dear Madam:

    In the matter of the application for the enrollment of your minor child, Jessie Susan Moore, as a citizen by blood of the Creek Nation, You are advised that it will be necessary for you to furnish this office with proof of your marriage to Bob Moore, the alleged father of said child and a citizen of the Creek Nation; said proof may consist of either the original or a certified copy of the marriage license and certificate, but inasmuch as two former requests for same have been ignored by you, you are advised that if same cannot be procured you should furnish this office within ten days with proof in the nature of witnesses or affidavits as to whether said Bob Moore was in fact the father of said child.

    You are also requested to write this office as to whether said child is living and an explanation of the fact that you have done nothing further towards the enrollment of this child since the original application of April 3, 1905.

                Respectfully,

                              Commissioner.

(The letter below typed as given)

                Lenna Indian territory[sic] January the 14 1907

to the department of the interior

Dear sirs in answer to your letter conserning my minor child Jessie Susan Moore I do hereby say that the said Robert Moore is the Father of the said Jessie Susan Moore the

Applications for Enrollment of Creek Newborn
Act of 1905   Volume VIII

minor child though I when Susan was inroled Alex Posey being well acquainted with Robert Moore and wasyoust to calling him that he just put his name down Bob Moore whitch it should have ben Robert Moore that is I find in all of his deallings he signs his name Robert Moore so I will send you our marriage licens and I do say that the sead Robert Moore is in fact the father of the sead Jessie Susan Moore and she is still alive though I don nothing towards the enrolment asept I have answered all the letters conserning this child so please send me a plat of this township 10 range 14 range east so the sead Bob Moore as Robert Moore whitch is all the same man lives in Coeato town so I remain yours truly

Mary Moore
at Lenna I T

N. C. 649.

Muskogee, Indian Territory, March 7, 1907.

Bob Moore,
    Lenna, Indian Territory.

Dear Sir:

You are hereby advised that on March 2, 1907, the Secretary of the Interior approved the enrollment of your minor child Jennie[sic] Susan Moore as a citizen by blood of the Creek Nation, and that the name of said child appears upon the roll of new born citizens by blood of the Creek Nation enrolled under the Act of Congress approved March 3, 1905, as number 1231.

This child is now entitled to an allotment, and application therefor should be made without delay at the Creek Land Office, Muskogee, Indian Territory.

Respectfully,

Commissioner.

Applications for Enrollment of Creek Newborn
Act of 1905   Volume VIII

BIRTH AFFIDAVIT.

DEPARTMENT OF THE INTERIOR.
COMMISSION TO THE FIVE CIVILIZED TRIBES.

IN RE APPLICATION FOR ENROLLMENT, as a citizen of the Creek Nation, of Jessie Susan Moore , born on the 10 day of April , 1904

Name of Father: Bob Moore   a citizen of the   Creek   Nation.
Okfusky[sic] Canadian
Name of Mother: Mary Moore   a citizen of the United States Nation.

Postoffice   Lenna, Ind. Ter.

AFFIDAVIT OF MOTHER.

UNITED STATES OF AMERICA, Indian Territory,
Western   DISTRICT.   } Child is present

I, Mary Moore , on oath state that I am 18 years of age and a citizen ~~by~~ *(blank)* , of the United States ~~Nation~~; that I am the lawful wife of Bob Moore , who is a citizen, by blood of the Creek Nation; that a female child was born to me on 10 day of April , 1904 , that said child has been named Jessie Susan Moore , and was living March 4, 1905.

Mary Moore

Witnesses To Mark:

Subscribed and sworn to before me this 3 day of April , 1905.

Drennan C Skaggs
Notary Public.

AFFIDAVIT OF ATTENDING PHYSICIAN OR MID-WIFE.

UNITED STATES OF AMERICA, Indian Territory,
Western   DISTRICT.   }

I, Catherine Kelly , a midwife , on oath state that I attended on Mrs. Mary Moore , wife of Bob Moore on the 10 day of April , 1904 ; that there was born to her on said date a female child; that said child was living March 4, 1905, and is said to have been named Jessie Susan Moore

her
Catherine x Kelly
mark

Applications for Enrollment of Creek Newborn
Act of 1905   Volume VIII

Witnesses To Mark:
{ Alex Posey
{ DC Skaggs

    Subscribed and sworn to before me this 3 day of April, 1905.

                                       Drennan C Skaggs
                                         Notary Public.

(The above Birth Affidavit given again.)

CERTIFICATE OF RECORD

United States of America
Indian Territory
Western District   ss

    I, Robert P. Harrison, Clerk of the United States Court in the Western District, Indian Territory, do hereby certify that the instrument hereto attached was filed for record in my office the 3 day of Jan 1903, at --M, and duly recorded in Book O, Marriage Record Page 10.

    Witness my hand and seal of said Court at Muskogee, in said Territory this 3 day of Jan A D 1903

                                         R P Harrison Clerk

By J. Harlan Deputy

I, Anna Garrigues, on oath state that the above and foregoing is a true and correct copy of the original.

                                         Anna Garrigues

Subscribed and sworn to before me this 26 day of January 1907

                                       Edward Merrick
                                         Notary Public.

Applications for Enrollment of Creek Newborn
Act of 1905   Volume VIII

MARRIAGE LICENSE.

United States of America
Indian Territory
Northern District   SS   No. 17

TO ANY PERSON AUTHORIZED BY LAW TO SOLEMNIZE MARRIAGE-GREETING:

You are hereby commanded to Solemnize the Rite and Publish the Banns of Matrimony between Mr. Robert Moore of Eufaula, in the Indian Territory, aged 49 years, and Miss Mary Kelley, of Eufaula, in the Indian Territory, aged 17 years, according to law, and do you officially sign and return this License to the parties therein named.
WITNESS my hand and official seal at Eufaula, Indian Territory, this 27th day of October, A. D. 1902.

                                R.P Harrison
SEal[sic]   Clerk of the U.S. Court.

By CE. Wilcox Deputy.

CERTIFICATE OF MARRIAGE.

United States of America
Indian Territory
Northern District   ss

I, F.B. Morris, a Minister of the Gospel, Do Hereby Certify, that on the 2 day of November A.D. 1902, did duly and according to law as commanded in the foregoing license, solemnize the Rite and Publish the Banns of Matrimony between the parties therein named.
Witness my hand this 3 day of November, A. D. 1902.
My credentials are recorded in the office of the Clerk of the United States Court, Indian Territory, Third Judicial Division, Book C, Page 136.

                                F.B. Morris
                                A minister of the Gospel

Applications for Enrollment of Creek Newborn
Act of 1905   Volume VIII

NC-650.

Muskogee, Indian Territory, August 12, 1905

Ellen Wolf,
    c/o William Wolf,
        Fame, Indian Territory.

Dear Madam:

    In the matter of the application for the enrollment of your minor daughter Jennie Wolf, born the third Monday in January 1904, as a citizen by blood of the Creek Nation, it appears from your affidavit now in[sic] file with the records of this office that there was no attending physician or midwife at the birth of said child.

    It is necessary for you to furnish this office, in lieu of the affidavit of the attending physician or midwife at the birth of said child, the affidavits of two disinterested persons as to her birth, said affidavits must set forth said child's name, the date of her birth, the names of her parents and whether or not she was living on March 4, 1905.

    You are also requested to inform this office as to the name under which you were finally enrolled, the names of your parents and other members of your family, your age and your final roll number as the same appears upon your allotment certificate and deeds.

    Please give this matter your prompt attention.

        Respectfully,

        Acting Commissioner.

NC-650.

Muskogee, Indian Territory, October 17, 1905.

Ellen Wolf,
    c/o William Wolf,
        Fame, Indian Territory.

Dear Madam:

    In the matter of the application for the enrollment of your minor daughter Jennie Wolf you state in your affidavit executed April 3, 1905 that said child was born on the third Monday in January 1904, and that no one attended you in the capacity of physician or midwife at the birth of said child. On September 29, 1905, you forwarded to this office the affidavit of yourself and Yanner Richison a midwife in which it is stated that the said Jennie Wolf was born January 3, 1904.

Applications for Enrollment of Creek Newborn
Act of 1905 Volume VIII

In order that you may correct the discrepancy between the two sets of affidavits there is inclosed herewith a form of birth affidavit which has been partially filled out. You are requested to fill in the blank spaces giving the correct date of the birth of said child and if a midwife attended on you at the birth of said child you will have her execute the affidavit for the midwife. If no midwife was in fact present it will be necessary for you to furnish this office, in lieu of her affidavit, the affidavits of two disinterested persons as to the birth of Jennie Wolf. Said affidavits must set forth said child's name, the date of her birth, the names of her parents and whether or not she was living on March 4, 1905.

You are also requested to inform this office as to the name under which you were finally enrolled, the names of your parents and other members of your family, your age and your final roll number as the same appears upon your allotment certificate and deeds.

Respectfully,

Commissioner.

CTD-4
Env.

N C 650

Muskogee, Indian Territory, March 7, 1907.

Ellen Wolfe,
    Care of William Wolfe,
        Fame, Indian Territory.

Dear Madam:

You are hereby advised that on March 2, 1907, the Secretary of the Interior approved the enrollment of your minor child Jennie Wolfe as a citizen by blood of the Creek Nation, and that the name of said child appears upon the roll of new born citizens by blood of the Creek Nation, enrolled under the Act of Congress approved March 3, 1905 number 1232.

This child is now entitled to allotment and application therefor should be made without delay at the Creek Land Office, Muskogee, Indian Territory.

Respectfully,

Commissioner.

Applications for Enrollment of Creek Newborn
Act of 1905   Volume VIII

BIRTH AFFIDAVIT.

DEPARTMENT OF THE INTERIOR.
COMMISSION TO THE FIVE CIVILIZED TRIBES.

IN RE APPLICATION FOR ENROLLMENT, as a citizen of the Creek Nation, of Jennie Wolf, born on the third Monday in ~~day of~~ January, 1904

Name of Father: William Wolf   a citizen of the   Creek   Nation.
Artussee Town
Name of Mother: Ellen Wolf (nee Washington)   a citizen of the   Creek   Nation.
Arbeka Deep Fork Town
                    Postoffice   Fame, Ind. Ter.

AFFIDAVIT OF MOTHER.

UNITED STATES OF AMERICA, Indian Territory,
    Western   DISTRICT.   } Child is present

    I, Ellen Wolf, on oath state that I am about 40 years of age and a citizen by blood, of the Creek Nation; that I am the lawful wife of William Wolf, who is a citizen, by blood of the Creek Nation; that a female child was born to me on the third Monday ~~day of~~ in January, 1904, that said child has been named Jennie Wolf, and was living March 4, 1905. That no one attended on me as midwife or physician at the birth of the child.
                                           her
                            Ellen x Wolf
Witnesses To Mark: mark
{ Alex Posey
{ DC Skaggs

    Subscribed and sworn to before me this 4 day of April, 1905.

                            Drennan C Skaggs
                               Notary Public.

Applications for Enrollment of Creek Newborn
Act of 1905 Volume VIII

BIRTH AFFIDAVIT.

DEPARTMENT OF THE INTERIOR.
COMMISSION TO THE FIVE CIVILIZED TRIBES.

IN RE APPLICATION FOR ENROLLMENT, as a citizen of the Creek Nation, of Jennie Wolf, born on 3 day of Jan , 1904

Name of Father: William Wolf   a citizen of the   Creek   Nation.
Name of Mother: Ellen Wolf   a citizen of the   Creek   Nation.

Postoffice   Fame, I T

AFFIDAVIT OF MOTHER.

UNITED STATES OF AMERICA, Indian Territory,
     Western   DISTRICT.

35 years of age and a citizen by
I, Ellen Wolf , on oath state that ~~I am years of age and a citizen by~~ blood , of the Creek Nation; that I am the lawful wife of William Wolf , who is a citizen, by blood of the Creek Nation; that a Female child was born to me on *(blank)* day of Jan, 1904 , that said child has been named Jennie Wolf , and was living March 4, 1905. That no one attended on me as midwife or physician at the birth of the child.

                               her
                         Ellen x Wolf
Witnesses To Mark: mark
   { Jacob Cole
   { *(Illegible)* Richard

Subscribed and sworn to before me 25 day of Sep , 1905.

                         M. Y. Killingsworth
                             Notary Public.
             My Com expires Apr 10, 07

AFFIDAVIT OF ATTENDING PHYSICIAN OR MID-WIFE.

UNITED STATES OF AMERICA, Indian Territory,
     Western   DISTRICT.

I, Yanner Richison , a midwife , on oath state that I attended on Mrs. Ellen Wolf , wife of William Wolf on the 3 day of Jan , 1904 ; that there was born to her on said date a female child; that said child was living March 4, 1905, and is said to have been named Jennie Wolf

Applications for Enrollment of Creek Newborn
Act of 1905   Volume VIII

Witnesses To Mark:
{ Jacob Cole
{ *(Illegible)* Richard

her
Yanner x Richison
mark

Subscribed and sworn to before me 25 day of Sep , 1905.

M. Y. Killingsworth
Notary Public.
My Com expires Apr 10, 07

NC 650.   FHW
DEPARTMENT OF THE INTERIOR,
COMMISSIONER TO THE FIVE CIVILIZED TRIBES.

In the matter of the application for the enrollment of Jennie Wolf as a citizen by blood of the Creek Nation.

DECISION

The record shows that an application was filed, in affidavit form, on April 7, 1905, for the enrollment of Jennie Wolf as a citizen by blood of the Creek Nation. A supplemental affidavit filed September 29, 1905, is attached to and made a part of the record herein.

The evidence in this case shows that the said Jennie Wolf is the child of William Wolf and Ellen Wolfe[sic], whose names appear on a partial schedule of citizens by blood of the Creek Nation approved by the Secretary of the Interior March 28, 1902, opposite Nos. 7410 and 7486 respectively.

It appears that the said Jennie Wolf was born in January, 1904 and was living March 4, 1905.

The Act of Congress approved March 3, 1905 (33 Stat., 1048) provides in part as follows:

"That the Commission to the Five Civilized Tribes is authorized for sixty days after the date of the approval of this Act to receive and consider applications for enrollments of children born subsequent to May twenty five, nineteen hundred and one, and prior to March fourth, nineteen hundred and five, and living on said latter date, to citizens of the Creek tribe of Indians whose enrollment has been approved by the Secretary of the Interior prior to the approval of this Act; and to enroll and make allotments to such children."

It is therefore, ordered and adjudged that said Jennie Wolf is entitled to enrollment as a citizen by blood of the Creek Nation in accordance with the provisions of

Applications for Enrollment of Creek Newborn
Act of 1905 Volume VIII

the law above quoted, and the application for her enrollment as such is accordingly granted.

Tams Bixby Commissioner.

Muskogee, Indian Territory.
JAN 17 1907

NC-651.

Muskogee, Indian Territory, August 12, 1905.

Lizzie Frank,
    c/o Austin Frank,
        Catoose[sic], Indian Territory.

Dear Madam:

    There is on file with this office application for the enrollment of your minor son Austin Frank, Jr., as a citizen by blood of the Creek Nation. It appears therefrom that you are a citizen by blood of the Creek Nation but this office is unable to identify you upon the final roll of citizens by blood of said nation. It is necessary that you be so identified before the rights of said son can be finally determined.

    You are therefore requested to immediately inform this office as to the name under which you were finally enrolled, the names of your parents and other members of your family and your final roll number as the same appears upon your allotment certificate and deeds.

Respectfully,

Acting Commissioner.

NC-651.

Muskogee, Indian Territory, October 17, 1905.

Lizzie Frank,
    c/o Austin Frank,
        Catoosa, Indian Territory.

Dear Madam:

    There is on file with this office application for the enrollment of your minor son Austin Frank, Jr., as a citizen by blood of the Creek Nation from

Applications for Enrollment of Creek Newborn
Act of 1905 Volume VIII

which it appears that you are a citizen of the Creek Nation but this office is unable to identify you upon the final roll of citizens by blood of the Creek Nation. It is necessary that you be so identified before the rights of said son can be finally determined.

You are therefore requested to immediately inform this office as to the name under which you were enrolled, the names of your parents and other members of your family and your final roll number as the same appears upon your allotment certificate and deeds.

Respectfully,

Commissioner.

BIRTH AFFIDAVIT

DEPARTMENT OF THE INTERIOR,
COMMISSION TO THE FIVE CIVILIZED TRIBES.

IN RE Application for Enrollment, as a citizen of the Muskogee Nation, of Austin Frank, born on the 12 day of Jan, 1903

Name of Father: Austin Frank   a citizen of the Muskogee Nation.
Name of Mother: Lizzie Frank   a citizen of the Muskogee Nation.

Post-office: Catoosa, Ind. T.

AFFIDAVIT OF MOTHER.

UNITED STATES OF AMERICA,
   INDIAN TERRITORY.
   Northern District.

I, Lizzie Frank, on oath state that I am 20 years of age and a citizen by blood, of the Muskogee Nation; that I am the lawful wife of Austin Frank, who is a citizen, by blood of the Muskogee Nation; that a male child was born to me on 12 day of Jan, 1903, that said child has been named Austin Frank, and is now living.

Lizzie Frank

WITNESSES TO MARK:

Subscribed and sworn to before me this 28 day of March, 1905.

WWWhitman

My Com Ex Nov 5 1907   NOTARY PUBLIC.

Applications for Enrollment of Creek Newborn
Act of 1905   Volume VIII

AFFIDAVIT OF ATTENDING PHYSICIAN OR MID-WIFE.

UNITED STATES OF AMERICA, }
INDIAN TERRITORY.
Northern   District.

I, Ellen Harrison , a midwife , on oath state that I attended on Mrs. Lizzie Frank, wife of Austin Frank on the 12 day of Jan , 1903 ; that there was born to her on said date a male child; that said child is now living and is said to have been named Austin Frank

                            Ellen Harrison
WITNESSES TO MARK: Her x mark
   { Eli Harrison
     Myrtle Witherspoon

Subscribed and sworn to before me this 28 *day of*   March , *1905.*

                            WWWhitman
My Com Ex Nov 5 1907   *NOTARY PUBLIC.*

NC-652.

                       Muskogee, Indian Territory, August 12, 1905.

A. W. Brown,
     Eufaula, Indian Territory.

Dear Sir:

       In the matter of the application for the enrollment of your minor daughter Eva May Brown, born April 3, 1902, as a citizen by blood of the Creek Nation, it will be necessary for you to furnish this office the affidavits of two disinterested persons as to the birth of said child. Said affidavits must set forth said child's name, the date of her birth, the names of her parents, and whether or not she was living on March 4, 1905.

       Please give this matter your immediate attention.

                     Respectfully,

                        Acting Commissioner.

Applications for Enrollment of Creek Newborn
Act of 1905   Volume VIII

BIRTH AFFIDAVIT.

DEPARTMENT OF THE INTERIOR.
COMMISSION TO THE FIVE CIVILIZED TRIBES.

IN RE APPLICATION FOR ENROLLMENT, as a citizen of the Creek Nation, of Eva May Brown, born on the 3rd. day of April, 1902

Name of Father: Almon W. Brown a noncitizen   a citizen of the   *(blank)*   Nation.
Name of Mother: Ada J. Brown   a citizen of the   Creek   Nation.

Postoffice   Eufaula   Ind. Tery.

AFFIDAVIT OF MOTHER.

UNITED STATES OF AMERICA, Indian Territory,
Western   DISTRICT.

I, Ada J. Brown, on oath state that I am Twenty-six years of age and a citizen by Blood, of the Creek Nation; that I am the lawful wife of Almon W. Brown, who is a non citizen, by *(blank)* of the *(blank)* Nation; that a female child was born to me on 3rd. day of April, 1902, that said child has been named Eva May Brown, and was living March 4, 1905.

Ada J. Brown

Witnesses To Mark:
{   My Commission Expires Jan. 30, 1909.

Subscribed and sworn to before me this 18th. day of August, 1905.

Frank W. Rushing
Notary Public.

AFFIDAVIT OF ATTENDING PHYSICIAN OR MID-WIFE.

UNITED STATES OF AMERICA, Indian Territory,
Western   DISTRICT.

I, Almon W. Brown, a physician, on oath state that I attended on Mrs. Ada J. Brown my, wife of ----------------- on the 3rd. day of April, 1902; that there was born to her on said date a female child; that said child was living March 4, 1905, and is said to have been named Eva May Brown

Almon W. Brown

Witnesses To Mark:
{

Applications for Enrollment of Creek Newborn
Act of 1905 Volume VIII

Subscribed and sworn to before me this 18th. day of August, 1905.

             Frank W. Rushing
My Commission Expires Jan. 30, 1909.   Notary Public.

United States of America, ((
           ((
Western District, Indian Territory. ((
           ((

W. A. Tolleson Being duly sworn states on oath that he is acquainted with Mrs. Ada J. Brown, a citizen by blood of the Creek Nation and Dr. Almon W. Brown her husband, a non citizen; That there was born to the said Mrs. Ada J. Brown, on the 3rd. day of April, 1902, a girl child which was named Eva May Brown and that said child as living on the 4th. day of March, 1904[sic].

                W.A. Tolleson

Subscribed and sworn to before me on this 18th. day of August, 1905.

             Frank W Rushing
    My Commission Expires Jan. 30, 1909.   Notary Public.

United States of America,
Western District, Indian Territory.

W.C. Grayson , being first duly sworn, states on his oath that he is acquainted with Mrs. Ada J. Brown, a citizen by blood of the Creek Nation, and Dr. Almond[sic] W. Brown, her husband; a non citizen; that there was born to the said Mrs. Ada J. Brown, on the 3rd. day of April, 1902, a girl child which was named Eva May Brown and that said child was living on the 4th. day of March, 1904.

                W.C. Grayson

Subscribed and sworn to before me on this 18th. day of August, 1905.

             Frank W Rushing
    My Commission Expires Jan. 30, 1909.   Notary Public.

Applications for Enrollment of Creek Newborn
Act of 1905   Volume VIII

BIRTH AFFIDAVIT.

DEPARTMENT OF THE INTERIOR.
COMMISSION TO THE FIVE CIVILIZED TRIBES.

IN RE APPLICATION FOR ENROLLMENT, as a citizen of the Creek Nation, of Eva May Brown , born on the 3 day of April , 1902

Name of Father: A. W. Brown   a citizen of the United States   Nation.
Name of Mother: Ada J. Brown   a citizen of the   Creek   Nation.

Postoffice   Eufaula, Ind. Terr.

AFFIDAVIT OF MOTHER.

UNITED STATES OF AMERICA, Indian Territory, ⎫
    Western   DISTRICT.   ⎬

I, Ada J. Brown , on oath state that I am 26 years of age and a citizen by blood, of the Creek Nation; that I am the lawful wife of A.W. Brown , who is a citizen, ~~by~~ *(blank)* of the United States ~~Nation~~; that a female child was born to me on 3rd day of April , 1902 , that said child has been named Eva May Brown , and was living March 4, 1905.

                                Ada J. Brown

Witnesses To Mark:
{

Subscribed and sworn to before me this 24 day of March , 1905.

                              Drennan C Skaggs
                              Notary Public.

AFFIDAVIT OF ATTENDING PHYSICIAN OR MID-WIFE.

UNITED STATES OF AMERICA, Indian Territory, ⎫
    (blank)   DISTRICT.   ⎬

I, A.W. Brown, M.D. , a Physician , on oath state that I attended on Mrs. Mrs[sic] A.W. Brown , wife of A.W. Brown (self) on the 3$\underline{rd}$ day of April , 1902 ; that there was born to her on said date a female child; that said child was living March 4, 1905, and is said to have been named Eva May Brown

                              A.W. Brown, M.D.

Applications for Enrollment of Creek Newborn
Act of 1905   Volume VIII

Witnesses To Mark:
{ Jno M. Byrd
{ A.A. Belding

Subscribed and sworn to before me 31st day of March, 1905.

My Commission Expires   C G Bush
Sept. 27, 1906   Notary Public.

BIRTH AFFIDAVIT.
DEPARTMENT OF THE INTERIOR.
COMMISSION TO THE FIVE CIVILIZED TRIBES.

IN RE APPLICATION FOR ENROLLMENT, as a citizen of the Creek Nation, of Maggie Shepherd, born on the 13th day of April, 1904

Name of Father: K. H. Shepherd   a citizen of the United States Nation.
Name of Mother: Addie M. Shepherd   a citizen of the Creek Nation.

Postoffice   Brush Hill I. T.

AFFIDAVIT OF MOTHER.

UNITED STATES OF AMERICA, Indian Territory, }
    Western   DISTRICT.   }

I, Addie M. Shepherd, on oath state that I am 26 years of age and a citizen by Blood, of the Creek Nation; that I am the lawful wife of K. H. Shepherd, who is a citizen, by *(blank)* of the United States Nation; that a Female child was born to me on 13th day of April, 1904, that said child has been named Maggie Shepherd, and was living March 4, 1905.

                              Addie M. Shepherd
Witnesses To Mark:
{ Warren Ruie
{

Subscribed and sworn to before me this 20th day of March, 1905.

                              M Y Killingsworth
My Com expires Apr 20th 1907   Notary Public.

Applications for Enrollment of Creek Newborn
Act of 1905   Volume VIII

AFFIDAVIT OF ATTENDING PHYSICIAN OR MID-WIFE.

UNITED STATES OF AMERICA, Indian Territory,
   Western   DISTRICT.

I, N. P. Lee, a Physician, on oath state that I attended on Mrs. Addie M Shepherd, wife of K. H. Shepherd on the 13th day of April, 1904; that there was born to her on said date a Female child; that said child was living March 4, 1905, and is said to have been named Maggie Shepherd

N.P. Lee

Witnesses To Mark:

Subscribed and sworn to before me this 20th day of March, 1905.

M Y Killingsworth

My Com expires Apr 20th 1907   Notary Public.

DEPARTMENT OF THE INTERIOR,
COMMISSION TO THE FIVE CIVILIZED TRIBES.

IN RE Application for Enrollment, as a citizen of the Creek Nation, of May Shepherd, born on the 16th day of February, 1902

Name of Father: K.H. Shepherd   a citizen of the United States Nation.
Name of Mother: Addie M Shepherd   a citizen of the   Creek   Nation.

Post-office: Brush Hill I.T.

AFFIDAVIT OF MOTHER.

UNITED STATES OF AMERICA,
   INDIAN TERRITORY.
   Western   District.

I, Addie M. Shepherd, on oath state that I am 26 years of age and a citizen by Blood, of the Creek Nation; that I am the lawful wife of K.H. Shepherd, who is a citizen, by *(blank)* of the United States Nation; that a Female child was born to me on 16th day of February, 1902, that said child has been named May Shepherd, and is now living.

Addie M. Shepherd

Applications for Enrollment of Creek Newborn
Act of 1905   Volume VIII

WITNESSES TO MARK:
{ Warren Ruie

Subscribed and sworn to before me this 20th day of March , 1905.

My Com expires Apr 20th 1907

M Y Killingsworth
Notary Public.

AFFIDAVIT OF ATTENDING PHYSICIAN OR MID-WIFE.

UNITED STATES OF AMERICA,
INDIAN TERRITORY.
Western   District.

I, W. J. Ford , a Physician , on oath state that I attended on Mrs. Addie M. Shepherd , wife of K. H. Shepherd on the 16th day of February , 1902 ; that there was born to her on said date a Female child; that said child is now living and is said to have been named May Shepherd

Dr. W. J. Ford

WITNESSES TO MARK:
{ DY Crowell M.D.

Subscribed and sworn to before me this 20 day of March , 1905.

My Com expires Apr 20th 1907

M Y Killingsworth
Notary Public.

BIRTH AFFIDAVIT.

Department of the Interior,
COMMISSION TO THE FIVE CIVILIZED TRIBES.

IN RE APPLICATION FOR ENROLLMENT, as a citizen of the Creek or Muskogee Nation, of David Jefferson Nelson , born on the *(blank)* day of *(blank)* , 190*(blank)*

Name of Father: William W. Nelson   a citizen of the U.S. Nation.
Name of Mother: Mary S. Nelson   a citizen of the Muskogee Nation.

Post-Office: Eufaula, I.T.

Applications for Enrollment of Creek Newborn
Act of 1905   Volume VIII

AFFIDAVIT OF MOTHER.

UNITED STATES OF AMERICA, }
   INDIAN TERRITORY,
   Western   District.

    I, Mary S. Nelson , on oath state that I am 27 years of age and a citizen by birth , of the Muskogee Nation; that I am the lawful wife of William W. Nelson , who is a citizen, by birth of the U.S. Nation; that a male child was born to me on 8th day of March , 1904 , that said child has been named David Jefferson Nelson, and is now living.

Mary S. Nelson

WITNESSES TO MARK:

{

    Subscribed and sworn to before me this 23^{d} *day of* March, 1905.

R.H. Searcy
Notary Public.

AFFIDAVIT OF ATTENDING PHYSICIAN OR MID-WIFE.

UNITED STATES OF AMERICA, }
Oklahoma ~~INDIAN~~ TERRITORY,
   ~~Western~~ County District.
Oklahoma

    I, R. M. Counterman MD , a Physician , on oath state that I attended on Mrs. Mary S. Nelson , wife of William W. Nelson on the eighth day of March , 1904 ; that there was born to her on said date a male child; that said child is now living and is said to have been named David Jefferson Nelson

R.M. Counterman, M.D.

WITNESSES TO MARK:

{

    Subscribed and sworn to before me this 25th *day of* March, 1905.

Edwin G. Bedford
Notary Public.

My commission expires
May 15 1907

Applications for Enrollment of Creek Newborn
Act of 1905   Volume VIII

BIRTH AFFIDAVIT.

DEPARTMENT OF THE INTERIOR.
COMMISSION TO THE FIVE CIVILIZED TRIBES.

IN RE APPLICATION FOR ENROLLMENT, as a citizen of the Creek Nation, of El Louisa Post, born on the 10 day of May, 1903

Name of Father: Thomas Post   a citizen of the   Creek   Nation.
Tuskegee Town
Name of Mother: Laura Post   a citizen of the United States ~~Nation~~.

Postoffice   Eufaula, Ind. Terr.

Child present.

AFFIDAVIT OF MOTHER.

UNITED STATES OF AMERICA, Indian Territory, }
   Western   DISTRICT.

I, Laura Post, on oath state that I am 28 years of age and a citizen by ~~(blank)~~, of the United States ~~Nation~~; that I am the lawful wife of Thomas Post, who is a citizen, by blood of the Creek Nation; that a female child was born to me on 10 day of May, 1903, that said child has been named El Louisa Post, and was living March 4, 1905.

Laura Post

Witnesses To Mark:
{

Subscribed and sworn to before me this 6 day of April, 1905.

Drennan C Skaggs
Notary Public.

AFFIDAVIT OF ATTENDING PHYSICIAN OR MID-WIFE.

UNITED STATES OF AMERICA, Indian Territory, }
   Western   DISTRICT.

I, Judy Grayson, a mid-wife, on oath state that I attended on Mrs. Laura Post, wife of Thomas Post ~~on the~~ about 2 ~~day of~~ years ago, ~~1~~; that there was born to her on said date a female child; that said child was living March 4, 1905, and is said to have been named El Louisa Post

her
Judy x Grayson
mark

Applications for Enrollment of Creek Newborn
Act of 1905 Volume VIII

Witnesses To Mark:
- DC Skaggs
- Alex Posey

Subscribed and sworn to before me 6 day of April, 1905.

           Drennan C Skaggs
           Notary Public.

BIRTH AFFIDAVIT.

Department of the Interior,
COMMISSION TO THE FIVE CIVILIZED TRIBES.

IN RE APPLICATION FOR ENROLLMENT, as a citizen of the Creek Nation, of Samantha Post, born on the 14 day of October, 1901

Name of Father: Thomas Post   a citizen of the Creek Nation. Tuskegee Town
Name of Mother: Laura Post   a citizen of the United States Nation.

      Post-Office: Eufaula, Ind. Terr.

AFFIDAVIT OF MOTHER.
        Child present

UNITED STATES OF AMERICA,
 INDIAN TERRITORY,
  Western   District.

I, Laura Post , on oath state that I am 28 years of age and a citizen ~~by~~ *(blank)* , of the United States ~~Nation~~; that I am the lawful wife of Thomas Post , who is a citizen, by blood of the Creek Nation; that a female child was born to me on 14 day of October , 1901 , that said child has been named Samantha Post , and ~~is now~~ was living. on March 4, 1905.

           Laura Post

WITNESSES TO MARK:

Subscribed and sworn to before me this 3 day of April, 1905.

           Drennan C Skaggs
           Notary Public.

Applications for Enrollment of Creek Newborn
Act of 1905   Volume VIII

AFFIDAVIT OF ATTENDING PHYSICIAN OR MID-WIFE.

UNITED STATES OF AMERICA,
   INDIAN TERRITORY,
  Western   District.

I, Adeline White , a mid-wife , on oath state that I attended on Mrs. Laura Post , wife of Thomas Post on the sometime in day of October , 1901 ; that there was born to her on said date a female child; that said child is now was living on March 4, 1905 and is said to have been named Samantha Post

                            her
                       Adeline x White

WITNESSES TO MARK: mark
{ DC Skaggs
  Alex Posey

Subscribed and sworn to before me this 3 *day of* April, *1905.*

                         Drennan C Skaggs
                            Notary Public.

NC-657.
DEPARTMENT OF THE INTERIOR,
COMMISSIONER TO THE FIVE CIVILIZED TRIBES.
Muskogee, I. T., February 8, 1906.

In the matter of the application for the enrollment of Clarence Roberson as a citizen by blood of the Creek Nation.

NANCY ROBERSON, being duly sworn, testified as follows:

BY THE COMMISSIONER:
Q What is your name? A Nancy Roberson.
Q What was your name before it was Roberson? A Nancy James.
Q What is your father's name? A Chotkey James.
Q What is the name of your mother? A Betsey James.
Q How old are you? A Twenty-three.
Q What is your post office address? A Checotah.
Q Have you a child named Clarence Roberson? A Yes, sir.
Q Can you read or write?   No, Sir.
Q Can you spell? A I spell a little.

Applications for Enrollment of Creek Newborn
Act of 1905 Volume VIII

Q We have two affidavits executed by you in which the first name of this child is spelled different ways. It is just plain Clarence, is it? A Yes, sir.
Q The usual way of spelling it is C-l-a-r-e-n-c-e? A Yes, sir. I didn't done that.
Q Is this child, Clarence Roberson, living? A Yes, sir.
Q When was he born? A He was born in December.
Q What year? A---------------1901
Q How old is the child.[sic] How old was it last December? A It was two years old.
Q What is the matter with you; don't you know anything at all. How old was it last December? A He was a year old.
Q And will be two years old next December? A Yes, sir.
Q That would make it 1904--is that right--instead of 1901? A Yes, sir.
Q What Creek Indian Town do you belong to? A Arbeka.

Witness is identified as Nancy James opposite Creek Indian Roll No. 7023.

HENRY ROBERSON, being duly sworn, testified as follows:

BY THE COMMISSIONER:
Q What is your name? A Henry Roberson?[sic] A[sic]
Q How old are you? A Twenty-six.
Q What is your post office address? A Checotah.
Q Are you the father of Clarence? A That is what she says. (indicating Nancy Roberson)
Q Are you her husband? A Supposed to be.
Q You know about that. You might not know whether or not you are the father of the child, but you know whether or not you are her husband, don't you? A Yes, sir.
Q Are you a citizen of any nation in Indian Territory? A No, sir.
Q Are you a United States citizen? A Yes, sir.
Q Can you read and write? A A little.
Q How do you spell that child's name? A C-l-a-r-e-n-c-e.
Q The regular way. A Yes, sir. You could spell it different.
Q You want it spelled the correct way? A Yes, sir.
Q C-l-a-r-e-n-c-e Roberson? A Yes, sir.

---oooOOOooo---

I, D. C. Skaggs, on oath state that the above and foregoing is a full and true transcript of my stenographic notes as taken in said cause on said date.

DC Skaggs

Subscribed and sworn to before me this 8" day of Feb. 1906.

J McDermott
Notary Public.

Applications for Enrollment of Creek Newborn
Act of 1905   Volume VIII

NC. 657.

DEPARTMENT OF THE INTERIOR,
COMMISSIONER TO THE FIVE CIVILIZED TRIBES.
MUSKOGEE, INDIAN TERRITORY.
MAY 28, 1906.

In the matter of the application for the enrollment of Clarence Roberson, deceased, as a citizen by blood of the Creek Nation.

Nancy Roberson, being duly sworn, testified as follows:

Q What is your name? A Nancy Roberson.
Q What is your age? A 24.
Q What is your post office address? A Checotah.
Q Is your child Clarence Roberson living? A No sir.
Q When did he die? A In March, no, he was living March 4, 1905 in March.
Q How long did he live? A He lived two years.
Q How many months did he live? A He lived three months before he died.
Q Three months? A Yes sir.
Q Did he live as much a six months? A No sir.
Q Are you sure of that? A Yes sir. He didn't live six months, he would have been two years old and six months if he had lived.
Q Would have been that old? A Yes sir, if he had lived.
Q When was he born? A He was born Christmas month, same as yes baby did.
Q Was he living when this child Joe T. Robinson[sic] was born, on December 18, 1905? A Yes sir.
Q Was he dead when this baby you have here was born? A Yes sir.
Q How long had he been dead? A About five years before this baby was born.

Witness apparently had no idea at all of dates as will be shown by the testimony.

Q You appeared here last February, about three months ago, and testified about Clarence, and you were asked then if he was living March 4, 1905 and you said Yes. Was he living this last spring? A Yes sir.
Q Are you sure of that? A I made a mistake right there.
Q Are you sure Clarence was living March 4, 1905 this last gone February? A He was dead, he was living.
Q If the child was living, how long after was it that you came in here, just three months ago, that he died? A I didn't tell that.
Q It is only three months ago? A Yes sir.
Q Did he die this month? A No sir.
Q Did he die last month? A I can't hardly tell that.

Henry Roberson, being duly sworn, testified as follows:

Q What is your name? A Henry Roberson.

Applications for Enrollment of Creek Newborn
Act of 1905   Volume VIII

Q What is your age? A About 26.
Q What is your post office address? A Checotah.
Q Can you read and write? A No sir.
Q Can't? A No sir.
[sic] Do you know how to spell your last name? A Yes sir, R-o-b-s-o-n.
Q That doesn't spell Roberson or Robinson, that spells Robson? A Thats[sic] the way my name is spelled.
Q Have you any papers, copy of your marriage license or any record matter that you have showing the correct spelling of your name? A No sir. My name is Henry Robson.
Q Cane[sic] you write your name? A Witness writes on a slip of paper, hereto attached, something looks like Henry Robson.
Q That has an "m" to it? A That "m" is meant to be "n".
Q You are advised that you must furnish your marriage license which shows the proper spelling of your name, or anything else which would give us authority to spell the correct name for these children that you wish to have enrolled.
Q When did Clarence die? A Last part of August, I don't know the date.
Q What August? A This last year.
Q How old was he when he died? A He was something little over a year old, not much.
Q The best of your recollection is how much over was he a year old? A I don't know exactly. I might have made a mistake, I don't know.
Q I didn't ask you if you knew exactly, I asked you about how he old[sic] when he died? A I don't know exactly, I guess he was a month or a couple of months over a year old.
Q What do you mean, -- you mean a month over a year? A Yes sir.
Q When was he born? A I don't know what year it was. It[sic] got it in a book but I couldn't tell you now.
Q You said he died in August of last year? A Yes sir, he died in August alright
Q Have you anyway of showing the exact date of the birth and death of Clarence, have you any witnesses to introduce or have you any written proof? A I have witnesses.
Q Are they here now? A No sir.
Q You had better bring them in. Didn't you say you had it written down somewhere? A Yes sir.
Q Did you write it? A No sir.
Q who wrote it? A Her father did.
Q When did he write it,[sic] A When it was birthed.
Q Did he write down the date of the death of Clarence? A I don't know whether he did no not.
Q Did anybody write it down anywhere for you? A I don't think so.
Q Did you by a coffin for Clarence? A No sir, we made one.
Q You made the coffin? A Yes sir.
Q ~~Have~~ Did you have the lumber or did you buy it? A Bought it.
Q From Whom? A From Tibbett.
Q At Checotah? A No sir in the country.
Q What is his first name? A Douglass Tibbett.
Q He lives out in country from Checotah? A Yes sir.
Q Did you have preaching at the house or at the grave? A Yes sir.
Q Who did the preaching? A Sam Woodford.

Applications for Enrollment of Creek Newborn
Act of 1905   Volume VIII

Q Were there any white people there either at the house or at the graveyard? A Bray lives right close to me, he was there.
Q How do you spell that? A I don't know.
Q Do you know his full name? A I don't know.
Q Did you have a doctor when the child died? A Yes sir yes I had a doctor waiting on him. Dr. Harris.
Q White man? A Yes sir.
Q You are a negro, aren't you? A Yes sir.
Q And this Doctor's name was Harris, do you know his given name? A No sir.
Q Is he a practicing physician? A Yes sir.
Q What is his post office? A Hoffman.
Q Dr. Harris of Hoffman, was he there when the child died? A No sir.
Q Was he there shortly before he died? [sic] He started there and was told the child was dead, and he returned back.
Q He was not there when the child died? A No sir. He returned back before he got there.
Q What did you father-in-law write in that book.[sic] [sic] The date of the birth.
Q Did he write that with a pencil or in ink? A Pencil.
Q What kind of a book? A Tablet.
Q You are advised that you should have him appear with that book, and you should have this doctor, or any other witnesses, you can furnish, appear at this office to testify about the birth and death of this child, and you should also furnish proof as to which is your correct name, whether it is Robinson, Roberson or Robson.

Lona Merrick, being duly sworn, states that the above and foregoing is a true and correct transcript of her stenographic notes as taken in said cause on said date.

Lona Merrick

Subscribed and sworn to before me this 28th day of May, 1906.

Henry G. Hains
Notary Public.

N.C. 657.

DEPARTMENT OF THE INTERIOR,
COMMISSIONER TO THE FIVE CIVILIZED TRIBES.
Muskogee, Indian Territory, October 16, 1906.

In the matter of the application for the enrollment of CLARENCE ROBERSON as a citizen by blood of the Creek Nation.

Applications for Enrollment of Creek Newborn
Act of 1905 Volume VIII

APPEARANCE:

    JOHN G. LIEBER appears for M. L. Mott, attorney for the Creek Nation.

    NANCY ROBERSON, being first duly sworn by Henry G. Hains, a Notary Public, testifies as follows:

BY THE COMMISSIONER:

Q What is your name? A Nancy Roberson.
Q How old are you? A I forget; I was eighteen when I married.
Q What is your post office address? A Checotah.
Q What Creek Indian town do you belong to? A Arbeka.
Q What is the name of your father? A Chotkey James.
Q What is the name of your mother? A Betsy James.
Q You say that you were eighteen when you married? A Yes sir.
Q When you were married, how long ago? A It was three years ago going on four.
Q In what month were you married? A I cant[sic] hardly tell that.
Q Was it this time of the year, or in the spring, or summer? A It was in the fall.
Q Must be about this time was it? A Yes sir.
Q Three years ago? A Yes sir.
Q What is the name of your husband? A Henry Roberson.
Q Have you your marriage license with you? A Yes sir.

    There is exhibited a marriage license and certificate between Henry Robinson and Nancy James. The license is dated January 21, 1903, and the certificate is dated January 23, 1903, showing they were married on January 21, 1903, by B. F. McElvain, a minister of the gospel.

Q Were you married to anybody else before Henry? A No sir, never have been married before.
Q Did you ever have any children by anybody else than Henry? A No sir.
Q How many children have you had by henry or anyone else? A Two.
Q Name these? A Clarence.
Q Is he living? A No sir dead.
Q What is the name of the other one? A Name was Joe and Papa gave him Thompson.
Q That would make him Joe T. we have here in the affidavit? A Yes sir.
Q How long had you been married to Henry Before[sic] your oldest child Clarence was born? A I don't know how old, cant[sic] hardly tell you.
Q Had you been married as much as a year? A Nearly a year.
Q How old was Clarenc[sic] when he died? A He was a year old, if I aint[sic] mistaken, I cant[sic] hardly tell that, I don't know how old he was.
Q When was he born? A Born in November.
Q What time? A Cant[sic] tell.

Applications for Enrollment of Creek Newborn
Act of 1905   Volume VIII

Q What year, when was your child Clarence born? A I cant[sic] tell.
Q Know the month? A Know the month all right.
Q What is it? A November.
Q Know the date of the month? A No sir.
Q Know the year? A No sir.
Q Next month is November; how many years ago is it? A Dont[sic] know.
Q Can you read or write? A No sir, cant[sic] read or write, write my name, but cant[sic] write.
Q When did Clarence die? A Died in August.
Q What year? A Dont[sic] know sir, cant[sic] say.

BY MR. LIEBER:

Q How long after you was[sic] married was it before Clarence was born? A Well I cant[sic] hardly tell that, but anyhow he was born in November.
Q Now you was[sic] married in January wasnt[sic] you? A Yes sir.
Q How old was he when he died? Clarence? A I cant[sic] hardly tell you, he was a year if I aint[sic] mistaken.
Q Was he more than a year old Nancy? A I dont[sic] know sir; anyhow he was a year old.
Q In what time of the year did he die, what month? A He died in August.
Q Was it the August after he was born that he died, or was it the second August after he was born that he died? A Second August.
Q He was born in November, was a year old the net November and the next August he died? A Yes sir.
Q How long has it been since Clarence died? A Just a year.
Q How many winters have we had since Clarence died? A Not but one winter since I remember of.
Q Just had one winter since Clarence died? A Yes sir.
Q Then he died during August of last year, is that right? A yes sir.

(Statement on behalf of the commissioner).

The witness does not appear to have any sense of dates in order to give intelligent answers, as will be shown by reference to testimony taken on earlier occasions, she having stated that this child was born in 1901; she also having stated that he was living March 4, 1905 in February, 1906, at the time of her last testimony on May 28, 19o6[sic], and that he died before her child Joe T. Robinson was born on December 18, 1905. It seems impossible to elicit an intelligent answer from the witness on any point touching the birth or death of this child.

There is also on file in this office various affidavits, among others, one executed by the witness before A. Jackson Temple on January 23, 1906, in which it is stated that Clarence Robinson was living on March 4, 1906.

Applications for Enrollment of Creek Newborn
Act of 1905   Volume VIII

It is also noted that in previous testimony the family name is variously given Roberson, Robinson and other ways.

The marriage license is returned to the witness.

BY THE COMMISSIONER:

Q Do you know what day of the week this is? A No sir.
Q Dont[sic] know that this is Tuesday? A I know this is Tuesday.
Q Why didnt[sic] you say so? A I know what the day of the week is.
Q What day was yesterday? A Monday.
Q What day will tomorrow be? A I done forgot.
Q What day do people go to church usually? A go to church on Sunday.
Q What month is this? A I dont[sic] know sir.
Q Dont[sic] know what month this is now? A No sir.
Q Do you know what month last month was? A No sir.
Q You are under oath to tell the truth? A I am telling the truth, because I done forgot it.
Q How much Indian blood have you, do you knoe[sic]? A No sir, I dont[sic] know.
Q Have you been to school? A I went to school a while, never went long.
Q Where did you go to school? A I went to school near Eufaula.
Q Did you ever go to school in Eufaula, Indian Territory high school? A No sir.
Q Do you mean to day that you dont[sic] know how long it has been since your child died? A Done forgot.
Q Did you ever know? A Used to remember, but done forgot.
Q Do you mean to say that you dont[sic] know how old he was when he died? A No.
Q Was he a week old Nancy? A No sir.
Q He wasnt[sic] that old? A He was older than that.
Q Was he a month old? A He was older than that.
Q Was he six months old? A He was older than that.
Q How do you know? Did you make any record of his birth or death, write it down anywhere? A My fatherinlaw[sic] wrote it down in the bible.
Q What is his name? A George Robinson.
Q Negro or white man? A Colored.
Q Your husband a colored man? A Yes sir, colored.
Q Did you ever read what he wrote down in the bible? A No sir.
Q Did anyone ever read it to you? A No sir.
Q Cant[sic] you tell whether this child died the same year it was born or not? A I cant[sic] hardly tell that, but if I aint[sic] mistaken I think it was a year old, if I aint[sic] mistaken.
Q Could you be mistaken? A I might be mistaken, cant[sic] tell.

WITNESS EXCUSED.

JAMES A SCOTT, being first duly sworn by Henry G. Hains, a Notary Public, testifies as follows:

Applications for Enrollment of Creek Newborn
Act of 1905   Volume VIII

BY THE COMMISSIONER:

Q Give your age, postoffice address and occupation? A Age 59, postoffice Muskogee, occupation, employed by M. L. Mott, Creek attorney, in investigating Creek enrollment cases.

BY MR. LIEBER:

Q Mr. Scott, did you examine into the case of Clarence Roberson, a child of Henry and Nancy Roberson? A I did.
Q Did you see a Bible record of the birth of that child? A I did.
Q What did the record say Mr. Scott? A Record says that the child, just as I do here, that he was born November 22, 1903; in a large family Bible.
Q Did the record show the date of the death of that child? A No sir.
Q You made an investigation with reference to the date of the death of that child? A I did.
Q What did you find Mr. Scott? A I asked for Henry Roberson, and his sister, Maria Roberson, who seemed to have the best idea in regard to the matter of any of them as to when it died and Maria, stated, I think it was, that he died on the 15th of August.
Q What year? A 1905. Henry Roberson I believe testified to the same thing; Chotkey, the grandfather, also stated that he knew of the death of the child. I then went to Mary McIntosh'S[sic], one of the neighbors, and a colored man Owens, another one of the neighbors, two very intelligent negros; I think both confirmed the death of the child as the month of August.
Q This last August or August a year ago? A 1905.
Q From your investigation are you satisfied that that child died after the 4th of March, 1905? A I am.
Q Satisfied that he was born prior to the 4th day of March, 1905? A I am satisfied that the child was born just about the date from that, and mind you in my investigation in this matter I examined neighbors ten or fifteen miles apart.

WITNESS EXCUSED.

HENRY ROBERSON, being first duly sworn by Henry G. Hains a Notary Public testified as follows:

BY THE COMMISSIONER:

Q What is your name? A Henry Roberson.
Q Have you testified before i the matter of the enrollment of your child, Clarence Roberson? A Yes sir.

Applications for Enrollment of Creek Newborn
Act of 1905   Volume VIII

BY MR. LIEBER:

Q You are the father of Clarence Roberson are you? a Yes sir.
Q How do you spell your name Henry? A I cant[sic] spell it good myself.
Q Can you read or write? A No sir, I can write my name that is all.
Q Spell it the way you write it? A H-e-n-r-by R-o-b-i-s-o-n. That is the only way I spell it.
Q Do you know when your child Clarence was born? A Yes sir.
Q When? A Born in November.
Q What time in November? A I dont[sic] know, would not be positive.
Q What year? A I don't know that.
Q When were you married to Nancy your wife? A I dont[sic] know sir what day of the month it was, year it was.
Q Marriage license shows you were married on the 21st day of January, 1903, which was three years ago last January; how long had you been married before Clarence was born? A About a year I reckon.
Q Well, was you married more than a year or less than a year? A We was married about a year before he was born, about a year.
Q Well now, you say-- he was born in November, and the record says you were married in January? A Yes sir, married in January.
Q Did one November pass after you were married and then another November come around before this child, Clarence, was born, or was he born the November after you were married in January? A We married in January, and this child was born that following November.
Q Sure that is right now Henry? A Think that is about right, I would not be positive.
Q What is your occupation? A I farm.
Q How many crops did you raise after you were married before Clarence was born? A Made the first crop after I was married; made one for my father, and stayed with my father all time before I was married; after I married made a crop; then made a crop across Deep Fork.
Q How many crops did you make from the time you were married until Clarence was born, between the time you were married and the time Clarence was born? A I made, this makes three crops.
Q I am not asking how mahy[sic] crops you have made since you were married, I am asking how many crops you made between the time you were married and the time that Clarence was born? A Just one.
Q Certain of that are you Henry? A Yes sir, one crop.
Q And you made a crop the same year that you were married did you? A Yes sir.
Q When did Clarence die? A He died in August.
Q What year? A 1905.
Q How long has it been since he died? A It has been a year this last August.
Q Sure of that are you Henry? A Yes sir.

Applications for Enrollment of Creek Newborn
Act of 1905   Volume VIII

BY THE COMMISSIONER:

Now if you dont[sic] know the year in which your child was born how is it that you can give the year in which he died? A My father-- had a brother die the same time that he died.
Q If your testimony up to date is true it shows that this child was born in 1903? A Yes sir.
Q And you mean to say that you could not tell that year until I mentioned it here now, and you told the year in which it died? A I told the reason I can tell how it died: I had a brother died the same week he died.
Q That fact would impress on you the date of the the death better than the fact that the date of birth was in the same year that you were married: you mean to say that you are so ignorant that you couldnt[sic] tell the year in which your child was born? A I couldnt[sic] tell that.
Q How long did your child Clarence live? A He lived until he was mighty near a year old.
Q Wasnt[sic] he mighty near a year old when he died? A No sir I couldnt[sic] say.
Q Dont[sic] you know if he was less than a year old when he died or more than a year old; was he over a year old or less than a year? A I couldnt[sic] be positive, I dont[sic] want to say, something like that.
Q Your own child and you couldnt[sic] tell whether he was less than a year or more than a year? A I couldnt[sic] tell you something I dont[sic] know.
Q Dont[sic] know whether your child was not as much as a year old or not? A Mighty near a year old.
Q You mean that he didnt[sic] reach his first birthday? A No answer.

BY MR. LIEBER:

Q Was that child walking before it died? A Just begin to walk.
Q Was he sickly when he was a baby or fairly in good health? A Sickly all the time.
Q How long had he been walking when he died? A Just begin to walk.
Q Do you know A. Jackson Temple, a Notary Public? A At Checotah?
Q Yes. A Yes sir.
Q Did your wife make affidavit before him regarding the birth of Clarence Roberson? A Yes sir.
Q Were you present when the affidavit was made? A Yes sir.
Q Did you tell the Notary Public when Clarence was born? A Yes sir.
Q Tell him when he died? A Yes sir, told him when he died, about when I thought he died, wouldnt[sic] be sure of it.
Q What did you tell him? A Told him died in August, day of the month I dont[sic] know, 1905, I think.
Q Now this affidavit is made before Temple on the 23rd day of June, 1906; in that affidavit your wife testified that Clarence was born on the 11 day of December, 1904, and was living on the 4th day of March, 1906? Was he living on the 4th day of this last March? A This last March, yes sir; last March he wasnt[sic] living, this last March he was living March 4, 1905, this last March a year ago.

Applications for Enrollment of Creek Newborn
Act of 1905   Volume VIII

WITNESS EXCUSED.

NANCY ROBERSON, recalled, testifies as follows:

BY MR. LIEBER:

Q Nancy, how old did you say Clarence was when he died? A I said I cant[sic] tell how old he was when he died.
Q Well was he more than a year old, or less than a year old? A I said, if I aint[sic] mistaken, he was a year old, if I aint[sic] mistaken.
Q How long was he sick before he died? A He was sick a good while, but I cant[sic] tell how many months.
Q Was he sick more than a month? A Yes sir for more than a month.
q Did he get old enough to walk? A He could stand alone, he couldnt[sic] walk.
Q Never did get old enough to walk around? A No sir, never did get old enough to walk around.
Q What sort of health did he have from the time that he was born until he died? A He had bad health, sickly little thing.
Q Did you have a doctor with you when Clarence was born? A No sir.
Q Did he have any spell of sickness from the time that he was born up to the time that he took sick and died? A He never had any bad sickness, sometimes well and sometimes sick.
Q Did you ever have a doctor with him from the time that he was born up to the time that he was taken sick and died? A Yes sir, I had a doctor at the time he died.
Q Before the time he took sick and died? A Yes sir, I had a doctor.
Q Did you ever have a doctor with him before that time? A Yes sir, I had a doctor with him before that time.
Q Do you mean to say that you had two doctors? A He got over this spell of sickness, the I got him another time.
Q What doctor did you have? A I had Dr. Ford, he is dead, he got killed.
Q Was he a married man? A Yes sir, married man.
Q Do you know where his wife is now? A His wife went back home.
Q Dont[sic] live in the Territory? A No sir, she went back.
Q Where did Dr. Ford live? A Had lived near Brushy Hill.

WITNESS EXCUSED.

GEORGE ROBERSON, being first duly sworn by Henry G. Hains, a Notary Public, testifies as follows:

BY THE COMMISSIONER:

Q What is your name? A George Roberson.
Q How old are you? A Am 45.

Applications for Enrollment of Creek Newborn
Act of 1905   Volume VIII

Q What is your postoffice address? A Fame.
Q Are you a citizen of any of the five tribes? A No sir, United States nigger.
Q Have you a son named Henry? A Yes sir.
Q Can you read or write? A No sir.
Q You dont[sic] know how you would spell your last name do you? A No sir, cant[sic] read or write.

BY MR. LIEBER:

Q George, did you son Henry have a child by Nancy Roberson by the name of Clarence? A Yes sir.
Q Do you know when that child was born? A Born in November.
Q What year? A I dont[sic] exactly know what year it was.
Q Remember when they were married? A Yes sir, married at my house, the child was born that year at my house.
Q Was the child born the same year that they were married? A Yes sir, I believe it was, it I aint[sic] mistaken he was born the same year.
Q What time of the year were they married? A Married in January
Q Did your son raise a crop the year that he was married? A Yes sir.
Q How many crops did he raise between the time that he was married and the time that Clarence was born? A Never raised any; born the same year.
Q Satisfied of that? A Yes sir.
Q How long did Clarence Live? A I couldnt[sic] tell you exactly, he died long the next August after they were married that year.
Q Died the next August after they were married? A Born in November, Clarence was, and he died the last of the next August.
Q Clarence was born in November and lived until the next August, is that right now George? A If I aint[sic] mistaken, that is the way it was.
Q Was she old enough to walk at the time that he died? A Yes sir, he could walk around a chair.
Q I mean, could he walk alone, without holding himself up to anything? A Yes sir, put him down on the floor, stand up and walk.
Q Would he walk all over the house by himself? A He could if he wanted to, would act like he was kind of scared.
Q He wasnt[sic] old enough? A He was old enough; I know children as old as he was walk all about.
Q Now you are certain he was born the same year that Henry and Nancy were married? A I wont[sic] be positive of that, I just know when he was born, the names of his parents and whether or not he was living on March 4, 1905, and know when they was married, he and Nancy: they were staying there picking cotton, in the Fall.
Q Did Nancy and Henry live with you the year they were married? A Yes sir, lived there that whole year.
Q How long did they live with you after they were married? A Stayed there all that year.
Q Where did they go the next year? A Come to a place on Deep Fork.

Applications for Enrollment of Creek Newborn
Act of 1905   Volume VIII

Q Then they didnt[sic] live with you only during the year they were married? A Yes sir, come back and forth, stay a while, never lived there, just come back and forth.
Q Now were they making their home at your house at the time that Clarence was born? A Yes sir, that was their home, living there.
Q Then the child must have been born the same year they were married, is that right? A Yes sir.
Q Isnt[sic] that your best recollection George? A That is my best recollection; he was born the same year; I know Henry was making a crop there that fall, I know he had some people there picking cotton there.
Q You say Henry made one crop at your place? A Yes sir.
Q Then he moved on Deep Fork? A Yes sir.
Q Whose place did he move on? A His wife's place.
Q How many crops did he make there? A He made one crop.
Q Then where did he go? A Never went anywhere then.
Q Has Henry moved more than once since he left your house? A Yes sir, lived with his grandpa, down at Morie's.
Q When? A The next year.
Q The year after he left your house? A Yes sir, he never lived there a whole year.
Q Did he live there that year at Morie's? A Yes sir.
Q Where did he move? A Moved up there.
Q Clarence still living? A Clarence still living.
Q Left your house and moved on whose place? A At Morie's.
Q How long did he stay at Morie's? A I couldnt[sic] tell, Henry was ten miles from me, never would go over there much.
Q Did he make a crop at Morie's? A Never did make any crop there.
Q About how long did he stay there? A I couldnt[sic] tell you how long he stayed there.
Q Where did he go to from Morie's? A Up there where he is living now, on his wife's place.
Q Has he been living there since? A Living there since.
Q Where did this child Clarence die; at the place where he is now living? A Place where he is living now.
Q Did Henry Leave[sic] your house of the same year? A He left there in the fall, long towards Christmas.
Q How old was Clarence when he left there? A I don't know sir he wasnt[sic] very old.
Q Year old or a few months old? A Couldnt[sic] have been a year old then.
Q Was he just a month or so old? A I didnt[sic] keep up with that part.
Q George how long have you been living where you are living now? A I have been living there two years.
Q When will it be three years? A Be three years long in February.
Q This coming February? A Yes sir.
Q How many crops have been made since you been living there? A Two crops.
Q This crop makes the third crop? A Yes sir.
Q Then when this crop is gathered it will be the third crop that has been made since you have been living where you live? A Yes sir.

Applications for Enrollment of Creek Newborn
Act of 1905   Volume VIII

Q Then did Clarence die the first year that you moved where you are living now, or the second year? A I couldnt[sic] tell exactly whether the first or second year, couldnt[sic] be positive in it.
Q Which year do you think it was? A I dont[sic] know sir.
Q I am asking you now, which one you think it was; was it the first year you moved there that Clarence died on the sedond[sic]? A Must have been the first year.
Q That is your recollection of it, is it? A Yes sir.

WITNESS EXCUSED.

HENRY ROBERSON, recalled, testifies as follows:

BY MR. LIEBER:

Q Henry, where did you live the first year you were married? A I lived across North Fork.
Q Who lived with you? A My father.
Q All that year? A Yes sir.
Q When did you move away from your father's house? A I moved away that winter after Christmas.
Q Made one crop on your father's place did you and moved away? A Yes sir.
Q Was Clarence born while you were living at your father's house? A Yes sir.
Q Where did you move to when you left Deep Fork? A Moved on wife's place.
Q Ever live on a fellow's place by the name of Morie? A Why I stayed over there a while, never did live there.
Q How long did you stay there? A Something about a month after my crops were laid by.
Q Moved on your wife's place? A Moved on my wife's place; left there.
Q When you left your father's house did you move on your wife's place? A Yes sir.
Q Long in the winter? A Yes sir.
Q How many crops have you made on your wife's place? A Made two crops.
Q This makes two crops does it, or three crops? A I had another fellow staying there the first year; I think this makes two crops.
Q You have been farming ever since you left your father's house? A Yes sir.
Q Raised a crop each year have you? A Yes sir. I had a white fellow living there that first year, year I moved there and he made a crop there and I had a crop; farmed in the same field; then I had a fellow there this last going year.
Q He made a crop? A Yes sir.
Q Who lived with you there this year? [sic] Nobody; just me and my brother; this makes three crops now.
Q This makes three crops? A Yes sir.
Q Now then did Clarence die the first year that you moved on your wife's place or the second year that you moved there? A He died-- he lived the first year we went over there; he didn't die then I dont[sic] think.

Applications for Enrollment of Creek Newborn
Act of 1905   Volume VIII

Q Now what is the name of this white fellow that was living March 4, 1905 in your house the first year you made a crop there? A Bob Ackers.
Q Where does he live now Henry? A He lives two miles east of Council Hill.
Q What was the mans[sic] name that cropped with you last year? A John Owens.
Q White man or colored man? A Colored man.
Q Where did John Owens live? A He lived, I reckon, about ten miles, no it wasnt[sic] that fur[sic], about eight miles on west of Checotah.
Q Now did Clarence die when Ackers was cropping with you or Owens was cropping with you? A Yes sir, when Owens was cropping with me.
Q Sure of that? A Yes sir, Owens' wife was there when he died.
Q Where did Owens live the year that Ackers cropped with you? A Lived on the Morie McIntosh place.
Q How far from your place? A About three and a half miles.
Q Know Owens at that time? A Yes sir I know[sic] him.
Q Knew his wife? A Yes sir.
Q Where did Owens raise a crop the year before he cropped on your place. A On Morie McIntosh place.
Q How many children have you and Nancy had Henry? A Two.

BY THE COMMISSIONER:

Q Did you bring in Chotkey James today as a witness? A Yes sir.
Q Do you know whether he brought in that book you claimed he wrote down that date of birth in? A No answer.

WITNESS EXCUSED.

———

CHOTKEY JAMES, being first duly sworn by Henry G. Hains, a Notary Public, testifies as follows:

Examined through Lona Merrick, official interpreter.

BY THE COMMISSIONER:

Q What is your name? A Chotkey James.
Q How old are you? A 48.
Q What is your postoffice address? A Fame.
Q Are you the father of Nancy Roberson? A Yes sir.

BY MR. LIEBER:

Q You know Henry Roberson? A Yes sir.
Q He is the husband of your daughter, Nancy? A Yes sir.

Applications for Enrollment of Creek Newborn
Act of 1905   Volume VIII

Q Did they have a child born to them by the name of Clarence? A Yes sir, it is dead now.
Q Where was Clarence born, at whose house? A George Roberson.
Q Do you know when Clarence was born? A I dont[sic] know.
Q Do you know what year it was? A I dont[sic] know.
Q How old was the child when you first saw it? this Clarence? A If it was a sickly child it must have been two years old; if it was a healthy child it must have been a young child; was just beginning to walk when I first saw it; might have been young dont[sic] know.
Q Do you know how old Clarence was when he died? A Dont[sic] know.
Q How far did you live from your daughter Nancy at the time Clarence was born? A I dont[sic] know how far it was.
Q Well was it in the same neighborhood or several miles away? A About a mile.
Q Did she come to see you often after she married Henry Robberson[sic]? A No sir.
Q And you say she lived about a mile from you at that time? A Yes sir, then after the child was born they moved across Deep Fork.
Q Where they are living now? A Yes sir.
Q How far are they living from you now Chotkey? A I dont[sic] know.
Q About how far? A I dont[sic] know.
Q How long does it take you to ride from your house to where Nancy lives now? A On horseback you leave home after breakfast and get there for dinner in the afternoon.
Q How long have you been living where you are living now? A Ben there a long time, dont[sic] know.
Q Well you lived where you are living now before Nancy was married didnt[sic] you? A Yes sir.
Q And you say she lived about one mile from you at the time Clarence was born? A Yes sir.
Q And you didnt[sic] see the child until it got up to be quite a baby, several months old? A Yes sir, they left Robersons[sic] house soon after the child was born; that was the reason I didnt[sic] see it any sooner.
Q Then you didnt[sic] see the child while they were living at Roberson's house? A No sir.
Q How often did you see the child before it died? A I didnt[sic] see it very often.
Q Were you present when the child died? A No sir.
Q Did you go to the funeral? A No sir.
Q How long had it been dead when you first learned that it was dead? A The child died on the 14th of August; he was buried on the 15th and I heard it on the 15th.
Q What year was it that the child died? A Last year, 1905.
Q How long has the child been dead? A Over a year.
Q Are you certain that the child died in the year 1905? A Yes sir; I guess if I was a lawyer I would know when the child was born and died.
Q How long before the child died was it that you last saw it? A I cant[sic] answer that, I dont[sic] know just how long I had seen it before it died.
Q Had you seen it as much as a month before it died? A I guess about a month.
Q Was it walking around when you last saw it alive? A Yes sir.

Applications for Enrollment of Creek Newborn
Act of 1905   Volume VIII

Q Did it walk all over the house, any place it wanted to? A No just stand up to chairs and things like that, couldnt[sic] walk very well.
Q Now can you tell the Commissioner how old the child was when it died? A I don't know, said a while ago dont[sic] know how old it was.
Q It wasnt[sic] old enough to walk alone was it? A No sir.
Q Are you a farmer? A Yes sir, I am a farmer; dont[sic] see what business of the Commission that is.
Q How many crops have you raise Chotkey since Clarence died? A That is outside of the record; came up here to tell what I know about the death of the child; didnt[sic] come to answer all those questions.
Q I am asking you now how many crops you have raised since that child died?
A Twice.
Q Does this make the second crop you have raised since the child died, or the third crop?
A Second.
Q Now do you mean to say that this will make the second crop that you have gathered since the child died, or the second crop that you have raised since the child died?
A Busy gathering the crops when I was summoned to appear here.
Q Does this make the second crop that you have gathered since the child died, or does it make the third crop since the child died? A Second crop. Second crop I was gathering; I was picking cotton.

BY THE COMMISSIONER:

Q Did you make any record of the date of birth of this child Clarence? A No sir.
Q Did you write it down on a piece of paper anywhere? A No sir.
Q Did you make any record of the date of the death of this child; did you write that down anywhere? A No sir.

WITNESS EXCUSED.

Cora Moore, being first duly sworn, states that as stenographer to the Commissioner to the Five Civilized Tribes she reported the proceedings had in the above entitled cause on October 16, 1906, and that the above and foregoing is a true and correct transcript of her stenographic notes taken in said cause on said date.

Cora Moore

Subscribed and sworn to before me October 17, 1906.

Edward Merrick
Notary Public.

Applications for Enrollment of Creek Newborn
Act of 1905   Volume VIII

N.C. 657.

DEPARTMENT OF THE INTERIOR,
COMMISSIONER TO THE FIVE CIVILIZED TRIBES.
Muskogee, Indian Territory, October 20, 1906.

In the matter of the application for the enrollment of CLARENCE ROBERSON as a citizen by blood of the Creek Nation.

APPEARANCE:
JOHN G. LIEBER appears for M. L. Mott,
Attorney for the Creek Nation.

LEVI LOVE, being first duly sworn by Henry G. Hains, a Notary Public, testifies as follows:

BY THE COMMISSIONER:

Q What is your name? A Levi Love.
Q How old are you? A 25 years old.
Q What is your postoffice? A Brush Hill, I. T.
Q Do you know Henry Roberson? A Yes sir.
Q Are you a citizen of any of the five tribes? A No sir.
Q State man? A Yes sir.
Q Is Henry Roberson a citizen of any of the five tribes? A No sir.
Q He is a state man too is he? A Yes sir.
Q Do you know the name of his wife? A No sir; I do know her name; aint[sic] well acquainted with her.
Q What is her name? A Nancy, Nancy Roberson.
Q Know what her name was before she married Henry? A No sir.
Q How long have you been acquainted with them? A About four years.
Q You know a child of theirs by the name of Clarence? A I know the child, but didnt[sic] know the child's name.
Q Boy was it? A Yes sir.
Q When was it born? A Dont[sic] know.
Q When did it die, do you know? A Died August the 11th. Q What year? A 1905.
Q How do you know it died-- how do you fix the date? A I know it because I helped to bury it.
Q Did they have a child before Clarence? A Not as I know of.
Q Did they have a child after Clarence? A Yes sir.
Q What was its name, do you know? A Dont[sic] know.
Q At the time you helped to bury Clarence, was this other child born yet? A No sir.
Q He died before this younger child was born, did he? A Yes sir.

Applications for Enrollment of Creek Newborn
Act of 1905   Volume VIII

BY MR. LIEBER:

Q Are you sure that Clarence has only been dead a little over a year? A Yes, he died last August the 11th, buried him on the 12th.
Q This last gone August? A 1905.
Q That would be this last August a year ago then, wouldnt[sic] it? A Yes sir.
Q Right sure that he didnt[sic] die two years ago last August? A Yes sir, I am sure of that.
Q Whose place were you living on at the time the child died? A Staying with Sam Brown.
Q How long have you been staying altogether with Sam Brown? A I am not staying there now.
Q How long did you stay with Sam Brown? A I stayed there about two months.
Q About two months? A Yes sir.
Q What year was it that you stayed with Sam Brown? A 1905.
Q Sure you are not making any mistake about that now, love, are you? A Sure of that.

WITNESS EXCUSED.

WILLIE WOODFORK, being first duly sworn by Henry G. Hains, a Notary Public, testifies as follows:

BY THE COMMISSIONER:

Q What is your name? A Willie Woodfork.
Q How old are you? A 22 years old.
Q What is your postoffice address? A Checotah, I.T.
Q Do you know Henry Roberson? A Yes sir.
Q How long have you known him? A Been knowing Henry Roberson for about eight years.
Q What is the name of his wife? A Nancy Roberson.
Q What was her name before she was married? A Nancy James.
Q You have know them both about eight years? A Yes sir.
Q Did they have a child born about two years ago or thereabouts? A I know they had a child born; dont[sic] know just how long.
Q What was its name? A Clarence.
Q That child living? A Nos ir.
Q How old was it when it died? A Dont[sic] know sir.
Q Know when it died? A Died last August a year ago.
Q In August of 1905? A Yes sir.
Q How do you know that? A Know the same day we come back from Okmulgee Henry Roberson met us and told us his child had died.

Applications for Enrollment of Creek Newborn
Act of 1905   Volume VIII

BY MR. LIEBER:

Q And all you know about it is what has been told you? A Yes sir.
Q When was it that you were coming from Okmulgee? A Last August, a year ago.
Q Did you go to the funer? A No sir, I wasnt[sic] there.
Q Didnt[sic] go there any time? A No, sir wasnt[sic] there at all.
Q How long was it before that that you had seen this child? A I think about the 4th day of August.
Q Did you see it on August 4, 1905? A Yes sir.
Q Sure of that? A Yes sir.
Q Where, picnic? A Yes sir, Creek picnic.
Q Nancy had it there, did she? A Yes sir, she had baby there.
Q You are sure you saw iton picnic day, the 4th of August, 1905? A Yes sir.
Q How old was it then, about? A I dont[sic] know, just how old.
Q Was she carrying it around in her arms? A Yes sir, she was packing it around.
Q Do you know when the child was born? A No sir.
Q Look like it was about eight months old, something like that? A I am afrid to say, I dont[sic] know.

BY THE COMMISSIONER:

Q After the 4th of August, 1905, where did you go? A Went to Okmulgee.
Q Who went with you? A My father.
Q Anyone else? A Joe Johnson, Leshie Woodfork, my brogher; my father's name is Shep.
Q How long did you stay there? A Stayed out there as near as I can recollect we were out there--
Q Just about now, month or week? A We stayed out there about three days.
Q When you were coming back, is that what you testified, Henry met you and told you that Clarence was dead? A Yes sir.
Q Sure of that now? A Yes sir, Henry met us.
Q Couldnt[sic] have been two years ago this last August, in 1904, when you saw this child at the picnic? A As near as I can recollect it was last August a year ago.

WITNESS EXCUSED.

HENRY ROBERSON, being first duly sworn by Henry G. Hains, a Notary Public, testifies as follows:

BY THE COMMISSIONER:

Q What is your name? A Henry Roberson.
Q Can you spell your name? A I cant[sic] spell it good.
Q You testified here the other day about the birth and death of Clarence, your child?
A Yes sir, but I couldnt[sic] tell exactly.

Applications for Enrollment of Creek Newborn
Act of 1905   Volume VIII

Q Couldnt[sic] tell at that time? A No sir.
Q Can you tell now? A Yes sir.
Q What time was Clarence born? A He was born in November.
Q Give the whole date? A He was born in November on the 22nd day.
Q 22nd? A Yes sir, think it was the 22nd.
Q Sure it was the 22nd? A Yes sir.
Q Well now, we have testimony here before that said it was December, which is correct? A One of them months.
Q You dont[sic] know which? A No sir, wouldnt[sic] be positive.
Q What year? A 1903.
Q What makes you think it was 1903? A I was married in 1903, and that following fall he was born.
Q What time in 1903 were you married? A Married on the 27th day of January.
Q 1903? A Yes sir.
Q And that following fall your child, Clarence, was born? A Yes sir.
Q How long did Clarence live? A Clarence live after he was born?
Q Yes? A He lived until he was pretty near three year[sic] old.
Q Three year[sic] old? A Think he was; wouldnt[sic] be positive to it. I know when he died.
Q When did he die? A He died in August.
Q What year? A This last August, was a year ago.
Q How do you know that? A Because I know it by this; it was after the 4th of August when he died, sick during the 4th, never died on the 4th; what date I dont[sic] know, what day it was, wouldnt[sic] be sure of it.
Q Sometime after the 4th of August, a year ago? A Yes sir.
Q How do you know it was a year ago? A Because this last going August would make it a year ago.
Q It wasnt[sic] this last going August? A No sir.
Q Are you sure it wasnt[sic] a year before this last going August? A That would make it two years ago, would it?
Q I am asking you if you are sure it wasnt[sic] two years ago this last going August? A would make it a year I think; I am not sure.

WITNESS EXCUSED.

Cora Moore, being first duly sworn, states that as stenographer to the Commissioner to the Five Civilized Tribes she reported the proceedings had in the above entitled cause on October 16, 1906, and that the above and foregoing is a true and correct transcript of her stenographic notes taken in said cause on said date.

Cora Moore

Subscribed and sworn to before me November 16, 1906.
Edward Merrick
Notary Public.

Applications for Enrollment of Creek Newborn
Act of 1905 Volume VIII

nc-657

DEPARTMENT OF THE INTERIOR,
COMMISSIONER TO THE FIVE CIVILIZED TRIBES.
MUSKOGEE, INDIAN TERRITORY.
NOVEMBER 20, 1906.

In the matter of the application for the enrollment of <u>Clarence Roberson</u>, as a citizen of the Creek Nation.

The Creek Nation here offers in evidence the affidavit of A. W. Harris, M. D. Exhibit "A", which shows that he attended Clarence Roberson during his last illness and that he died sometime in August, 1905.

The Creek Nation now here rests this case.

I, Julia C. Laval on my oath state that the above and foregoing is a true and correct transcript of my stenographic notes as taken by me on said date in said cause.

Julia C. Laval

Subscribed and sworn to before
me this 27 day of November, 1906.

Edward Merrick
Notary Public.

NC-657.

FHW
JWH

DEPARTMENT OF THE INTERIOR,
COMMISSIONER TO THE FIVE CIVILIZED TRIBES.

In the matter of the application for the enrollment of Clarence Roberson, deceased, as a citizen by blood of the Creek Nation.

DECISION.

The record in this case shows that application was made, in affidavit form, on March 31, 1905, for the enrollment of Clarence Roberson, deceased, as a citizen by blood of the Creek Nation. Supplemental affidavits as to the birth and death of said applicant, executed November 7, 1905, February 8, June 23 and November 12, 1906, also a certified copy of marriage license of Henry Robinson and Nancy James, are attached to

Applications for Enrollment of Creek Newborn
Act of 1905 Volume VIII

and made part of the record herein. Further proceedings were had on February 8, May 28, October 16, and October 20, 1906.

The evidence shows that Clarence Roberson, deceased, was the son of Henry Roberson, a non-citizen, and of Nancy Roberson, whose name appears as Nancy James on a partial schedule of citizens by blood of the Creek Nation approved by the Secretary of the Interior March 28, 1902, opposite roll No. 7023.

The evidence further shows that the name of the applicant is variously spelled but the weight of testimony establishes it as Clarence Roberson and as such the said applicant is herein considered.

It further appears that the testimony is conflicting as to the exact date of the birth and death of the said applicant, but it is clearly established by the evidence that the said Clarence Roberson was born not later than December 27, 1904, and died during the month of August, 1905.

The Act of Congress approved March 3, 1905 (33 Stat. L., 1048), provides in part as follows:

"That the Commission to the Five Civilized Tribes is authorized for sixty days after the date of the approval of this Act to receive and consider applications for enrollments of children born subsequent to May twenty five, nineteen hundred and one, and prior to March fourth, nineteen hundred and five, and living on said latter date, to citizens of the Creek tribe of Indians whose enrollment has been approved by the Secretary of the Interior prior to the approval of this act; and to enroll and make, nineteen hundred and five, and living on said latter date, to citizens of the Creek tribe of Indians whose enrollment has been approved by the Secretary of the Interior prior to the approval of this act; and to enroll and make allotments to such children."

It is therefore, ordered and adjudged that the said Clarence Roberson, deceased, is entitled to be enrolled as a citizen by blood of the Creek Nation, in accordance with the provisions of law above quoted, and the application for his enrollment as such is accordingly granted.

                                         Tams Bixby Commissioner.

Muskogee, Indian Territory.
JAN 18 1907

Applications for Enrollment of Creek Newborn
Act of 1905   Volume VIII

BIRTH AFFIDAVIT

DEPARTMENT OF THE INTERIOR,
COMMISSION TO THE FIVE CIVILIZED TRIBES.

IN RE Application for Enrollment, as a citizen of the Creek Nation, of Clerence[sic] Roberson , born on the 27 day of December , 1904

Name of Father: Henry Roberson   a citizen of the   U.S.   ~~Nation~~.
Name of Mother: Nancy Roberson   a citizen of the   Creek Nation.

Post-office: Checotah I.T.

AFFIDAVIT OF MOTHER.

UNITED STATES OF AMERICA, }
  INDIAN TERRITORY.
  Western   District.

                                                              Twenty
I, Nancy Roberson , on oath state that I am ~~Twenty-three~~ years of age and a citizen by blood , of the Creek Nation; that I am the lawful wife of Henry Roberson , who is a non citizen, ~~by (blank) of the (blank)~~ Nation; that a boy male child was born to me on 27 day of December , 1904 , that said child has been named Clerence Roberson , and is now living.
                                                    her
                                         Nancy x Roberson
WITNESSES TO MARK: mark
  { S.J. Logan
  { D.F. Patterson

Subscribed and sworn to before me this 27 day of   March , 1905.

My Com. expires   Bunnie McIntosh
May 16/1908   NOTARY PUBLIC.

AFFIDAVIT OF ATTENDING PHYSICIAN OR MID-WIFE.

UNITED STATES OF AMERICA, }
  INDIAN TERRITORY.
  Western   District.

I, Henry Roberson , a Husband , on oath state that I attended on Mrs. Nancy Roberson , wife of Henry Roberson on the 27th day of December , 1904 ; that there was born to her on said date a male child; that said child is now living and is said to have been named Clerence Roberson
                                         Henry roberson[sic]

Applications for Enrollment of Creek Newborn
Act of 1905 Volume VIII

WITNESSES TO MARK:
{ S.J. Logan
{ D.F. Patterson

Subscribed and sworn to before me this 27 *day of* March , 1905.

My Com. expires May 16/1908   Bunnie McIntosh
                                  NOTARY PUBLIC.

Nancy Robertson[sic] was in about
Nancy James   Role[sic] no 7023   Creek Indian
fathers[sic] name   Chostke James
mothers[sic] name   Betsey James
town of Arbeka

BIRTH AFFIDAVIT.

DEPARTMENT OF THE INTERIOR.
COMMISSION TO THE FIVE CIVILIZED TRIBES.

    IN RE APPLICATION FOR ENROLLMENT, as a citizen of the Creek Nation, of Clarence Roberson , born on the 27 day of December, 1904

		U.S.	
Name of Father: Henry Roberson	a citizen of the	~~Creek~~	Nation.
Name of Mother: Nancy Roberson	a citizen of the	Creek	Nation.

                    Postoffice   Checotah, I.T.

AFFIDAVIT OF MOTHER.

UNITED STATES OF AMERICA, Indian Territory, }
    Western   **DISTRICT.**   Child not present

    I, Nancy James nee Roberson , on oath state that I am 22 years of age and a citizen by blood , of the Creek Nation; that I am the lawful wife of Henry Roberson , who is a citizen, by *(blank)* of the United States Nation; that a male child was born to me on 27 day of December , 1904 , that said child has been named Clarence Roberson, and was living March 4, 1905.   her
                                Nancy James nee Roberson x
Witnesses To Mark: mark
{ Preston Janway
{ Wm Simpson

Applications for Enrollment of Creek Newborn
Act of 1905   Volume VIII

Subscribed and sworn to before me this 7 day of November, 1905.
My Commission
expires May 14 1908

                      Preston Janway
                            Notary Public.

AFFIDAVIT OF ATTENDING PHYSICIAN OR MID-WIFE.

UNITED STATES OF AMERICA, Indian Territory, ⎫
    Western   DISTRICT.   ⎬

I, Faney Lasley, a midwife, on oath state that I attended on Mrs. Nancy Roberson James nee, wife of Henry Roberson on the 27 day of December, 1904; that there was born to her on said date a male child; that said child was living March 4, 1905, and is said to have been named Clarence Roberson

                                      her
                        Faney Lasley x
Witnesses To Mark: mark
  { P. Janway
    Wm Simpson

Subscribed and sworn to before me 7 day of November, 1905.

                      Preston Janway
                          Notary Public.

BIRTH AFFIDAVIT.
                      DEPARTMENT OF THE INTERIOR.
                  COMMISSION TO THE FIVE CIVILIZED TRIBES.

IN RE APPLICATION FOR ENROLLMENT, as a citizen of the Creek Nation, of Clarence Roberson, born on the 27 day of December, 1904

Name of Father: Henry Roberson   a citizen of the   U.S.   Nation.
Name of Mother: Nancy Roberson   a citizen of the   Creek Nation.

                  Postoffice   Checotah, Ind Ter

Applications for Enrollment of Creek Newborn
Act of 1905 Volume VIII

AFFIDAVIT OF MOTHER.

UNITED STATES OF AMERICA, Indian Territory, }
Western DISTRICT.

I, Nancy James , on oath state that I am 22 years of age and a citizen by blood , of the Creek   Nation; that I am the lawful wife of Henry Roberson , who is a citizen, by *(blank)* of the United States ~~Nation~~; that a male   child was born to me on 27 day of December , 1904 , that said child has been named Clarence Roberson, and was living March 4, 1905.

                                                her
                                    Nancy x Roberson

Witnesses To Mark: mark
{ H.G. Hains
  Alex Posey

Subscribed and sworn to before me this 8 day of February , 1906.

                                    HG Hains
                                      Notary Public.

BIRTH AFFIDAVIT.

DEPARTMENT OF THE INTERIOR,
COMMISSIONER TO THE FIVE CIVILIZED TRIBES.

ENROLLMENT OF MINORS. ACT OF CONGRESS, APPROVED APRIL 26, 1906.

IN RE APPLICATION FOR ENROLLMENT, as a citizen of the Creek Nation, of Clarence Robinson , born on the 11th day of December , 1904

Name of Father: Henry Robinson   Not a citizen of the   Creek   Nation.
Name of Mother: Nancy Robinson nee James   a citizen of the   Creek   Nation.

Tribal enrollment of father   non   Tribal enrollment of mother   7025

                             Postoffice   Checotah, I.T.

AFFIDAVIT OF MOTHER.

UNITED STATES OF AMERICA, Indian Territory, }
Western   District.

I, Nancy Robinson nee James , on oath state that I am Twenty four years of age and a citizen by birth , of the Creek   Nation; that I am the lawful wife of   Henry Robinson , who is not a citizen, by birth of the Creek Nation; that a male child was

Applications for Enrollment of Creek Newborn
Act of 1905   Volume VIII

born to me on   11th   day of December , 1904 , that said child has been named   Clarence Robinson , and was living March 4, 1906.
her
Nancy x Robinson

WITNESSES TO MARK:
{ S.E. Temple
{ J.C. Sutton

Subscribed and sworn to before me this   23   day of   June   , 1906.

A. Jackson Temple
Notary Public.

My commission expires Sept 9th, 1909.

AFFIDAVIT OF ATTENDING PHYSICIAN OR MID-WIFE.

UNITED STATES OF AMERICA, Indian Territory,
   Western   District.

I, Fannie Lasley , a mid-wife , on oath state that I attended on Nancy Robinson nee James , wife of Henyr[sic] Robinson on the 11th day of December , 1904 ; that there was born to her on said date a   male   child; that said child was living March 4, 1906, and is said to have been named   Clarence Robinson

her
Fannie x Lasley

WITNESSES TO MARK:
{ Ella Lasley
{ Tom Wilson

Subscribed and sworn to before me this   23   day of   June   , 1906.

A. Jackson Temple
Notary Public.

My commission expires Sept 9th, 1909.

United States of America   )
     Indian Territory   ) SS
Western Judicial District.   )

My names is A. W. Harris I am a licenced[sic] practicing physician my Post Office address is Hoffman Indian Territory   I am Thirty years old   I was located at Hitchita I.T. During the Year of 1905. Enguaged[sic] in the practice of my profession and was the attending physician during the last ilness[sic] of Clarence Roberson. I do not know the exact date that Clarence Roberson died but know that it was some time after August 15th, 1905, and in the Month of August.

A.W. Harris M.D.

Applications for Enrollment of Creek Newborn
Act of 1905   Volume VIII

Subscribed and sworn to before me as a Notary Public this 12th. day of November 1906.

Ira E. Davis

My Commission expires the   7th   day of   April   1909

Exhibit "A"

MARRIAGE LICENSE

UNITED STATES OF AMERICA,
INDIAN TERRITORY,   SS.   No. 931.
WESTERN DISTRICT.

TO ANY PERSON AUTHORIZED BY LAW TO SOLEMNIZE MARRIAGE--GREETING:

YOU ARE HEREBY COMMANDED to solemnize the rite and publish the banns of matrimony between Mr. Henry Robinson, of Fame, in the Indian Territory, aged 21 years, and Miss Nancy James, of Fame, in the Indian Territory, aged 18 years, according to law, and of[sic] you officially sign and return this License to the parties therein named.

Witness my hand and official seal at Eufaula, Indian Territory, this 21st day of January, A. D. 1900.

R.P. Harrison, Clerk of the U.S. Court.

SEAL
By C.E. Wilcox, Deputy.

CERTIFICATE OF MARRIAGE.

UNITED STATES OF AMERICA,
INDIAN TERRITORY,   SS.
WESTERN DISTRICT.

I, B. F. McElwain, a Minister of the Gospel, do hereby certify that on the 21st day of January, A.D. 1903, did duly and according to law as commanded in the foregoing License, solemnize the rite and publish the Banns of matrimony between the parties therein named.

Witness my hand this 23rd day of January, A. D. 1903.

My credentials are recorded in the office of the Clerk of the United States Court, Indian Territory, Western District, Book C, Page 150.

B.F. McElwain,
A Minister of the Gospel.

Applications for Enrollment of Creek Newborn
Act of 1905   Volume VIII

CERTIFICATE OF RECORD.

UNITED STATES OF AMERICA,
INDIAN TERRITORY,   SS.
WESTERN DISTRICT.

 I, Robert P. Harrison, Clerk of the United States Court in the Western District, Indian Territory, do hereby certify that the instrument hereto attached was filed for record in my office the 7 day of Apr. 1903, at _____ M., and duly recorded in Book O, Marriage Record, Page 273.
 Witness my hand and seal of said Court at Muskogee, in said Territory this 7 day of Apr. A.D. 1903.

            R.P. Harrison, Clerk.
SEAL
By J. Harlan, Deputy.

 Lona Merrick, being duly sworn, states that the above and foregoing is a true and correct copy of the original Marriage License.

            Lona Merrick

Subscribed and sworn to before me this 16 day of October, 1906.

            Edward Merrick
            Notary Public.

NC-657.

         Muskogee, Indian Territory, August 14, 1905.

Henry Roberson,
 Checotah, Indian Territory.

Dear Sir:

 In the matter of the application for the enrollment of your minor son Clerence Roberson, born December 27, 1904, as a citizen by blood of the Creek Nation, it will be necessary for you to file with this office the affidavit of the attending physician or midwife as to the birth of said child and a blank for that purpose is inclosed herewith.

 However, if there was no attending physician or midwife when said child was born it will be necessary for you to furnish, in lieu of the affidavit of the attending physician or midwife, the affidavits of two disinterested persons as to the birth of said child, said affidavits must set forth said child's name, the date of his birth, the names of his parents, and whether or not he was living on March 4, 1905.

Applications for Enrollment of Creek Newborn
Act of 1905   Volume VIII

This office is unable to identify Nancy Roberson the mother of said child upon the final roll of citizens by blood of the Creek Nation. It is necessary that she be so identified before the rights of said child can be finally determined. You are, therefore, requested to inform this office of the name under which the said Nancy Roberson is finally enrolled, the names of her parents and other members of her family, the Creek Indian town to which she belongs and her roll number as the same appears upon her allotment certificate and deeds.

Respectfully,

Acting Commissioner.

NC-657.

Muskogee, Indian Territory, October 17, 1905.

Henry Roberson,
    Checotah, Indian Territory.

Dear Sir:

In the matter of the application for the enrollment of your minor son Clarence Roberson, born December 27, 1904, as a citizen by blood of the Creek nation it will be necessary for you to file with this office the affidavit of the attending physician or midwife as to the birth of said child and a blank for that purpose is inclosed herewith.

However, if there was no attending physician or midwife when said child was born it will be necessary for you to furnish, in lieu of the affidavit of the attending physician or midwife, the affidavits of two disinterested persons as to the birth of said child, said affidavits must set forth said child's name, the date of his birth, the names of his parents, and whether or not he was living on March 4, 1905.

This office is unable to identify Nancy Roberson the mother of said child upon the final roll of citizens by blood of the Creek Nation. It is necessary that she be so identified before the rights of said child can be finally determined. You are, therefore, requested to inform this office of the name under which the said Nancy Roberson is finally enrolled, the names of her parents and other members of her family, the Creek Indian town to which she belongs and her roll number as the same appears upon her allotment certificate and deeds.

Respectfully,

Commissioner.

CTD-3.

Applications for Enrollment of Creek Newborn
Act of 1905   Volume VIII

N.C. 657.
Muskogee, Indian Territory, March 7, 1907.

Nancy Roberson,
Checotah, Indian Territory.

Dear Madam:

You are hereby advised that on March 2, 1907 the Secretary of the Interior approved the enrollment of your minor child Clarence Roberson as a citizen by blood of the Creek Nation, and that the name of said child appears upon the roll of New Born citizens by blood of the Creek Nation, enrolled under the Act of Congress approved March 3, 1905, as number 1233.

This child is now entitled to allotment and application therefor should be made without delay at the Creek Land Office, Muskogee, Indian Territory.

Respectfully,

Commissioner.

BIRTH AFFIDAVIT.

DEPARTMENT OF THE INTERIOR.
COMMISSION TO THE FIVE CIVILIZED TRIBES.

IN RE APPLICATION FOR ENROLLMENT, as a citizen of the Creek Nation, of Hepsey Scott, born on the 16 day of November, 1902

Name of Father: Sam Scott   a citizen of the   Creek   Nation.
Eufaula Canadian
Name of Mother: Nancy Scott   a citizen of the   Creek   Nation.
Quasarte No. 1
Postoffice   Eufaula, Ind. Ter.

AFFIDAVIT OF MOTHER.

UNITED STATES OF AMERICA, Indian Territory,
Western   DISTRICT.

I, Nancy Scott, on oath state that I am 33 years of age and a citizen by blood, of the Creek Nation; that I am the lawful wife of Sam Scott, who is a citizen, by blood of the Creek Nation; that a female child was born to me on 16 day of

Applications for Enrollment of Creek Newborn
Act of 1905 Volume VIII

November , 1902 , that said child has been named Hepsey Scott , and was living March 4, 1905.

Nancy Scott

Witnesses To Mark:
{

Subscribed and sworn to before me this 3 day of April , 1905.

Drennan C Skaggs
Notary Public.

AFFIDAVIT OF ATTENDING PHYSICIAN OR MID-WIFE.

UNITED STATES OF AMERICA, Indian Territory, }
Western   DISTRICT.

I, Lucy Wesley , a midwife , on oath state that I attended on Mrs. Nancy Scott , wife of Sam Scott on the   16 day of   November , 1902 ; that there was born to her on said date a female child; that said child was living March 4, 1905, and is said to have been named   Hepsey Scott

her
Lucy x Wesley
mark

Witnesses To Mark:
{ Alex Posey
  DC Skaggs

Subscribed and sworn to before me 3 day of April, 1905.

Drennan C Skaggs
Notary Public.

NC-660.

Muskogee, Indian Territory, August 14, 1905.

Peter R. Ewing,
    Eufaula, Indian Territory.

Dear Sir:

In the matter of the application for the enrollment of your minor children, Ethel Ewing, born October 20, 1901, and Eulelia Ewing, born December 5, 1902, as citizens by blood of the Creek Nation, it will be necessary for you to furnish this office with the

Applications for Enrollment of Creek Newborn
Act of 1905 Volume VIII

affidavits of the attending physician or midwife at their birth and two blanks for that purpose are inclosed herewith.

However, if there was no attending physician or midwife at the birth of these children then it will be necessary for you to furnish, in lieu of the affidavits of the attending physician or midwife, the affidavits of two disinterested persons as to the birth of said children. Said affidavits must set forth the names of said children, the dates of their birth, the names of their parents and whether or not they were living on March 4, 1905.

Respectfully,

Acting Commissioner.

2 BC
Env.

AFFIDAVIT.

United States of America,
Western District, Indian Territory

   Miller McCombs, being duly sworn states on oath, that she is well acquainted with Peter R. Ewing and his wife Susie A. Ewing, have lived near them and have been at their residence frequently and am acquainted with their children; that there was born to the said Peter R. Ewing and Susie A. Ewing his wife, on or about the 20th. day of October, 1901, a girl child, and that said child was named Ethel; that said child was living on the 4th day of march[sic], 1905, and is still living.
And that Ther[sic] was born to the said Peter R. Ewing and Susie A. Ewing, his wife, on or about the 5th. day of December, 1902, a girl child and that said child was named Eulelia and that said last child was living on the 4th. day of March, 1905 and that she is still living.   her

Witness to mark.   Miller x McCombs
Frank W. Rushing   mark
Joe Grayson
   Subscribed and sworn to before me this 26th, day of August, 1905.

Frank W. Rushing
Notary Public.

Applications for Enrollment of Creek Newborn
Act of 1905   Volume VIII

AFFIDAVIT.

United States of America,
   Western District, Indian Territory.

David McCombs being by me first duly sworn states on his oath that he is acquainted with Peter R. Ewing and Susie A. Ewing, his wife and have lived near them and have been frequently at their residence and am acquainted with their children; that there was born to the said Peter R. Ewing and his wife, Susie A. Ewing a girl child, or about the 20 day of October, 1901; that said child was named Ethel and that said child was living in[sic] the 4th. day of March, 1905 and is still living. And that on or about the 5th. day of December 1902, there was born to the said Peter B. Ewing and Susie A. Ewing, a girl child; that said child was named Eulelia, and that said child was living on the 4th. day of March, 1905 and is still living.

   David McCombs

Subscribed and sworn to before me this 26th, day of August, 1905.

   Frank W Rushing
   Notary Public.

BIRTH AFFIDAVIT.

Department of the Interior,
COMMISSION TO THE FIVE CIVILIZED TRIBES.

IN RE APPLICATION FOR ENROLLMENT, as a citizen of the Creek Nation, of Eulelia Ewing , born on the 5 day of December , 1902

Name of Father: Peter R. Ewing   a citizen of the   Creek   Nation.
Hitchita Town
Name of Mother: Susie A. Ewing   a citizen of the   Creek   Nation.
Tuskegee Town

   Post-Office: Eufaula, Ind. Ter.

AFFIDAVIT OF MOTHER.

UNITED STATES OF AMERICA,
   INDIAN TERRITORY,   Child is present
   Western   District.

I, Susie A. Ewing   , on oath state that I am 36 years of age and a citizen by blood , of the Creek Nation; that I am the lawful wife of Peter R. Ewing , who is a citizen, by blood of the Creek Nation; that a female child was born to me on

Applications for Enrollment of Creek Newborn
Act of 1905   Volume VIII

5 day of December, 1902, that said child has been named Eulelia Ewing, and is now living.

Susie A. Ewing

WITNESSES TO MARK:
{

Subscribed and sworn to before me this 3 day of April, 1905.

Drennan C Skaggs
Notary Public.

AFFIDAVIT OF ATTENDING PHYSICIAN OR MID-WIFE.

UNITED STATES OF AMERICA,
  INDIAN TERRITORY,
Western   District.

my wife

I, Peter R. Ewing, a ~~(blank)~~, on oath state that I attended on ^ Mrs. Susie A. Ewing, ~~wife of (blank)~~ on the 5 day of December, 1902; that there was born to her on said date a female child; that said child is now living and is said to have been named Eulelia Ewing

PR Ewing

WITNESSES TO MARK:
{

Subscribed and sworn to before me this 3 day of April, 1905.

Drennan C Skaggs
Notary Public.

BIRTH AFFIDAVIT.

Department of the Interior,
COMMISSION TO THE FIVE CIVILIZED TRIBES.

IN RE APPLICATION FOR ENROLLMENT, as a citizen of the Creek Nation, of Ethel Ewing, born on the 20 day of October, 1901

Name of Father: Peter R. Ewing   a citizen of the   Creek   Nation.
Hitchita Town
Name of Mother: Susie A. Ewing   a citizen of the   Creek   Nation.
Tuskegee Town

Post-Office: Eufaula, Ind. Ter.

Applications for Enrollment of Creek Newborn
Act of 1905   Volume VIII

AFFIDAVIT OF MOTHER.

UNITED STATES OF AMERICA,
   INDIAN TERRITORY, } Child is present
  Western   District.

I, Susie A. Ewing , on oath state that I am 36 years of age and a citizen by blood , of the Creek Nation; that I am the lawful wife of Peter R. Ewing , who is a citizen, by blood of the Creek Nation; that a female child was born to me on 20 day of October , 1901, that said child has been named Ethel Ewing , and is now living.

                              Susie A. Ewing

WITNESSES TO MARK:

{

Subscribed and sworn to before me this 3 *day of* April, *1905.*

                              Drennan C Skaggs
                                  Notary Public.

Father
AFFIDAVIT OF ~~ATTENDING PHYSICIAN OR MID-WIFE.~~

UNITED STATES OF AMERICA,
   INDIAN TERRITORY, }
  Western   District.

                                                        my wife

I, Peter R. Ewing , ~~a (blank)~~ , on oath state that I attended on ^ Mrs. Susie A. Ewing , ~~wife of (blank)~~ on the 20 day of October , 1901 ; that there was born to her on said date a female child; that said child is now living and is said to have been named Ethel Ewing

                              PR Ewing

WITNESSES TO MARK:

{

Subscribed and sworn to before me this 3 *day of* April, *1905.*

                              Drennan C Skaggs
                                  Notary Public.

Applications for Enrollment of Creek Newborn
Act of 1905   Volume VIII

NC 661

DEPARTMENT OF THE INTERIOR
COMMISSIONER TO THE FIVE CIVILIZED TRIBES
MUSKOGEE, INDIAN TERRITORY.
SEPTEMBER 4, 1906.

In the matter of the application for the enrollment of Lucius Young as a citizen by blood of the Creek Nation.

APPEARANCES: John G. Lieber, acting for M. L. Mott attorney for Creek Nation.

Elizabeth Young being first duly sworn, testified as follows:

Questions by Commissioner:

Q: What is your name? A: Elizabeth Young.
Q: How old are you? A: 21.
Q: What is your post-office address? A: Eufaula, I.T.
Q: How long have you lived in Eufaula? A: About 15 years.
Q: Are you a citizen of any of the five tribes? A: No sir.
Q: You are a negro aren't you? A: Yes sir.
Q: Have you any other blood that you know of besides negro blood? A: No sir, not as I know of.
Q: Full blooded negro are you? A: Yes sir.
Q: Are you married? A: No sir, I have been married.
Q: To whom were you married? A: Harry Young.
Q: Is he living? A: Yes sir.
Q: Where is he now? A: He is a Canadian.
Q: When were you married to him? A: In 1900.
Q: What date? A: The 2nd. day of February 1900.
Q: How long did you live with him? A: We lived together 2 years.
Q: Then did you get a divorce? A: Yes sir.
Q: In 2 years after you married him? A: Yes sir.
Q: Then you must have gotten a divorce in 1902 didn't you? A: No, I didn't get the divorce in 1902, I got the divorce last year.
Q: 1905? A: Yes sir.
Q: What month? A: I got the divorce in March.
Q: Do you mean to say you were divorced from him 2 years after you married him? A: Two years after we were married.
Q: Do you still stick to that that it is 1905 as you say? You say you didn't get your divorce until March last year, that is five years from 1900? A: Yes sir, it was 5 years from 1900.
Q: It was five years after you were married before you got a divorce was it? A: Yes sir.
Q: Had you been separated before you got the divorce? A: Yes sir.

Applications for Enrollment of Creek Newborn
Act of 1905   Volume VIII

Q: How long did you live with him after your marriage before you separated? A: We lived together about a year before we separated.
Q: Did you have any children by him up to the time you first separated? A: Yes, I had a child after we separated.
Q: How long afterwards? A: It was about 2 months I expect.
Q: When did you separate the first time? A: We separated in February the first time.
Q: What year? A: It was in 1900 when we separated then we went back together again.
Q: Have you been to school, and can you read and write? A: Yes sir.
Q: Now don't you know if you were married in February of 1900 and lived with him a year before you separated you couldn't have separated in 1900, that is the same year you gave for the marriage.
Q:[sic] The next February after we married we separated.
Q: Then that would be February 1901, wouldn't it? A: Yes sir
Q: You say two months after that you had this child Lucius? A: Yes sir.
Q: Then you say that child was born in April of 1901, do you? A: Yes sir.
Q: Now are you sure of that? A: Yes sir.
Q: Well that would make it about June 1901, how long did you live with him that time? A: I stayed with him about 2 weeks I guess.
Q: Well that is still in June 1901, then did you live with him again after that? A: No sir.
Q: That is the last you lived with him, June 1901? A: Yes sir.
Q: Are you sure of that? A: Yes sir.
Q: How does it come that you didn't get your divorce until last year then? A: We just didn't put in for it.
Q: Where did you get your divorce, from the Eufaula Court there? A: Yes sir.
Q: Is your marriage license on file there too? A: Yes sir
Q: What is the name of this Harry Young's father? A: Joe Young.
Q: What is the name of his mother? Adeline Young.
Q: Is Harry Young living? A: Yes sri[sic].
Q: Do you know what Creek Indian town he belongs to? A: Yes I did know, he belonged to the Creek Nation.
Q: What Creek Indian Town? A: I disremember now.
Q: Did you ever have any other children by him? A: No sir.
Q: How long had you been married at this time did you say before this child was born? A: Oh it was pretty near a year before the child was born.
Q: Are you sure of that? A: Yes sir.
Q: Are you sure it wasn't 3 or 4 years? A: Yes sir.
Q: You are sure of that are you? A: Yes sir.
Q: Is that child living? A: Yes sir.
Q: Where is it? A: In Eufaula.
Q: Who had charge of it? A: Mamma.
Q: Do you live with your mother? A: Yes sir.
Q: How old is the child? A: Oh it is two years and 5 months old.
Q: Now you say you can read and write, don't you know that is that child is 2 years and 5 months old and this is 1906, that this child must have been born about the 4th. month of 1904? Instead of 1901 as you stated and indtead[sic] of one year after your marriage as you stated, it was born at least 4 years after your marriage, isn't that a fact? A: Yes sir.

Applications for Enrollment of Creek Newborn
Act of 1905   Volume VIII

Q: How do you account for the fact then that you stated minute ago that you were married just about a year when this child was born? A: It was about a year, because I was married in February and the child was born in April.
Q: The next April, a year afterwards? A: Yes sir.
Q: Therefore it was born about a year and a month after you married him was it? A: Yes sir.
Q: Never had any other child by him but this one did you? A: Yes sir.
Q: Now you have stated positively that you separated from this fellow Young sometime in that year after you married him didn't you? A: Yes sir.
Q: And never lived with him again the last time you separated from him? A: No sir not after the last time.
Q: Now you say you married him in February and lived with him until when? A: I lived with him up until the next February
Q: Then you separated? A: Yes sir.
Q: Then how long before you lived with him again? A: About 2 months.
Q: Then that would make it April of 1901 wouldn't it? A: Yes sir.
Q: Then how long did you live with him that time? A: About 2 weeks.
Q: Did you separate from him then? A: Yes sir.
Q: Did you ever live with him again after that? A: No sir.
Q: If that is the case, he was not the father then, of any child that was born as you stated the last time about a year and 5 months ago was he? A: No sir, I made a mistake
Q: You have made lots of mistakes, what is the correct age of this child? A: 2 years and 5 months old.
Q: Well two years and five months will take us back to about April 1904 now you say you separated from this man for the last time in April 1901? A: Yes sir.
Q: So you couldn't have had any child[sic] by him in April 1904 or 2 years and 5 months ago could you? A: No sir.
Q: How did you make that mistake? A: I counted too far back.
Q: The fact of the matter is that you never did have a child by him, did you? A: Yes sir.
Q: Did you ever live with anybody else? A: No sir.
Q: Did you ever have any child by any other man? A: No sir.
Q: Don't you go with any negroes[sic] down there? A: No sir.
Q: What is the name of your mother, who this child is with? A: Adeline Phillips.
Q: We have here an affidavit of yourself and Adeline Philips[sic] you signed it and Adeline Philips the midwife signed by mark, which says a child was born to you and Harry Young your lawful husband on April 6, 1904, how do you account for the fact that you swore to that affidavit as you did and you now swear you separated from Harry Young in April 1901, three years before this? A: Well I just made a mistake in this one.
Q: Which is a mistake? A: This one here.
Q: When were you married to Harry Young? A: I married Harry Young in 1903.
Q: Why did you say you were married to him in 1900 a while ago? A: I made a mistake.
Q: Your mother is a black woman is she? A: Yes sir.
Q: And she was the midwife? A: Yes sir.
Q: Did you have any doctor when this child was born? A: nobody but Mamma.
Q: Did you by any medicine from the stores any place at that time? A: No sir.

Applications for Enrollment of Creek Newborn
Act of 1905 Volume VIII

Q: What did you come in here today for? A: I came here to see about filing for the baby.
Q: Didn't you ever feceive[sic] any notice to file for this child? A: I got a notice that he was enrolled.
Q: You did? A: Yes sir.
Q: Have you got that notice with you? A: No sir, I didn't bring it with me.
Q: How long ago did you get that notice? A: I got the notice about 2 or 3 weeks after I enrolled.
Q: Wasn't that a notice that there was an application here for the enrollment of this child? A: Well I guess it was.
Q: It wasn't any notice that he was enrolled, was it?
A:[sic] This child wasn't enrolled until last November, and you made application in April of 1905, you never received any notice to come and file for this child did you?
A: No sir.
Q: Did you ever see any notice that Harry Young had to come in and file for this child? A: No sir.
Q: How long has he lived in Canadian? A: I don't know how long it has been.
Q: About how long since he went there? A: He went there I guess it has been about a month or a little longer. I think it is.
Q: Did he ever tell you he had received a notice to come and file for this child? A: He told me he was coming to file month before last.
Q: How long has it been since you separated from him the last time? A: Oh, it has been over a year.

Questions by John G. Lieber:

Q: When was it you separated from this man the last time? A: We separated it was about 2 weeks after the last time we separated.
Q: When was the last time you separated from him? A: The last time was in August.
Q: What year? A: It was 1903.
Q: How long did you live with him when you were first married[sic] A: I lived with him a year, just about a year.
Q: In what month were you married? A: We were married in February, the 2nd. day of February.
Q: What year? A: We were married in 1902.
Q: You were married in February? A: Yes sir.
Q: How long did you live with him? A: I lived with him about 2 years.
Q: You just stated you lived with him a year, a minute ago. A: I said I lived with him about a year before we separted[sic] the first time.
Q: How long did you live with him, after you were first married before you separated from him? A: About a year.
Q: What month did you leave him? A: In February about the last.
Q: How long did you stay apart then? A: We stayed apart about 2 months.
Q: Then you went back to him about April did you? A: Yes sir
Q: Then how long did you live with him? A: We stayed together two weeks.

Applications for Enrollment of Creek Newborn
Act of 1905   Volume VIII

Q: That would be along about April of the year you were married that you quit him the second time is that right? A: Yes sir.
Q: Have you ever lived with him since then? A: No sir.
Q: You are sure of that now are you? A: Yes sir.
Q: Never has been with you since that at all? A: Yes he came around and sat and talked with me.
Q: Has he slept with you since that time? A: No sir.
Q: You never got your divorce until last year you say? A: No sir.
Q: You haven't remarried since you got the divorce have you? A: No sir.
Q: What was your name before you married this fellow? Elizabeth Day.
Q: Ho[sic] does it come that your mother's name is Adeline Philips? A: My mother is dead, that is my grand-mother's name but I call her mother.
Q: Did you get yur[license] at Eufaula? A: Yes sir.
Q: How long has your mother been dead? A: Mamma has been dead since I was small, I can't remember.

This is all the evidence that was given in said cause on said date.

I, Julia C. Laval on my oath state that the above and foregoing is a true and complete transcript of my stenographic notes as taken by me in said cause on said date.

Julia C. Laval

Subscribed and sworn to before me this 18 day of September, 1906.

Edward Merrick
Notary Public.

DEPARTMENT OF THE INTERIOR,
COMMISSIONER TO THE FIVE CIVILIZED TRIBES.
MUSKOGEE, INDIAN TERRITORY.
SEPTEMBER 10, 1906.

N.C. 661.

In the matter of the application for the enrollment of Lucius Young as a citizen by blood of the Creek Nation.

APPEARANCES: John G. Lieber, acting for M. L. Mott, attorney for Creek Nation.

Harry Young, being first duly sworn by Henry G. Hains, testified as follows:

Q: What is your name? A: Harry Young.
Q: How old are you? A: 24.

Applications for Enrollment of Creek Newborn
Act of 1905   Volume VIII

Q: What is your post-office address? A: Eufaula.
Q: What is the name of your father? A: Joe Young.
Q: What is the name of your mother? A: Adeline Young.
Q: What Creek Indian town do you belong to? A: Tuskeegee[sic].
Q: What is the name of your brothers and sisters? A: Thomas Post, William Post, Nellie Post and Homer Post.
Q: Now what are you giving all of those Posts for? A: They are half brothers.
Q: I asked you for your sisters and Brothers, have you any? A: Yes sir I have.
Q: Go ahead and try to give some of the full ones. A: Polly Young, and Katie Young and Mary Ella and Fay Young.

Witness is identified as Harry Young, opposite roll number 3608.

Q: Your mother belonged to the same Creek Indian town as you do[sic] A: Yes sir.
Q: What town does your father belong to? A: He is a state man.
Q: Negro isn't he? A: Yes sir.
Q: Have you ever been married? A: Yes sir.
Q: Are you now married? A: Yes sir.
Q: To the same person? A: No sir.
Q: What was the name of your first wife? A: Elizabeth Day.
Q: How long was she your wife? A: About a year.
Q: When were you married to her? A: 1902.
Q: What time? A: It was in February 1902.
Q: Now are you sure of that? A: I don't know whether it was 1902 or 1903.
Q: Have you your marriage license with you? A: No sir.
Q: Where is it on file, what Court house? A: Eufaula.
Q: How long did you live with Elizabeth after you married her? A: Going on about a year.
Q: Was it a full year or less? A: It was about 11 months.
Q: You were married what time in 1902? A: February 15.
Q: You lived with her until the following January are you sure of that? A: Yes sir.
Q: Then what did you do, get a divorce? A: Yes sir.
Q: Where did you get that divorce? A: Eufaula.
Q: Are you sure you got that divorce in January 1903? A: I got the divorce in February 1906.
Q: You are telling us you married her in 1902 and got a divorce the following year?
A: No sir, I didn't get a divorce the next year?
Q: You separated from her the next year? A: Yes sir.
Q: Have you lived with her since? A: Yes sir. Yes sir.
Q: But you didn't get your divorce until 1906? A: No sir.
Q: Are you married now? A: Yes sir.
Q: What is the name of your second wife? A: Lillie Young.
Q: When did you marry her? A: March.
Q: In what year? A: 1906.
Q: So from the time 11 months after you married Elizabeth after you separated you never lived with her since? A: No sir.

Applications for Enrollment of Creek Newborn
Act of 1905   Volume VIII

Q: Now then Henry, if that is the case how does it come, you swear you had a child by her born in the spring of the year in 1904, how do you account for that? A: I must have been mistaken by that. It was in the spring of 1902 or 1903. A:[sic] I am not sure which year it was I forget now whether it was 1902 or 1903.
Q: Is this your handwriting on this affidavit you executed? A: Yes sir.
Q: Did you know what you were swearing to, when you swore to that and signed it? A: Yes sir, I think I do.
Q: When was this child born? A: The child was born in 1903 or 1904.
Q: Don't know what year? A: No sir, it slipped my memory.
Q: Were you living with her when it was born? A: No sir.
Q: How long had you been separated? A: About 3 months after I quit living with her.
Q: The child was born about three months after you quit living with her? A: Yes sir.
Q: Do you recognize this child as yours? A: Yes sir.
Q: Who was the midwife when this child was born, do you know? A: Adeline Philips.
Q: How do you know that? A: That is what they told me, I wasn't present.
Q: What month was this child born in? A: I think it was March or April, I forget which. It was either the last of March or the 1st. of April.
Q: What year? A: 1904 I think.
Q: A minute ago you said 1903 or 1904, now do you know which? A: I am not certain, but I think it was 1903.
Q: Well now you swore here in this affidavit it was born in the spring of 1904? A: We were married in 1903 and separated on the last of the year and the child was born along in March I think, in 1904.
Q: Now refreshing your mind that way you think it was 1904 like your affidavit states? A: Yes sir.
Q: Elizabeth and Adeline swear it was born April 6, 1904 do you know anything about that? A: Yes, I think it was along about April when it was born.

Questions by J. G. Lieber, acting for Creek Attorney.

Q: Now you say you were married in 1903, do you? A: Yes sir
Q: Now what makes you think that? [sic] Because I didn't think of it and it came to my rememberance[sic] now.
Q: Have you got your marraige[sic] license with you, that you got when you married this woman? A: No sir, I think she has got it, she did have it.
Q: Can you fursnish[sic] the Commissioner a certified copy of the license you got yourself? A: Yes sir.
Q: Will you do it? A: Yes sir.
Q: How much time do you want in order to send that certified copy to the Commissioner? A: About 30 days.
Q: You can get it in less time than that can't you? A: Yes, I can, I suppose, I will make it about 30 days and be sure of it.
Q: You can send them a dollar to Eufaula and tell them to send it up here.

Applications for Enrollment of Creek Newborn
Act of 1905   Volume VIII

Questions by Commissioner:

Q: Didn't you receive a notice to file for this child? A: No sir, I never did receive a notice.
Q: Where did you say your post-office was? A: Eufaula.
Q: A: notice was sent to you last winter to Eufaula, Indian Territory do you go to the post-office? A: Yes sir, I think somebody carries my letters away, I was waiting on the notice and never did get it.
Q: Is this child living? A: Yes sir.
Q: Where is it? A: Living with its grand-mother.
Q: What is her name? A: Adeline Philips.
Q: Is that where Elizabeth is living? A: No sir she is living up here at Eufaula.

This is all the testimony given in said cause on said date.

I, I, Julia C. Laval on my oath state that the above and foregoing is a true and complete transcript of my stenographic notes as taken by me in said cause on said date.

Julia C. Laval

Subscribed and sworn to before
me this 22 day of September, 1906.

Edward Merrick

DEPARTMENT OF THE INTERIOR.
COMMISSION TO THE FIVE CIVILIZED TRIBES.

IN RE APPLICATION FOR ENROLLMENT, as a citizen of the Creek Nation, of Lucius Young, born on the 6 day of April, 1904

Name of Father: Harry Young   a citizen of the   Creek   Nation.
Tuskegee Town
Name of Mother: Elizabeth Young   a citizen of the United States Nation.

Postoffice   Eufaula, Ind. Ter.

AFFIDAVIT OF MOTHER.

UNITED STATES OF AMERICA, Indian Territory, }   Child is present
    Western   DISTRICT.

I, Elizabeth Young, on oath state that I am 18 years of age and a citizen ~~by~~ *(blank)*, of the United States ~~Nation~~; that I am the lawful wife of Harry Young,

299

Applications for Enrollment of Creek Newborn
Act of 1905   Volume VIII

who is a citizen, by blood of the Creek Nation; that a male child was born to me on 6 day of April , 1904 , that said child has been named Lucius Young , and was living March 4, 1905.

Elizabeth Young

Witnesses To Mark:
{

Subscribed and sworn to before me this 3 day of April , 1905.

Drennan C Skaggs
Notary Public.

AFFIDAVIT OF ATTENDING PHYSICIAN OR MID-WIFE.

UNITED STATES OF AMERICA, Indian Territory,
    Western   DISTRICT. }

I, Adaline Phillips , a midwife , on oath state that I attended on Mrs. Elizabeth Young , wife of Harry Young on the 6 day of April , 1904 ; that there was born to her on said date a male child; that said child was living March 4, 1905, and is said to have been named Lucius Young

her
Adaline x Phillips
mark

Witnesses To Mark:
{ Alex Posey
  DC Skaggs

Subscribed and sworn to before me 3 day of April, 1905.

Drennan C Skaggs
Notary Public.

SUPPLEMENTAL PROOF.

DEPARTMENT OF THE INTERIOR,
COMMISSION TO THE FIVE CIVILIZED TRIBES.

IN RE Application for Enrollment, as a citizen of the Creek (or Muskogee) Nation, of Lucius Young, born on ~~the~~ in the Spring ~~day of~~ of , 1904

Name of Father:	Harry Young	a citizen of the	Creek	Nation.
Name of Mother:	Elizabeth "	a citizen of the	U.S.	Nation.

Postoffice   Eufaula

Applications for Enrollment of Creek Newborn
Act of 1905 Volume VIII

AFFIDAVIT OF PARENT.
(To be made if child is now living)

UNITED STATES OF AMERICA,
    Indian Territory,
Western   DISTRICT.

    I, Harry Young, on oath state that I am 23 years of age and a citizen by blood, of the Creek (or Muskogee) Nation; that I am the father of Lucius Young a male child who was born on the in the ~~day of~~ Spring of, 1904, that said child is now living.

                                  Harry Young

Witnesses To Mark:

    Subscribed and sworn to before me this 20" day of September, *1905*.

                                  Henry G. Hains
                                      Notary Public.

NC-661.

                        Muskogee, Indian Territory, August 14, 1905.

Elizabeth Young,
    c/o Harry Young,
        Eufaula, Indian Territory.

Dear Madam:

    In the matter of the application for the enrollment of your minor son, Lucius Young, as a citizen by blood on the Creek Nation, it will be necessary for you to file with this office either the original or a certified copy of the marriage license and certificate showing marriage between you and Harry Young the father of said child.

                              Respectfully,

                              Acting Commissioner.

Applications for Enrollment of Creek Newborn
Act of 1905   Volume VIII

NC-662

Muskogee, Indian Territory, August 12, 1905.

Nobe Watts,
    Eufaula, Indian Territory.

Dear Sir:

    In the matter of the application for the enrollment of your minor daughter, Minnie Watts, born July 6, 1904, as a citizen by blood of the Creek Nation, it will be necessary for you to furnish this Office with the affidavits of two disinterested persons as to the birth of said child. Said affidavits must set forth said child's name, the date of its birth, the names of its parents, and whether or not he was living on March 4, 1905.

    Please give this matter your immediate attention.

        Respectfully,

        Acting Commissioner.

Indian Territory
Western District.

Personally appeared before me, a Notary Public of the above named District, Billy Jesse and John Londigan, who being duly sworn depose and say, We are well acquainted with Nobe Watts and Susie Watts, parents of Minnie Watts, and that the said Minnie Watts was born on the 6th day of July 1o04[sic], and was living on March 4th 1o05[sic].

        Billy Jesse
        John Londigan

Subscribed and sworn to before me this 26th day of Aug. 1o05.

        Thos F. *(Illegible)*
        Notary Public.

Applications for Enrollment of Creek Newborn
Act of 1905 Volume VIII

DEPARTMENT OF THE INTERIOR.
COMMISSION TO THE FIVE CIVILIZED TRIBES.

IN RE APPLICATION FOR ENROLLMENT, as a citizen of the Creek Nation, of Minnie Watts, born on the 6 day of July, 1904

Name of Father: Nobe Watts   a citizen of the United States Nation.
Name of Mother: Susie Watts (nee Jesse)   a citizen of the Creek Nation.
Tulmochussee Town

           Postoffice   Eufaula, Ind. Ter.

AFFIDAVIT OF MOTHER.

UNITED STATES OF AMERICA, Indian Territory,
    Western   DISTRICT.   Child is present

    I, Susie Watts, on oath state that I am 21 years of age and a citizen by blood, of the Creek Nation; that I am the lawful wife of Nobe Watts, who is a citizen, by blood of the Creek Nation; that a female child was born to me on 6 day of July, 1904, that said child has been named Minnie Watts, and was living March 4, 1905.

                                        Susan Watts

Witnesses To Mark:
{

    Subscribed and sworn to before me this 3 day of April, 1905.

                                   Drennan C Skaggs
                                           Notary Public.

                            Father
AFFIDAVIT OF ~~ATTENDING PHYSICIAN OR MID-WIFE~~.

UNITED STATES OF AMERICA, Indian Territory,
    Western   DISTRICT.

                                                     my wife
    I, Nobe Watts, ~~a (blank)~~, on oath state that I attended on ^ Mrs. Susie Watts, ~~wife of (blank)~~ on the 6 day of July, 1904; that there was born to her on said date a female child; that said child was living March 4, 1905, and is said to have been named Minnie Watts

                                       Nobe Watts

Witnesses To Mark:
    { Alex Posey

Applications for Enrollment of Creek Newborn
Act of 1905   Volume VIII

Subscribed and sworn to before me 3 day of April, 1905.

                                  Drennan C Skaggs
                                  Notary Public.

DEPARTMENT OF THE INTERIOR.
COMMISSION TO THE FIVE CIVILIZED TRIBES.

IN RE APPLICATION FOR ENROLLMENT, as a citizen of the Creek Nation, of Lonie Givens, born on the 25 day of June, 1904

Name of Father: Choctaw Givens   a citizen of the   Creek   Nation.
Thlopthlocco Town
Name of Mother: Kizzie Givens   a citizen of the   Creek   Nation.
Tuckabatche Town
                      Postoffice   Eufaula, Ind. Ter.

AFFIDAVIT OF MOTHER.

UNITED STATES OF AMERICA, Indian Territory,
    Western   DISTRICT.   Child is present

    I, Kizzie Givens, on oath state that I am about 30 years of age and a citizen by blood, of the Creek Nation; that I am the lawful wife of Choctaw Givens, who is a citizen, by blood of the Creek Nation; that a female child was born to me on 25 day of June, 1904, that said child has been named Lonie Givens, and was living March 4, 1905.
                                  her
                          Kizzie x Givens
Witnesses To Mark: mark
    Alex Posey
    DC Skaggs

Subscribed and sworn to before me this 3 day of April, 1905.

                                Drennan C Skaggs
                                Notary Public.

Applications for Enrollment of Creek Newborn
Act of 1905 Volume VIII

AFFIDAVIT OF ATTENDING PHYSICIAN OR MID-WIFE.

UNITED STATES OF AMERICA, Indian Territory, ⎫
    Western   DISTRICT.   ⎭

      I, Jennie Bender , a midwife , on oath state that I attended on Mrs. Kizzie Givens , wife of Choctaw Givens on the 25 day of June , 1904 ; that there was born to her on said date a female child; that said child was living March 4, 1905, and is said to have been named Lonie Givens

                                           her
                                     Jennie x Bender

Witnesses To Mark: mark
  ⎰ Alex Posey
  ⎱ DC Skaggs

      Subscribed and sworn to before me 3 day of April, 1905.

                                Drennan C Skaggs
                                  Notary Public.

DEPARTMENT OF THE INTERIOR.
COMMISSION TO THE FIVE CIVILIZED TRIBES.

      IN RE APPLICATION FOR ENROLLMENT, as a citizen of the Creek Nation, of Minnie Givens, born on the 7 day of Jan , 1902

Name of Father: Choctaw Givens   a citizen of the Creek   Nation.
Thlopthlocco Town
Name of Mother: Kizzie Givens   a citizen of the Creek   Nation.
Tuckabatche Town

                     Postoffice   Eufaula, Ind. Ter.

AFFIDAVIT OF MOTHER.

UNITED STATES OF AMERICA, Indian Territory, ⎫
   Western   DISTRICT.   ⎭   Child is present

      I, Kizzie Givens , on oath state that I am about 30 years of age and a citizen by blood , of the Creek Nation; that I am the lawful wife of Choctaw Givens , who is a citizen, by blood of the Creek Nation; that a female child was born to me on 7 day of January , 1902 , that said child has been named Minnie Givens , and was living March 4, 1905.   her
                                    Kizzie x Givens
                                        mark

Applications for Enrollment of Creek Newborn
Act of 1905   Volume VIII

Witnesses To Mark:
{ Alex Posey
{ DC Skaggs

Subscribed and sworn to before me this 3 day of April, 1905.

                Drennan C Skaggs
                Notary Public.

AFFIDAVIT OF ATTENDING PHYSICIAN OR MID-WIFE.

UNITED STATES OF AMERICA, Indian Territory, }
    Western   DISTRICT.

I, Jennie Bender, a midwife, on oath state that I attended on Mrs. Kizzie Givens, wife of Choctaw Givens on the 7 day of January, 1902; that there was born to her on said date a female child; that said child was living March 4, 1905, and is said to have been named Minnie Givens

                   her
              Jennie x Bender
Witnesses To Mark: mark
{ Alex Posey
{ DC Skaggs

Subscribed and sworn to before me 3 day of April, 1905.

                Drennan C Skaggs
                Notary Public.

BIRTH AFFIDAVIT.

DEPARTMENT OF THE INTERIOR.
COMMISSION TO THE FIVE CIVILIZED TRIBES.

IN RE APPLICATION FOR ENROLLMENT, as a citizen of the Creek Nation, of Helen M. Murray, born on the 26th day of May, 1904

Name of Father: John Murray   a citizen of the Creek Nation.
Name of Mother: Lucy Murray (nee Macabey) a citizen of the Creek Nation.

            Postoffice   Checotah, Ind. Ty.

Applications for Enrollment of Creek Newborn
Act of 1905   Volume VIII

AFFIDAVIT OF MOTHER.

UNITED STATES OF AMERICA, Indian Territory, ⎱
    Western   DISTRICT.   ⎰

    I, Lucy Murray , on oath state that I am 23 years of age and a citizen by Blood, of the Creek Nation; that I am the lawful wife of John Murray , who is a citizen, by Blood of the Creek Nation; that a female child was born to me on 26th day of May, 1904 , that said child has been named Helen M Murray , and is now living.

Lucy Murray

Witnesses To Mark:
{

    Subscribed and sworn to before me this 27th day of March , 1905.

My Commission Expires Feb. 24, 1907.   AA Smith
Notary Public.

AFFIDAVIT OF ATTENDING PHYSICIAN OR MID-WIFE.

UNITED STATES OF AMERICA, Indian Territory, ⎱
    Western   DISTRICT.   ⎰

    I, J M Lanning , a Physician , on oath state that I attended on Mrs. Lucy Murray , wife of John Murray on the 26th day of May , 1904 ; that there was born to her on said date a female child; that said child is now living and is said to have been named Helen M. Murray

J.M. Lanning M.D.

Witnesses To Mark:
{

    Subscribed and sworn to before me this 27th day of March , 1905.

My Commission Expires Feb. 24, 1907.   AA Smith
Notary Public.

Applications for Enrollment of Creek Newborn
Act of 1905   Volume VIII

HGH

REFER IN REPLY TO THE FOLLOWING:

NC-665

DEPARTMENT OF THE INTERIOR,
COMMISSIONER TO THE FIVE CIVILIZED TRIBES.

Muskogee, Indian Territory, August 14, 1905.

Monday Bean,
  Eufaula, Indian Territory.

Dear Sir:

In the matter of the application for the enrollment of your minor children, Supsie Bean and John Bean, as citizens by blood of the Creek Nation, it will be necessary for you to furnish this Office with the affidavits of the mother of said children as to their birth. For that purpose, there are enclosed herewith blank proofs, which are properly filled out. You are requested to have the mother of said children appear before a notary public and swear to same, and when they are sworn to, return them to this Office in the enclosed envelope.

Respectfully,

Wm O. Beall
Acting Commissioner.

JYM-14-1
Env

N.C. 665.

Muskogee, Indian Territory, October 31, 1905.

Alex Posey,
  Clerk in Charge Creek Field Party,
    Okemah, Indian Territory.

Dear Sir:

There are herewith enclosed affidavits of William and Hagie Sullivan, in the matter of the application for the enrollment of John and Susie[sic] Bean, as citizens by blood of the Creek Nation. Said affidavits were executed before Drennan C Skaggs, notary public, and the seal of the notary was not affixed in either case.

A notarial seal has this day been expressed to Mr. Skaggs and you will request him to affix his seal to the affidavits herewith enclosed and to all other affidavits sworn to before him, before same are sent to this office.

Respectfully,

Commissioner.

Applications for Enrollment of Creek Newborn
Act of 1905 Volume VIII

BIRTH AFFIDAVIT.

DEPARTMENT OF THE INTERIOR.
COMMISSION TO THE FIVE CIVILIZED TRIBES.

IN RE APPLICATION FOR ENROLLMENT, as a citizen of the Creek Nation, of Supsie Bean , born on the 5 day of Jan , 1903

Name of Father: Monday Bean   a citizen of the   Creek   Nation.
Hutchechuppa
Name of Mother: Lena Bean   a citizen of the   Creek   Nation.
Eufaula Canadian

         Postoffice   Eufaula I.T.

AFFIDAVIT OF ATTENDING PHYSICIAN OR MID-WIFE.

UNITED STATES OF AMERICA, Indian Territory,
     Western   DISTRICT.

we[sic] were personally acquainted I, We the undersigned , a ~~(blank)~~ , on oath state that ~~I attended on~~ Mrs. Lena Bean , wife of Monday Bean ~~on the (blank) day of~~ , 190 ; that there was born to her on Jan 5, 1903 ~~said date~~ a female child; that said child was living March 4, 1905, and is said to have been named Supsie Bean

                           Wm Sullivan
                               her
Witnesses To Mark: Hagie x Sullivan
   { DC Skaggs   mark
     Alex Posey

Subscribed and sworn to before me 9 day of Sept., 1905.

                           Drennan C Skaggs
                              Notary Public.

Applications for Enrollment of Creek Newborn
Act of 1905 Volume VIII

BIRTH AFFIDAVIT.

DEPARTMENT OF THE INTERIOR.
COMMISSION TO THE FIVE CIVILIZED TRIBES.

IN RE APPLICATION FOR ENROLLMENT, as a citizen of the Creek Nation, of Supsie Bean, born on the 5 day of January, 1903

Name of Father: Monday Bean   a citizen of the   Creek   Nation.
Hutchechuppa Town
Name of Mother: Lena Bean   a citizen of the   Creek   Nation.
Eufaula Canadian Town

                 Postoffice   Eufaula, Ind.Ter.

AFFIDAVIT OF ~~MOTHER~~. Father

UNITED STATES OF AMERICA, Indian Territory,   not
    Western   DISTRICT.   Child is ^ present

      I, Monday Bean, on oath state that I am 29 years of age and a citizen by blood, of the Creek Nation; that I am the lawful ~~wife~~ husband of Lena Bean, who is a citizen, by blood of the Creek Nation; that a female child was born to ~~me~~ her on 5 day of January, 1903, that said child has been named Supsie Bean, and was living March 4, 1905. That the mother cannot appear personally to make application on account of sickness.   his
                                                     Monday x Bean
Witnesses To Mark: mark
   { Alex Posey
   { DC Skaggs

      Subscribed and sworn to before me this 3 day of April, 1905.

                                               Drennan C Skaggs
                                                 Notary Public.

AFFIDAVIT OF ATTENDING PHYSICIAN OR MID-WIFE.

UNITED STATES OF AMERICA, Indian Territory,
    Western   DISTRICT.

      I, Lucy Wesley, a midwife, on oath state that I attended on Mrs. Lena Bean, wife of Monday Bean on the 5 day of January, 1903; that there was born to her on said date a female child; that said child was living March 4, 1905, and is said to have been named Supsie Bean

Applications for Enrollment of Creek Newborn
Act of 1905   Volume VIII

                                    her
                                Lucy x Wesley
Witnesses To Mark: mark
  { Alex Posey
    DC Skaggs

Subscribed and sworn to before me 3 day of April, 1905.

                                  Drennan C Skaggs
                                  Notary Public.

DEPARTMENT OF THE INTERIOR.
COMMISSION TO THE FIVE CIVILIZED TRIBES.

IN RE APPLICATION FOR ENROLLMENT, as a citizen of the Creek Nation, of John Bean, born on the 3 day of Nov., 1904

Name of Father: Monday Bean   a citizen of the   Creek   Nation.
Hutchechuppa Town
Name of Mother: Lena Bean (nee Thomas)   a citizen of the   Creek   Nation.
Eufaula Canadian Town
                      Postoffice   Eufaula, Ind.Ter.

AFFIDAVIT OF ~~MOTHER~~. Father

UNITED STATES OF AMERICA, Indian Territory,
    Western   DISTRICT.   Child is present

    I, Monday Bean, on oath state that I am 29 years of age and a citizen by blood, of the Creek Nation; that I am the lawful ~~wife~~ husband of Lena Bean, who is a citizen, by blood of the Creek Nation; that a male child was born to ~~me~~ her on 3 day of November, 1904, that said child has been named John Bean, and was living March 4, 1905.
                                  his
                            Monday x Bean
Witnesses To Mark: mark
  { Alex Posey
    DC Skaggs

Subscribed and sworn to before me this 3 day of April, 1905.

                                Drennan C Skaggs
                                Notary Public.

Applications for Enrollment of Creek Newborn
Act of 1905   Volume VIII

AFFIDAVIT OF ATTENDING PHYSICIAN OR MID-WIFE.

UNITED STATES OF AMERICA, Indian Territory,
Western   DISTRICT.

I, Lucy Wesley, a midwife, on oath state that I attended on Mrs. Lena Bean, wife of Monday Bean on the 3 day of November, 1904 ; that there was born to her on said date a male child; that said child was living March 4, 1905, and is said to have been named John Bean

                              her
Witnesses To Mark: Lucy x Wesley
  { Alex Posey   mark
    DC Skaggs

Subscribed and sworn to before me 3 day of April, 1905.

                        Drennan C Skaggs
                           Notary Public.

BIRTH AFFIDAVIT.

DEPARTMENT OF THE INTERIOR.
COMMISSION TO THE FIVE CIVILIZED TRIBES.

IN RE APPLICATION FOR ENROLLMENT, as a citizen of the Creek Nation, of John Bean, born on the 3 day of Nov, 1904

Name of Father: Monday Bean   a citizen of the   Creek   Nation.
Hutchechuppa
Name of Mother: Lena Bean   a citizen of the   Creek   Nation.
Eufaula Canadian
                      Postoffice   Eufaula I.T.

AFFIDAVIT OF ATTENDING PHYSICIAN OR MID-WIFE.

UNITED STATES OF AMERICA, Indian Territory,
Western   DISTRICT.

                                  were personally acquainted with
~~I~~, We the undersigned, ~~a (blank)~~, on oath state that ~~I attended on~~ Mrs. Lena Bean, wife of Monday Bean ~~on the (blank) day of (blank), 190~~ ; that there was born to her on Nov 3 1904 ~~said date~~ a male child; that said child was living March 4, 1905, and is said to have been named John Bean
                            Wm Sullivan

Applications for Enrollment of Creek Newborn
Act of 1905   Volume VIII

Witnesses To Mark:
    { DC Skaggs
       Alex Posey

                  her
              Hagie x Sullivan
                 mark

Subscribed and sworn to before me 9 day of Sept., 1905.

                        Drennan C Skaggs
                          Notary Public.

NC-666

                 Muskogee, Indian Territory, July 20, 1905.

Martha Meyers,
     Okmulgee, Indian Territory.

Dear Madam:

     There are on file in this office affidavits, executed by you and your husband, in which the date of the birth of your minor child, Herbert Meyers, is given as of July 20 and July 26, 1902.

     You are requested to advise this office as to the correct date of the birth of said child.

                 Respectfully,

                            Commissioner.

                   (Copy)

                 Okmulgee, July 31, 1905.

To Commissi*(ink stain)* Five Tribes,
             Muskogee *(ink stain)*
     With reference to N.C. -666
any other date than July 26, 1902 is an error regarding the birth of Herbert Meyers who was Born July 26" 1902

                 Respectfully,

                 (signed)   Martha Meyers
                 (signed)   Charles E. Meyers.

Applications for Enrollment of Creek Newborn
Act of 1905   Volume VIII

BIRTH AFFIDAVIT.

DEPARTMENT OF THE INTERIOR.
COMMISSION TO THE FIVE CIVILIZED TRIBES.

IN RE APPLICATION FOR ENROLLMENT, as a citizen of the Creek Nation, of Herbert Meyers, born on the 26 day of July, 1902

Name of Father: Charles E Meyers   a citizen of the United States Nation.
Name of Mother: Martha Meyers   a citizen of the   Creek   Nation.

                Postoffice   Okmulgee I.T.

AFFIDAVIT OF MOTHER.

UNITED STATES OF AMERICA, Indian Territory,
    Western   DISTRICT.

I, Martha Meyers, on oath state that I am 30 years of age and a citizen by Blood, of the Creek Nation; that I am the lawful wife of Charles E Meyers, who is a citizen, by *(blank)* of the United States Nation; that a male child was born to me on 26 day of July, 1902, that said child has been named Herbert, and was living March 4, 1905.

                                Martha Meyers

Witnesses To Mark:

    {

Subscribed and sworn to before me this 28 day of March, 1905.

                              Wm P Manley
                                    Notary Public.

My Com. Ex. July 23-06

AFFIDAVIT OF ATTENDING PHYSICIAN OR MID-WIFE.

UNITED STATES OF AMERICA, Indian Territory,
    Western   DISTRICT.

I, W. C. Mitchener, a Physician, on oath state that I attended on Mrs. Martha Meyers, wife of Charles E Meyers on the 26 day of July, 1902; that there was born to her on said date a male child; that said child was living March 4, 1905, and is said to have been named Herbert

                              W.C. Mitchener M.D.

Witnesses To Mark:

    {

Applications for Enrollment of Creek Newborn
Act of 1905   Volume VIII

Subscribed and sworn to before me this 28 day of March , 1905.

Wm P Manley
Notary Public.

My Com. Ex. July 23-06

BIRTH AFFIDAVIT.

DEPARTMENT OF THE INTERIOR,
COMMISSION TO THE FIVE CIVILIZED TRIBES.

In Re Application for Enrollment, as a citizen of the Creek Nation, of Herbert Myers, born on the 20 day of July , 1902

Name of Father: Charles E Myers   a citizen of the United States Nation.
Name of Father: Martha Myers   a citizen of the   Creek   Nation.

Post-office   Okmulgee

AFFIDAVIT OF <s>MOTHER</s>. Father

UNITED STATES OF AMERICA,
   INDIAN TERRITORY,
  Western   District.

    I, Charles E. Myers , on oath state that I am 47 years of age and a citizen <s>by</s> *(blank)* , of the United States <s>Nation</s>; that I am the lawful <s>wife</s> husband of   Martha Myers , who is a citizen, by blood of the Creek Nation; that a male child was born to <s>me</s> said Martha Myers on 20   day of July , 1902 , that said child has been named Herbert Myers , and is now living.

Charles E. Meyers

WITNESSES TO MARK:
{

Subscribed and sworn to before me this 30th day of August , 1904.

Edward Merrick
NOTARY PUBLIC.

Applications for Enrollment of Creek Newborn
Act of 1905 Volume VIII

NC-667

Muskogee, Indian Territory, August 14, 1905.

Watson Washington,
    Eufaula, Indian Territory.

Dear Sir:

    In the matter of the application for the enrollment of your minor children, Mandy Washington, born May 18, 1902, and Melah Washington, born July 18, 1904, as citizens by blood of the Creek Nation, it will be necessary for you to furnish this Office with the affidavits of two disinterested persons as to the birth of said children. Said affidavits must set forth the names of said children, the dates of their birth, the names of their parents, and whether or not they were living on March 4, 1905.

    Please give this matter your immediate attention.

                  Respectfully,

                            Acting Commissioner.

BIRTH AFFIDAVIT.

Department of the Interior,
COMMISSION TO THE FIVE CIVILIZED TRIBES.

    IN RE APPLICATION FOR ENROLLMENT, as a citizen of the Creek Nation, of Melah Washington, born on the 18 day of July, 1904

Name of Father: Watson Washington   a citizen of the   Creek   Nation.
Eucha Town
Name of Mother: Lucy Washington   a citizen of the   Creek   Nation.
Tulsa Little River Town
                  Post-Office: Eufaula, Ind. Ter.

AFFIDAVIT OF MOTHER.

UNITED STATES OF AMERICA,
    INDIAN TERRITORY,   Child is present
    Western   District.

    I, Lucy Washington, on oath state that I am about 30 years of age and a citizen by blood, of the Creek Nation; that I am the lawful wife of Watson Washington, who is a citizen, by blood of the Creek Nation; that a female

Applications for Enrollment of Creek Newborn
Act of 1905   Volume VIII

child was born to me on 18 day of July , 1904 , that said child has been named Melah Washington , and ~~is now~~ was living. on March 4, 1905

her
Lucy x Washington
mark

WITNESSES TO MARK:
{ Alex Posey
{ DC Skaggs

Subscribed and sworn to before me this 3 *day of* April, *1905.*

Drennan C Skaggs
Notary Public.

Father

AFFIDAVIT OF ~~ATTENDING PHYSICIAN OR MID WIFE~~.

UNITED STATES OF AMERICA,
INDIAN TERRITORY,
Western District.

my wife
I, Watson Washington , ~~a (blank)~~ , on oath state that I attended on ^ Mrs. Lucy Washington , ~~wife of (blank)~~ on the 18 day of July , 1904 ; that there was born to her on said date a female child; that said child is now living and is said to have been named Melah Washington

his
Watson x Washington
mark

WITNESSES TO MARK:
{ Alex Posey
{ DC Skaggs

Subscribed and sworn to before me this 3 *day of* April, *1905.*

Drennan C Skaggs
Notary Public.

BIRTH AFFIDAVIT.

DEPARTMENT OF THE INTERIOR.
COMMISSION TO THE FIVE CIVILIZED TRIBES.

IN RE APPLICATION FOR ENROLLMENT, as a citizen of the Creek Nation, of Melah Washington , born on the 18 day of July , 1904

Name of Father: Watson Washington   a citizen of the   Creek   Nation.
Eucha Town
Name of Mother: Lucy Washington   a citizen of the   Creek   Nation.
L. R. Tulsa Town

Postoffice   Eufaula I.T.

Applications for Enrollment of Creek Newborn
Act of 1905 Volume VIII

AFFIDAVIT OF ATTENDING PHYSICIAN OR MID-WIFE.

UNITED STATES OF AMERICA, Indian Territory,
Western DISTRICT.

I, We the undersigned , a (blank) , on oath state that I attended on we are personally acquainted with Mrs. Lucy Washington , wife of Watson Washington on the (blank) day of (blank) , 1 ; that there was born to her on July 18, 1904 said date a female child; that said child was living March 4, 1905, and is said to have been named Melah Washington

                              her
                         Liza x Barnett
Witnesses To Mark: mark
{ Alex Posey   *(Name Illegible)*
{ DC Skaggs

Subscribed and sworn to before 21 day of Sept., 1905.

                                Drennan C Skaggs
                                  Notary Public.

BIRTH AFFIDAVIT.

DEPARTMENT OF THE INTERIOR.
COMMISSION TO THE FIVE CIVILIZED TRIBES.

IN RE APPLICATION FOR ENROLLMENT, as a citizen of the Creek Nation, of Mandy Washington , born on the 18 day of May , 1902

Name of Father: Watson Washington	a citizen of the	Creek	Nation.
Eucha Town			
Name of Mother: Lucy Washington	a citizen of the	Creek	Nation.
L. R. Tulsa Town			

                         Postoffice   Eufaula I.T.

AFFIDAVIT OF ATTENDING PHYSICIAN OR MID-WIFE.

UNITED STATES OF AMERICA, Indian Territory,
Western DISTRICT.

I, We the undersigned , a (blank) , on oath state that I attended on we are personally acquainted with Mrs. Lucy Washington , wife of Watson Washington on the (blank) day of (blank) , 1 ; that there was born to her on May 18, 1902 said date a female child; that said child was living March 4, 1905, and is said to have been named Mandy Washington

Applications for Enrollment of Creek Newborn
Act of 1905   Volume VIII

Witnesses To Mark:
{ Alex Posey
  DC Skaggs

her
Liza x Barnett
mark
(Name Illegible)

Subscribed and sworn to before 21 day of Sept., 1905.

Drennan C Skaggs
Notary Public.

BIRTH AFFIDAVIT.

Department of the Interior,
COMMISSION TO THE FIVE CIVILIZED TRIBES.

IN RE APPLICATION FOR ENROLLMENT, as a citizen of the Creek Nation, of Mandy Washington, born on the 18 day of May, 1902

Name of Father: Watson Washington   a citizen of the   Creek   Nation.
Eucha Town
Name of Mother: Lucy Washington   a citizen of the   Creek   Nation.
Tulsa Little River Town

Post-Office: Eufaula, Ind. Ter.

AFFIDAVIT OF MOTHER.

UNITED STATES OF AMERICA,
  INDIAN TERRITORY,   Child is present
   Western   District.

I, Lucy Washington, on oath state that I am about 30 years of age and a citizen by blood, of the Creek Nation; that I am the lawful wife of Watson Washington, who is a citizen, by blood of the Creek Nation; that a female child was born to me on 18 day of May, 1902, that said child has been named Mandy Washington, and ~~is now~~ was living. on March 4, 1905

her
Lucy x Washington
mark

WITNESSES TO MARK:
{ Alex Posey
  DC Skaggs

Subscribed and sworn to before me this 3 day of April, 1905.

Drennan C Skaggs
Notary Public.

Applications for Enrollment of Creek Newborn
Act of 1905   Volume VIII

Father
AFFIDAVIT OF ~~ATTENDING PHYSICIAN OR MID WIFE~~.

UNITED STATES OF AMERICA,
INDIAN TERRITORY,
Western   District.

my wife
I, Watson Washington , ~~a (blank)~~ , on oath state that I attended on ^ Mrs. Lucy Washington , ~~wife of (blank)~~ on the 18 day of May , 1902 ; that there was born to her on said date a female child; that said child is now living and is said to have been named   Mandy Washington

his
Watson x Washington
mark

WITNESSES TO MARK:
{ Alex Posey
  DC Skaggs

Subscribed and sworn to before me this 3 *day of* April, *1905.*

Drennan C Skaggs
Notary Public.

NC-668

Muskogee, Indian Territory, August 22, 1905.

Polly Derrisaw,
    Care of William Derrisaw,
        Eufaula, Indian Territory.

Dear Madam:

In the affidavit now on file with the records of this Office in the matter of the application for the enrollment of your minor daughter, Carrie Derrisaw, as a citizen by blood of the Creek Nation, the surname of said child and yourself appears in the body of the affidavit as "Darisaw," while you signed the affidavit "Polly Derrisaw." Derrisaw seems to be the correct spelling of your surname, inasmuch as your husband, from whom the name is derived, is identified upon the final roll of citizens by blood of the Creek Nation as William Derrisaw.

For the purpose of correcting this discrepancy as to the surname of your said child, there is enclosed herewith blank for proof of birth, which has been filled out, and you are requested to have same executed, and when so executed, return it to this Office in the enclosed envelope.

Applications for Enrollment of Creek Newborn
Act of 1905   Volume VIII

You are requested to give this matter your immediate attention, and are advised that until the corrected affidavits have been filed, nothing further can be done in the matter of the enrollment of your said daughter, Carrie Derrisaw, as a citizen by blood of the Creek Nation.

Respectfully,

Commissioner.

JYM-22-1

BIRTH AFFIDAVIT.

Department of the Interior,
COMMISSION TO THE FIVE CIVILIZED TRIBES.

IN RE APPLICATION FOR ENROLLMENT, as a citizen of the Creek Nation, of Carrie Darisaw, born on the 16 day of December, 1903

Name of Father: William Darisaw   a citizen of the   Creek   Nation. Coweta Town
Name of Mother: Pollie Darisaw (nee Barnett) a citizen of the   Creek   Nation. Weogufke[sic] Town

Post-Office: Eufaula I.T.

AFFIDAVIT OF MOTHER.

UNITED STATES OF AMERICA,
   INDIAN TERRITORY,
   Western   District.

Child present

I, Pollie Darisaw, on oath state that I am 24 years of age and a citizen by blood, of the Creek Nation; that I am the lawful wife of William Darisaw, who is a citizen, by blood of the Creek Nation; that a female child was born to me on 16 day of December, 1903, that said child has been named Carrie Darisaw, and is now was living. on March 4, 1905.

Polly Derrisaw

WITNESSES TO MARK:

Subscribed and sworn to before me this 3 day of April, 1905.

Drennan C Skaggs
Notary Public.

Applications for Enrollment of Creek Newborn
Act of 1905 Volume VIII

AFFIDAVIT OF ATTENDING PHYSICIAN OR MID-WIFE.

UNITED STATES OF AMERICA,
INDIAN TERRITORY,
Western District.

I, Louina Stover , a mid-wife , on oath state that I attended on Mrs. Pollie Darisaw , wife of William Darisaw on or about the 18 day of December , 1903 ; that there was born to her on said date a female child; that said child is now living and is said to have been named Carrie Darisaw

Luina[sic] Stover

WITNESSES TO MARK:
{

Subscribed and sworn to before me this 3 day of April, 1905.

Drennan C Skaggs
Notary Public.

BIRTH AFFIDAVIT.

DEPARTMENT OF THE INTERIOR.
COMMISSION TO THE FIVE CIVILIZED TRIBES.

IN RE APPLICATION FOR ENROLLMENT, as a citizen of the Creek Nation, of Carrie Derrisaw , born on the 16th day of December , 1903

Name of Father: William Derrisaw	a citizen of the Creek	Nation.
Name of Mother: Polly Derrisaw	a citizen of the Creek	Nation.

Postoffice Eufaula, I.T.

AFFIDAVIT OF MOTHER.

UNITED STATES OF AMERICA, Indian Territory,
Western DISTRICT.

I, Polly Derrisaw , on oath state that I am 24 years of age and a citizen by blood , of the Creek Nation; that I am the lawful wife of William Derrisaw , who is a citizen, by blood of the Creek Nation; that a female child was born to me on 16th day of December , 1903 , that said child has been named Carrie Derrisaw , and was living March 4, 1905.

Polly Derrisaw

Witnesses To Mark:
{

Applications for Enrollment of Creek Newborn
Act of 1905 Volume VIII

Subscribed and sworn to before me this 12 day of September, 1905.

                                                     Preston Janway
                                                     Notary Public.

AFFIDAVIT OF ATTENDING PHYSICIAN OR MID-WIFE.

UNITED STATES OF AMERICA, Indian Territory,
   Western   DISTRICT.

    I, Luina Stover, a mid-wife, on oath state that I attended on Mrs. Polly Derrisaw, wife of William Derrisaw on the 16th day of December, 1903; that there was born to her on said date a female child; that said child was living March 4, 1905, and is said to have been named Carrie Derrisaw

                                                   her
                                        Luina Stover x
Witnesses To Mark: mark
  { E.H. Walker
    (Name Illegible)

Subscribed and sworn to before me this 12 day of September, 1905.

My Commission   Preston Janway
Expires May 19-1908   Notary Public.

DEPARTMENT OF THE INTERIOR,
COMMISSION TO THE FIVE CIVILIZED TRIBES.
Sapulpa, I.T. May 1st, 1905.

    In the matter of the application of Senora Jefferson for enrollment as a citizen by blood of the Creek Nation.

    Nancy W. Fanning, being duly sworn, by E.C. Griesel, a Notary Public, testified as follows:

By Commission:
Q What is your name? A Nancy W. Fanning.
Q What is the name of the child? A Its name is Senora Jefferson.
Q Walter Jefferson is the father? A Yes sir.
Q You saw this child yesterday, did you? A Yes sir.
Q ~~The child~~ Walter Jefferson is a Creek citizen? A Yes sir.
Q The mother's name is Annie, is it? A Yes sir.

Applications for Enrollment of Creek Newborn
Act of 1905   Volume VIII

Q The child is living with the grandmother is it? A Yes.
Q When was the mother born? A Don't know.
Q The child about two years old? A Born in the fall of 1903. Born the first day of August, 1903. Going on two years old.
Q The mother is dead? A yes sir.
Q Living with the grandmother, Lena? A Yes.
Q What is it[sic] post office? A Tulsa.
Q Do you know the town of the mother? A Lochopaka.
Q Your name is Nancy W. Fanning, is it not? A Yes.
Q Your husband's name is Bob? A Yes sir.
Q You are a citizen of the Creek Nation? A Yes sir.

--------oOo---- -

Nora Burgess, being duly sworn, by E.C. Griesel, a Notary Public, testified as follows:

By Commission:
Q What is your name? A Nora Burgess.
Q What town do you belong to? A Lochopaka.
Q You saw this child Senora? A Yes.
Q When did you see Senora last? A Last Saturday evening.
Q Whose the father of that child? A Walter Jefferson.
Q And who is the mother? A Annie Jefferson.
Q She id dead is she? A Yes sir.
Q About how old is that child? A About two years old.

E.C. Griesel, being duly sworn, states that the above and foregoing is a true and complete transcript of his stenographic notes as taken in said cause on said date.

Edw C Griesel

Subscribed and sworn to before me this 5 day of May, 1905.

(Name Illegible)
Notary Public.

Applications for Enrollment of Creek Newborn
Act of 1905   Volume VIII

N.C. 669.
DEPARTMENT OF THE INTERIOR,
COMMISSIONER TO THE FIVE CIVILIZED TRIBES.
Muskogee, Indian Territory, August 19, 1905.

In the matter of the application for the enrollment of Senora Jefferson as a citizen by blood of the Creek Nation.

Walter Jefferson, being duly sworn, testified as follows through Alex Posey, official interpreter.

Q What is your name? A Walter Jefferson
Q What is your age? A 24
Q What is your post office address? A Tulsa.
Q Are you a citizen of the Creek nation? A Yes, sir.
Q What is the name of your father? A Thomas Jefferson.
Q What is the name of your mother? A Lena Jefferson.
Q Have you a child named Senora Jefferson? A Yes, sir
Q Is it living? A Yes, sir
Q What was the name of this child's mother? A Annie
Q Annie what? A I presume she was enrolled under the name of her father Chesley Starr.

Annie Jefferson is identified on Creek Indian card 3698 as Annie Starr opposite 3807.

Q You executed two affidavits in one of them you state the child was born July 31, 1903, in the other you state in October 1903 which is correct? A I didn't make that mistake it was a mistake of the notary, July is correct
Q And in affidavit of the midwife she said July 31, 1904 that is incorrect of course as it was after the death of the mother? A Yes, sir
Q When did Annie die? A First of August 1903
Q Lena Jefferson makes a mistake in the year? A Yes, sir Lena Jefferson, my mother, is a full blood and dont[sic] know dates very well.

I, Anna Garrigues, on oath state that the above is a true and correct copy of my stenographic notes taken in said cause on said date.

Anna Garrigues

Subscribed and sworn to before
me this 19th day of August 1905   Henry G. Hains
                                                    Notary Public.

Applications for Enrollment of Creek Newborn
Act of 1905   Volume VIII

BIRTH AFFIDAVIT.

See Dup App

DEPARTMENT OF THE INTERIOR.
COMMISSION TO THE FIVE CIVILIZED TRIBES.

IN RE APPLICATION FOR ENROLLMENT, as a citizen of the Creek Nation, of Senora Jefferson, born on the 31 day of July, 1903

Name of Father: Walter Jefferson   a citizen of the   Creek   Nation.
(Illegible Tallahassa)
Name of Mother: Annie   "   (de'c.)   a citizen of the   "   Nation.
Lochapocha
                              Postoffice   Tulsa

AFFIDAVIT OF ~~MOTHER~~. Father

Child Present

UNITED STATES OF AMERICA, Indian Territory, }
   Western   DISTRICT.

I, Walter Jefferson, on oath state that I am 23 years of age and a citizen by blood, of the Creek Nation; that I am the lawful ~~wife~~ Husband of Annie Jefferson (de'c), who is a citizen, by blood of the Creek Nation; that a female child was born to me on 31 day of July, 1903, that said child has been named Senora Jefferson, and was living March 4, 1905.

                                     Walter Jefferson
Witnesses To Mark:
{

Subscribed and sworn to before me this 2 day of May, 1905.

    (Seal)   Edw C Griesel
                                         Notary Public.

AFFIDAVIT OF ATTENDING ~~PHYSICIAN OR MID-WIFE~~.
Grandmother

UNITED STATES OF AMERICA, Indian Territory, }
   Western   DISTRICT.

I, Lena Jefferson, a midwife, on oath state that I attended on Mrs. Annie Jefferson, wife of Walter Jefferson on the 31 day of July, 1904; that there was born to her on said date a female child; that said child was living March 4, 1905, and is said to have been named Senora Jefferson
                                     her
                              Lena x Jefferson
                                 mark

Applications for Enrollment of Creek Newborn
Act of 1905   Volume VIII

Witnesses To Mark:
{ *(Name Illegible)*
{ Jesse McDermott

Subscribed and sworn to before me 2 day of May, 1905.

(Seal)   Edw C Griesel
                                    Notary Public.

BIRTH AFFIDAVIT.

DEPARTMENT OF THE INTERIOR.
COMMISSION TO THE FIVE CIVILIZED TRIBES.

IN RE APPLICATION FOR ENROLLMENT, as a citizen of the Creek Nation, of Senora Jefferson, born on the 31 day of July , 1904

Name of Father: *(Smudge)* Jefferson   a citizen of the   Creek   Nation.
Name of Mother: Annie *(Illegible)*   a citizen of the   Unknown   Nation.

Postoffice   *(Illegible)*

                              Father
AFFIDAVIT OF ~~MOTHER~~.

UNITED STATES OF AMERICA, Indian Territory, ⎫
        Western   DISTRICT.   ⎭

I, *(Smudge)* Jefferson , on oath state that I am 24 years of age and a citizen by Blood, of the Creek Nation; that I am the lawful ~~wife~~ Husband of Annie Jefferson Decd" , who is a citizen, by Blood of the Blood[sic] Nation; that a Male[sic] child was born to me on 31 day of October , 1905 , that said child has been named Senora Jefferson   , and is now living.

                                    Walter Jefferson

Witnesses To Mark:
{

Subscribed and sworn to before me this 18" day of March, 1905.

        My Com Ex 7/3/1906   Robert E Lynch
                                    Notary Public.

327

Applications for Enrollment of Creek Newborn
Act of 1905   Volume VIII

AFFIDAVIT OF ATTENDING PHYSICIAN OR MID-WIFE.

UNITED STATES OF AMERICA, Indian Territory, ⎱
    Western   DISTRICT. ⎰

    I, Lena Jefferson, a Midwife, on oath state that I attended on Mrs. Annie Jefferson, wife of Walter Jefferson on the 31 day of July, 1904 ; that there was born to her on said date a Male child; that said child is now living and is said to have been named Senora Jefferson

                                                 her
                                          Lena x Jefferson
Witnesses To Mark: mark
  ⎰ Wm ? Bruner
  ⎱ R E Lynch

    Subscribed and sworn to before me this 18 day of March, 1905.

    My Com Ex 7/3/1906   Robert E Lynch
                                          Notary Public.

NC-669

                                    Muskogee, Indian Territory, August 14, 1905.

Walter Jefferson,
    Tulsa, Indian Territory.

Dear Sir:

    In the matter of the application for the enrollment of your minor daughter, Senora Jefferson, as a citizen by blood of the Creek Nation, the date of the birth of said child is stated in different affidavits as October 31, 1903, and July 31, 1903, and July 31, 1904.

    You are requested to immediately inform this Office as to which of the aforesaid dates, if any, is the correct one of the birth of said child.

    This Office is unable to identify Annie Jefferson (deceased), the mother of said child upon the final roll of the citizens by blood of the Creek Nation. You are therefore requested to state the name under which said Annie Jefferson is finally enrolled, the names of her parents and other members of her family, and, if possible, her final roll number as the same appears upon her allotment certificates and deeds.

    Please give these matters your immediate attention.

                                Respectfully,

                                              Acting Commissioner.

Index

ACKERS
Bob 269
ALLEN
R C 78, 79
ANSIEL
Albert Robert 137, 138
Charlie 134, 135, 136, 137
Mary 134, 135, 136, 137
Robert Lee 137, 138
Robert Leroy 134, 135
Statie Ann 137, 138
William F. 134, 136, 137
ASBURY
Jim 127, 133
AUSTIN
Ora M 53

BAKER
Marion 54
BANTON
R 64, 65, 66, 67, 68
BARBER
Nettie G 64, 67
BARNETT
Austin 167, 168, 169, 170, 171, 172, 173
Edmund .. 167, 170, 171, 172, 173
Hammer .. 167, 168, 169, 172, 173
Hannah 172
Jennie 84, 85
Liza 167, 168, 169, 170, 171, 173, 318, 319
Lizanna 172
Pollie 321
Sis 223
Sissie 145
Sissy 148
BARNETTE
Sissie 96
BARRY
Wm 58
BASTABLE
John 52

BAYNE
R S 101
BEALL
Wm O ... 28, 75, 76, 155, 173, 308
BEAN
John 308, 311, 312
Lena 309, 310, 311, 312
Monday .. 308, 309, 310, 311, 312
Supsie 308, 309, 310
Susie 308
BEAVER
B J 191
Byer 106, 109
Lecus 107
Mulsie 106, 107, 108, 109
Poyer 107, 108, 109
Rhoda 111, 113
Walter 106, 108, 109
BEAVERS
B J 79, 80, 190
BEDFORD
Edwin G 251
BELDING
A A 248
BELL
Rebecca 187
BENDER
Jennie 305, 306
BERRYHILL
Sarah 161, 162
BEST
Jason L 158, 159
BIXBY
Tams 6, 36, 37, 155, 181, 212, 213, 242, 277
BLAKE
Simon 127, 132
Wm P 187
BLAND
John C W 55
John C W, MD 55
BRASHER
A T 99

Index

BRAY 258
BRENNAN
  Francis R 157, 158, 159
BRIGHT
  John 125, 126, 127, 128,
    129, 130, 131, 132, 133, 134
  Lafa 125, 126, 127, 128, 129, 130
  Lena 127, 132, 133
  Reubin 130, 133, 134
  Reugin 125
  Rhebin 131
  Rheubin 131, 132, 133
  Rhoda 126, 129, 130, 131, 133
  Rhody 126, 127, 128, 129, 131,
    132, 133, 134
  Sander 134
BRITT
  Mittie B 175
BROWN
  Ada J 245, 246, 247
  Almon W 245
  C W 184
  Clarence W 181, 182, 183, 184,
    185, 187, 188
  Clarence William ... 180, 181, 182,
    183, 185, 186
  Cleler 61
  Cleller 56, 57, 58, 60
  Dr Almon W 246
  Dr Almond W 246
  Eva May 244, 245, 246, 247
  Eve May 246
  Jack 59
  Jackson 56, 57, 58, 60, 61
  John William . 180, 181, 182, 184,
    185, 186, 188
  Laura 43, 56, 57, 58, 60
  Mrs A W 247
  Rebecca . 180, 182, 183, 184, 185,
    186, 188
  Rosanna 52
  Ruth 181, 182, 183, 184, 188
  Sam 273

A W 244, 247
A W, MD 247
BRUCE
  Irene E 184
BRUNER
  Berry 8
  Mary 78
  Mattie 10
  Miller 22
  Plly 8
  Pollie 8, 12, 13
  Polly 7
  Wm ? 328
BUFORD
  Charles 100
BURGESS
  Nora 324
BURTON
  Mary 75
  Rugus Cheestell 75
BUSH
  C G 248
BYRD
  Jno M 248

CALDWELL
  L P 118
CARR
  Limbo 94, 95, 96, 97, 149
  Mille 96
  Millie 95, 96, 97
  Washington 94, 95, 96, 97
CASSINGHAM
  John R 28, 29, 31
CAZAD
  S C 220, 221
CHANDLER
  T A 53
CHOTKEY 262
CHUPCO
  Cilla 14, 15, 16, 18, 19
  Katie 16
  Micco 16

Index

Toney 16, 18, 19
CHUPSO
   Toney 15
CLARENCE 257
CLARKSTON
   Alex 165, 166
   Maggie J 164, 165, 166
   Mollie 165
   Raymond 164, 165, 166
CLIFTON
   N B 97
COLBERT
   Sam 216
COLE
   Jacob 240, 241
COLLINS
   Lewis 103, 104, 105, 106
   Louis 149
   Noah 103, 104, 105, 106
   Sophie 103, 104, 105, 106
COLMON
   Gladdys 63
   Gladdys Leuna 63, 67, 68
   Gladdys May 63
   Gladys May 66
   Nettie Alice 63, 64, 65
   Nettie G 63, 64, 65, 66, 67, 68
   W E 63, 64, 65, 66, 67, 68
COLVARD
   W H 102
   Wm H 102
COMPIER
   Millie 20
   Mitchell 20, 21, 23, 24, 25, 26
   Willie 20, 21, 22, 23, 24, 25, 26, 27
COOK
   Will 126, 130
COPPEDGE
   C E, MD 229
CORBOY
   Kate 174, 175, 177, 178, 179
CORNELL
   David 61, 62
   Manie 61, 62
   Willie 61, 62
CORSAR
   Cinthia 107
COSAR
   Cynthia 107
COUNTERMAN
   R M, MD 251
COZAD
   S C 228
CRANSTON
   O G 186
CREWS
   Tom 126, 130
CROSBY
   Berry Martin 158, 159
   Charles E 157, 158, 159
   Elizabeth A 157, 158, 159
   Ferdinand Wilber 157
   Mary Ann 159
CROWELL
   D Y, MD 250
CULLY
   William 204
CULP
   A H 77
   A H, MD 77
CURTIS
   Lydia 178
DARISAW 320
   [Ollie 321
   Carrie 321, 322
   Pollie 321, 322
   William 321, 322
DAVIDSON
   Charles A 53
   Chas A 53
DAVIS
   Bettie 89, 90, 91
   Fanny 89, 90
   Ira E 283

Index

Minie 91
Minnie 90
Sampson 89, 90, 91
DAY
   Elizabeth 296, 297
DEERE
   Lawyer 16
DEERISAW
   Emma 150
   Polly 150
DEPRIEST
   Emily 229, 230
   James 228, 229, 230
   Luther 228, 229, 230
DERESAW
   Emma 145, 147, 148
   Polly 145
DERRISAW
   Carrie 320, 321, 322, 323
   Polly 320, 322, 323
   William 320, 322, 323
DILL
   W H 118
DIXON
   Della 191, 192, 193
   Ethel Luler 191, 192
   Henry Jefferson 192, 193
   Sam 191, 192, 193
DKAGGS
   D C 9
DOTSON
   M A 40
   Mrs M D 40
DRESBACK
   Nellie 40
   Ralph 40
DUNN
   Tupper 118
DUNSON
   L E 180
DYE
   Joe 44

ELLIOTT
   J H 57
ENGLISH
   A Z 101
EVERETT
   Elmer 74
EWING
   Ethel 287, 288, 290, 291
   Eulelia 287, 289, 290
   P R 290, 291
   Peter R 287, 288, 289, 290, 291
   Susie A 288, 289, 290, 291

FANNIN
   E J 59
FANNING
   Bob 324
   Nancy W 323, 324
FETTING
   Franklin T 177
FIELDS
   Leslie 47, 48, 50
   Monnah 48, 51
FISHER
   George 43
FLETCHER
   Caroline 38
FLOWERS
   Alice 37, 38, 39
   Joseph 37, 38, 39
   Willie Eva 36, 37, 38, 39
FORD
   Dr 265
   Dr W J 250
   W J 250
FOWLER
   J W 87
   Sam 87
FOX
   John 30
FRANCIS
   Menaffie 152
   Mennaffa 153

Mitchell 152, 153
Susie 152, 153
FRANK
   Austin 242, 243, 244
   Austin, Jr 242
   Jane 34
   Lizzie 242, 243, 244
   Mary 34
FRIDAY
   Joe 76
FULOTKA
   Susan 191
FUNK
   J F 165
   William A 157
   William Adam 157

GAMBLER
   Billy 140
   Hepsey 141, 144
   John 140, 141, 142, 143, 144
   Martin 140, 141, 142, 143, 144
GARRIGUES
   Anna 20, 45, 69, 80, 81, 235, 325
GILLIAM
   W C 201
GIRDNER
   Maggie A 164, 165
   Maggie J 166
GIVENS
   Annie 90, 91
   Choctaw 304, 305, 306
   Kizzie 304, 305, 306
   Lonie 304, 305
   Minnie 305, 306
GLENN
   Mrs E A 64, 65
GLOVER
   Lynn 58
GOAT
   Alfred F .. 23, 25, 82, 83, 123, 124
   John R 24, 25

Mardle 20
Millie 20, 21, 22, 23, 24, 25, 26, 27
Wardley 122
GOLD
   S M 126, 130
GRAY
   Siah 32, 33
GRAYSON
   Adeline 139
   Joe 288
   Judy 252
   W C 246
GREEN
   R L 41
GRIESEL
   E C 21, 48, 51, 69, 70, 71, 323, 324
   Edw C 10, 18, 39, 45, 46, 49, 65, 67, 69, 70, 71, 116, 145, 146, 163, 164, 208, 209, 210, 324, 326, 327
GROSS
   Ben D 30
GULLEY
   William 207

HAINS
   H G 19, 143, 281
   Henry G ... 75, 258, 259, 261, 262, 265, 269, 272, 273, 296, 301, 325
HAMILTON
   J O 52
HARJO
   Mary 62
HARLAN
   J 284
HARRINGTON
   A 57
   Laura 59
HARRIS
   Dr 258
   A W 282

A W, MD 276, 282
HARRISON
  Eli 244
  Ellen 244
  R P 235, 236, 283
  Robert P 101, 235, 284
HAWKINS
  Daniel 110, 111, 112, 113, 114
  Kate 110, 111, 112
  Liza 168, 169, 170, 171
  Melissa 110, 113, 114, 115
  Rhoda 111, 112, 113, 114
HENDRICKSON
  Eliza 40, 41, 42, 43, 44, 58
  James 41, 42, 43, 44
  Sarah Jane 41
  Sarrah 41, 42
  Sarrah Jane 42, 43, 44
HENRY
  Allen 161, 162
HENSLEY
  J W 165
HERROD
  David 83
  Rosanna 154
  Sophia 154, 156
  Susanna 154, 155, 156
HIBBARD
  L 9
HILL
  Dollie 57, 58, 60
  V E 104
HINKLE
  Oliver C 204
HODGES
  Mrs Tillie 157, 158
HOLT
  Z I J 38
HULSEY
  Ida 93
HUNKAPILLAR
  A B S 60
HUSHFIELD

  M H 77
HUTSON
  Ella 92, 93
INGRAM
  T J 97
ISLAND
  Lizzie 219, 220
  Maggie 219, 220, 221
  Napoleon B 219, 220, 221
  Susie 221
  Yeggues 221
  Yeggues Clarance 220
JACOBS
  Lean 199
JAMES
  Betsey 254, 279
  Betsy 259
  Chostke 279
  Chotkey .. 254, 259, 269, 270, 271
  Nancy 254, 255, 259, 273, 276,
    277, 279, 280, 281, 282, 283
JANWAY
  P280
  Preston 96, 97, 105, 112, 114,
    115, 201, 220, 221, 226, 227, 228,
    279, 280, 323
JEFFERSON
  Annie 323, 324, 325, 326, 327,
    328
  Lena 324, 325, 326, 328
  Senora 323, 325, 326, 327, 328
  Thomas 325
  Walter 323, 324, 325, 326, 327,
    328
JESSE
  Billy 302
  Susie 303
JOHNSON
  Bessie 119, 120
  Cullie 118
  Cully 118, 119, 120

Jennie 120
Joe 274
Mahala 117, 118, 119, 120
Sallie 195
Ulter 117, 118, 119
JONES
   Geo M 222

KELLER
   H O 176
   M O 175
KELLEY
   Gobey 188
   Mary 236
   Nancy 78
   Ned 190, 191
KELLY
   Catherine 234
   Nancy 77, 78, 79, 80
   Perry 77, 78, 79
   Reuben 77, 78, 79
KILLINGSWORTH
   M Y 240, 241, 248, 249, 250
KING
   Berry W 11, 12
   Charlie 6, 7, 8, 9, 10, 11, 12, 13
   Claudy J 10, 11
   Luther Lewis 6, 7, 8, 9, 12, 13
   Mary A 11
   Mattie 6, 7, 8, 9, 10, 11, 12, 13
   Mrs 9
KITE
   Jemima 201, 202
   A L 201, 202
   Lucy May 201, 202
KNIGHT
   Malinda 180

LANNING
   J M 307
   J M, MD 307
LARNEY
   Cilla 14, 15, 16, 17, 18

Micco 16
Rhoda 17
Toney 15, 16, 17
Tony 14, 18
LASLEY
   Ella 282
   Faney 280
   Fannie 282
LAVAL
   Julia C 276, 296, 299
LEE
   N P 249
LEWIS
   Cinda 195, 196
   Daniel 195
   Eddie 45, 46, 49, 50
   John 45, 46, 47, 48, 49, 50, 51,
      52, 194
   Johnson 194, 195, 196
   Lillie 47, 48, 49
   Lucinda 194, 195
   Lulu 194, 195, 196
   Manna 51, 52
   Mona 47, 49, 50
   Monnah 48, 51
   Mose 51
   Mosey 51, 52
   Nona 45, 46
LIEBER
   J G 298
   John G 259, 272, 292, 295, 296
   Mr ... 262, 264, 265, 266, 268, 273
LINN
   Charles P 184
LOGAN
   S J 32, 33, 198, 225, 279
   S L 278
LONDIGAN
   John 302
LONG
   Cilla 16
   Hannah 15
   Kizzie 15, 16, 18, 19

Index

Loday 14, 15, 16, 18, 19
Noah 21
Rhoda 14, 15, 16, 18
Sam 15
Thomas 21, 24, 25
Toney 16
Tony 15
LOVE
   Levi 272
LOVETT
   Manie 61
LUCAS
   J B 29, 30, 31
LUNSFORD
   Hattie 76, 77
   John C 76, 77
   Martha 76, 77
LYNCH
   R E 328
   Robert E 327, 328

MACABEY
   Lucy 306
MCCLUSKEY
   W S 55
MCCOMBS
   David 289
   Mary 103
   Miller 288
MCDERMOTT
   J 17, 20, 22, 33, 48, 51, 81, 82, 141, 167, 210, 255
   Jesse 15, 16, 48, 51, 140, 143, 327
MCELVAIN
   B F 259
MCELWAIN
   B F 283
MCGILBRA
   Cinda 159, 160
   Hepsey 143, 144
   Hepsie 141, 142
   Jackson 159

Jennie 111
Lizzie 141, 144, 153
Lucinda 160
Melissa 159, 160
MCGILBRAY
   Daniel 140
   Hepsey 140, 141, 142, 143
   Lizzie 140
MCGIRT
   Billy 121, 122, 123, 124, 125
   Emma 80, 81, 82, 83, 84, 85, 121, 122, 123, 124, 125
   Emma Smith 82
   George 81, 121, 122, 123, 124, 125
MCINTOSH
   Annie Lila 75
   Bennie 32, 33
   Bunnie ... 197, 198, 199, 225, 278, 279
   Cheesie 28, 29, 31
   D N, Jr 75
   Dick 153, 155, 156
   Ida 153, 154, 155, 156
   Ida M 222, 223, 224
   Jeanetta 197, 199
   L G 109, 127, 128, 129, 131, 132, 133, 134, 203, 204, 222, 223, 224
   Leah 198, 199
   Leona 223, 224
   Leonie 222, 223
   Leonie M 223
   Mary 262
   Morie 269
   Rosanna 154
   Susanna 153, 154, 155, 156
MCKENNEY
   John 22
MALANEY
   Annie 224, 225
   Jim 224, 225
   Lena 224, 225
MANELY

Melah 213
MANLEY
    Archie 204
    Idaac 211
    Isaac 203, 205, 206, 207, 208, 209, 211, 212, 213, 215, 216, 217, 218, 219
    Jacob 204
    Lentoce 207, 209, 211, 213
    Linda 213
    Linda Isaac 211, 213
    Lindy 203, 204, 205, 206, 210, 212, 218, 219
    Lindy Isaac 203, 207, 208, 209, 214, 215, 216, 217
    Martha ... 203, 205, 207, 208, 209, 210, 211, 212, 213, 214, 215, 216, 217, 218, 219
    Mela 211, 213
    Melah 208, 209, 210, 211, 212, 213, 214, 215
    Wm P 314, 315
MANLY
    Isaac 214
(MCINTOSH)
    Morie 267, 268
MERRCK
    Edward 299
MERRICK
    Edward .. 235, 271, 275, 276, 284, 296, 315
    Lona 19, 45, 46, 258, 269, 284
MEYERS
    Charles E 314
    Charley E 313
    Herbert 313, 314
    Martha 313, 314
MICKEY
    Palmer 82, 83, 124
MILLER
    Cilla 70, 71
    J Y 17, 69, 70, 71, 140
MILLS

B H 1, 2
MING
    Bessie 1, 2
MINGO
    Aggie 1, 2, 3, 4
    Bessie 1, 2, 3
    Billy 3, 4, 5, 6
    Joseph 1, 2, 3, 4, 5
MITCHELL
    Jennetta 79
    Warlecy 79
MITCHENER
    W C 314
    W C, MD 314
MOORE
    Bob 231, 232, 233, 234
    Cora 271, 275
    Jennie Susan 233
    Jessie Susan 231, 232, 233, 234
    Mary 231, 232, 233, 234
    Robert 232, 233, 236
    Susan 233
MORRIS
    F B 236
MORRISON
    Carrie 100, 102, 103
    Hettie Ola 100, 102, 103
    Louisa 81
    Louise 105
    Major 100, 101, 102, 103
MORTON
    Leo Britt 174, 177, 178
    Mittie B 174, 177, 178
    O A 177
    Osborn 174
    Osborn A 175, 177, 178
    T W 120
MOTT
    M L 259, 262, 272, 292, 296
MURRAY
    Ada 98, 99, 100
    Helen M 306, 307
    John 306, 307

Index

Lucy............................ 306, 307
MURRELL
   Mary.............................. 145, 151
MUSTON
   James A................................ 187
MYERS
   Charles E.............................. 315
   Herbert................................. 315
   Martha................................. 315
NAX
   E R...................................... 124
NELSON
   David Jefferson............. 250, 251
   Mary S............................ 250, 251
   William W...................... 250, 251
NIX
   E K.. 82
   E R...................................... 123
NORMAN
   Tom... 8
OGLESBY
   Harry.................................... 41
   Sallie B................................. 58
   W J.............41, 42, 43, 44, 56, 58
O'REILLY
   E I....................................... 216
OTT
   Zun..................................... 104
OWEN
   F C..................................... 216
OWENS
   John................................... 269

PALMER
   Ella......................33, 34, 35, 36
   Jim......................33, 34, 35, 36
   Mary....................33, 34, 35, 36
   Mollie............................. 82, 123
PARKER
   E L.. 72
   Lucinda M............................ 72

PATTERSON
   D F.........................225, 278, 279
PECK
   O K.................................76, 77
PEIRCE
   C S.......................................174
PENSE
   Alice..................................39, 40
   J H....................................39, 40
   Malissa.............................39, 40
PERRYMAN
   Phillip...................................79
PHILIPS
   Adeline..........294, 296, 298, 299
PHILLIPS
   Adaline...............................300
   Adeline...............................294
   J H......................................180
   John H...........119, 120, 179, 180
PITMAN
   Florence........................200, 201
   Lewis..............................200, 201
   Vonnie............................200, 201
PORTORA
   Geo M 222
POSEY
   Alex...3, 4, 11, 12, 13, 17, 18, 20,
   21, 45, 46, 47, 48, 50, 62, 81, 89,
   90, 91, 95, 106, 109, 138, 139,
   144, 146, 149, 151, 152, 153, 156,
   160, 167, 168, 169, 170, 171, 196,
   205, 206, 207, 208, 209, 215, 217,
   218, 219, 233, 235, 239, 253, 254,
   281, 287, 300, 303, 304, 305, 306,
   308, 309, 310, 311, 312, 313, 317,
   318, 319, 320, 325
   Mr..206
POST
   El Louisa 252
   Homer..................................297
   Laura 252, 253, 254
   Nellie....................................297
   Samantha.....................253, 254

Index

Thomas 252, 253, 254, 297
William 297
POSTOAK
   Arthur E 161, 163, 164
   Hattie L 162, 163
   Lillie 161, 162, 163, 164
   Lilly 163
   Lincoln 161, 162, 163
POWELL
   Charles 52
PRICE
   Louvina 225

RED
   D J 116, 117
REED
   Jennie 88
   John 88
   Liester 88
   Porter 88
REYNOLDS
   Aa 99
   Ada 98, 99, 100
   Charle 99
   Charley 98, 99, 100
   Charlie 97, 99
   Clarence Andrew .. 97, 98, 99, 100
RICH
   Marry 220, 221
   Mary 227, 228
RICHARD
   Sam 29
RICHARDSON
   Sam 28
RICHISON
   Yanner 237, 240, 241
RIDER
   Chas 23, 25, 82, 83, 122, 123, 124
RILEY
   Emma 146, 147, 150
   Leah 144, 145, 146, 147, 150, 151

Thomas .. 145, 146, 147, 149, 150, 151
Tootie 144, 145, 146, 147, 148, 149
ROBBERSON
   Henry 270
ROBERSON 257, 258, 261
   Clarence 254, 255, 256, 258, 259, 260, 262, 263, 264, 265, 266, 267, 268, 269, 270, 271, 272, 273, 275, 276, 279, 280, 281, 282, 285, 286
   Clerence 278, 284
   Ella 68
   George 265, 267, 270
   Henry 255, 256, 259, 262, 266, 267, 268, 269, 272, 273, 274, 277, 278, 279, 280, 281, 284, 285, 298
   Joe 259
   Joe T 259
   Leo 68
   Maria 262
   Mary 68, 69, 71
   Nancy 254, 255, 256, 259, 260, 261, 262, 265, 266, 269, 270, 272, 273, 274, 277, 278, 279, 280, 285, 286
   Philip 68
ROBERTSON
   Nancy 279
ROBINSON 257, 258, 261
   Clarence 260, 281, 282
   Ellen 70, 71
   George 261
   Henry 276, 281, 283
   Henyr 282
   Joe T 256, 260
   Leo 69, 70
   Mary 69, 70, 71
   Nancy 281, 282
   Philip 69, 70, 71
ROBISON
   Henry 263

Index

ROBSON 258
  Henry 257
ROGERS
  Harry H 188
RUIE
  Warren 248, 250
RUSHING
  Frank W 198, 245, 246, 288, 289
RYAN
  W J 184, 186

SANDS
  Martha 86, 87
  Nettie 86, 87
  Philip H 86
  Phillip H 86, 87
SARTY
  Emanuel 142
SAWYER
  Charles H 205, 206
SCOTT
  Hepsey 286, 287
  James A 261
  Mr 262
  Nancy 286, 287
  Sam 286, 287
SEARCY
  R H 251
SELF
  America 115, 116
  Clark 72
  Delila 71, 72, 73
  Della 191, 192
  Golie Ray 74, 75
  Maggie Ophelia 71, 72, 74, 75
  Rolie Ray 73
  William J 71, 72, 73
  William O 75
SERAN
  Arthur M 183, 185
SHAVER
  Will 198

SHEPHERD
  Addie M 248, 249, 250
  K H 248, 249, 250
  Maggie 248, 249
  May 249, 250
SHERRILL
  Chas M 229
SIMPSON
  R L 223
  Wm 279, 280
SITTON
  Anna M 97
  Anna Margaret 97
SKAGGS
  D C 3, 4, 11, 12, 13, 17, 22, 33, 47, 49, 50, 62, 89, 90, 91, 95, 106, 109, 139, 144, 145, 146, 149, 151, 152, 153, 156, 160, 167, 168, 169, 170, 171, 196, 205, 206, 208, 209, 210, 215, 217, 218, 219, 235, 239, 247, 253, 254, 255, 287, 300, 304, 305, 306, 309, 310, 311, 312, 313, 317, 318, 319, 320
  Drennan C 3, 4, 5, 10, 11, 12, 13, 18, 24, 34, 35, 47, 50, 62, 72, 73, 84, 88, 89, 90, 91, 92, 93, 95, 98, 99, 103, 106, 107, 108, 109, 110, 111, 113, 114, 121, 122, 129, 130, 135, 136, 137, 138, 139, 144, 148, 149, 150, 151, 152, 153, 156, 160, 168, 169, 170, 171, 192, 193, 196, 199, 200, 215, 217, 218, 219, 224, 230, 234, 235, 239, 252, 253, 254, 287, 290, 291, 300, 303, 304, 305, 306, 308, 309, 310, 311, 312, 313, 317, 318, 319, 320, 321, 322
SMITH
  A A 307
  Charles S 80
  Edna 138, 139
  Emma ... 81, 82, 83, 122, 123, 124
  F L 226
  John 82, 83, 122, 123, 124

    Loisa 82, 83
    Louisa 122, 123, 124
    Martha 138, 139
    Wade 138, 139
STARR
    Annie 325
    Chesley 325
STEWART
    America 115, 116
    Floyd Lee 115, 116, 117
    William 115, 116
    William H 116
STOVER
    Louina 322
    Luina 322, 323
STUBBLEFIELD
    Ida 91, 92, 93
    John 91, 92, 93
    Johnnie 91, 92
    Minnie 92, 93
STUTSMAN
    N 73
    N, MD 73
    Nettie 74
SULLIVAN
    Bettie 90
    Hagie 169, 171, 207, 209, 215,
        216, 217, 218, 219, 308, 309, 313
    W M 169, 171
    William 206, 308
    Wm 309, 312
SUTTON
    J C 282

TAYLOR
    M D 66, 68, 116
    M D, MD 66, 68, 117
TEMPLE
    A Jackson 260, 264
    S E 282
TEMPLS
    A Jackson 282
THOMAS

    Bipacy 24
    Harley 205
    Katie 20
    Lena 311
    Millie 20, 23, 24, 26
    Minnie 20
THOMPSON
    Legus 27, 28, 29, 30, 31, 32
    Lena 28, 29, 30, 31, 32
    Lenna 28
    Ollie 28, 29, 30, 31, 32
    Simma 29
TIBBETT
    Douglass 257
TIGER
    Barney 1
    Cinda 159
    Jane 135, 138
    Jas 190, 191
    Katie 2
    Sallie 160
TILEY
    Emma 148
    Thomas 148
    Tootie 148
TODD
    J W 122, 123
    James 8
    Jim 8
TOLLESON
    W A 137, 192, 193, 202, 246
    W A, MD 137, 192, 193
TURNER
    G S 41, 42, 43, 44
    G S, MD 42, 43
TYLER
    Tom 8

VANCE
    Joseph 53, 54, 55
    Mellette 55
    Ora Myrtle 54, 55
    William Mellette 54, 55

Index

VANN
  Emma 188, 189, 190, 191
  Harbey 188
  Lydia 188, 189, 190, 191
  Wadley 190, 191
  Watlie 189

WALKER
  E H 323
  Edith 226
  Edward H 112, 114, 115, 226, 227
  Eula 226, 227
  George Washington 227, 228

WARLECY
  Jennetta 79
  Jimmie 80
  Nancy 79, 80

WASHINGTON
  Dave 30
  Ellen 239
  Lucy 316, 317, 318, 319, 320
  Mandy 316, 318, 319, 320
  Melah 316, 317, 318
  Watson 316, 317, 318, 319, 320

WATSOBN
  Aurora 85

WATSON
  Aurora 80, 81, 84
  D H 77
  Holmer 82
  Homer 83, 84
  J W V 87
  Nora 80, 81, 82, 83, 85, 86, 122
  Senora 80

WATSON 80

WATTS
  Minnie 302, 303
  Nobe 302, 303
  Susie 302, 303

WESLEY
  Lucy 106, 109, 287, 310, 311, 312

WEST
  Annie 118, 119

WHITE
  Adeline 254

WHITMAN
  W W 243, 244

WILCOX
  C E 195, 236

WILEY
  A J 100

WILLIAMS
  Nat 1, 2

WILLINGHAM
  Dock 145
  Emma 144, 145, 146, 148, 149, 151

WILSON
  Tom 282

WIND
  George 179, 180
  Jesse 179, 180
  Millie 179, 180

WINSTON
  James A 175, 176, 186
  Jas A 176, 186

WITHERSPOON
  Myrtle 244

WITMORE
  H 74

WOLF
  Ellen 237, 239, 240
  Jennie 237, 238, 239, 240, 241
  William 237, 239, 240, 241

WOLFE
  Ellen 238, 241
  Jennie 238
  William 238

WOODFORD
  Sam 257

WOODFORK
  Leshie 274
  Willie 273

WOODS
   Carrie 101
WRIGHT
   Lawrence 166

YAHOLA
   Aggie 2, 3
YARHOLA
   Mulliah 87
YOUNG
   Adeline 293
   Adline 297
   Elizabeth.292, 298, 299, 300, 301
   Fay 297
   Harry 292, 293, 294, 295, 296, 297, 299, 300, 301
   Joe 293, 297
   Katie 297
   Lcius 300
   Lillie 297
   Lucius....292, 293, 296, 299, 300, 301
   Marion D 158
   Marion F 159
   Mary Ella 297
   N S 187
   Polly 297
   S J 177
   Simon J 177

www.ingramcontent.com/pod-product-compliance
Lightning Source LLC
Chambersburg PA
CBHW020241030426
42336CB00010B/579